Nick Middleton teaches geography at Oxford University and is a fellow of St Anne's College. He is a Royal Geographical Society award-winning writer, and author of seven travel books including *Going to Extremes* and *Surviving Extremes*. These both looked at some of the world's least hospitable environments and those who live there, and were filmed for major Channel 4 television series. The journeys in this book were also the subject of a Channel 4 prime-time series.

Also by Nick Middleton

The Last Disco in Outer Mongolia

Kalashnikovs and Zombie Cucumbers:
Travels in Mozambique

Travels as a Brussels Scout

Ice Tea and Elvis: A Saunter Through the Southern States

Going to Extremes: Mud, Sweat and Frozen Tears

Surviving Extremes: Ice, Jungle, Sand and Swamp

Extremes Along the Silk Road

Adventures Off the World's Oldest Superhighway

NICK MIDDLETON

JOHN MURRAY

© Nick Middleton 2005

First published in 2005 by John Murray (Publishers)
A division of Hodder Headline

Paperback edition 2006

A CIP catalogue record for this title is available from the British Library

ISBN 0 7195 6720 3

Typeset in Monotype Bembo
by Rowland Phototypesetting Ltd,
Bury St Edmunds, Suffolk

Printed and bound by
Clays Ltd, St Ives plc

Hodder Headline policy is to use papers that are natural,
renewable and recyclable products and made from wood
grown in sustainable forests. The logging and manufacturing
processes are expected to conform to the environmental
regulations of the country of origin.

John Murray (Publishers)
338 Euston Road
London NW1 3BH

For Lorraine

Contents

Acknowledgements

I am indebted to a large number of people for their assistance during my travels researching this book. Above all come those I met living in some of Asia's more remote localities. Their good nature and generous hospitality was an inspiration throughout. I would also like to thank many others whose names follow. They all helped logistically and in other ways they know how, both with the book and the accompanying television series.

In Mongolia and northwestern China: James Bates, Jacky Houdret, Guy Pugh, Roger Vernon, Paul Paragon, Simon Tindall, Batbayar, Kong Min, Wu Jinying (Jane), Ai Pu Er Ding, Susan Xu, Mrs Nabouyi and Bruno Baumann.

In Tibet: Andrew Palmer, Stephen Shearman, Doug Dreger, Donald Ng, Daniel Winkler, Topden Lama, Youyou, Gylsang Droma and Norbu Wangdan.

In Kazakhstan: Matt Dickinson, Jonathan Partridge, Ben Roy, Bayan Orumbayeva, Altay Zhatkanbayev, Zhannat Makhambetova, Nurbolat Beket, Renato Sala, Jean-Marc Deom and Dave Butler.

In Britain: Dr Paul Richards, William Anderson, Katherine Perry, Claire Hamilton, Zam Baring, Tom Beard, Adam Robinson, Toyin Ogunbiyi, Doreen Montgomery, Gordon Wise, Mark Carwardine and Lorraine Desai.

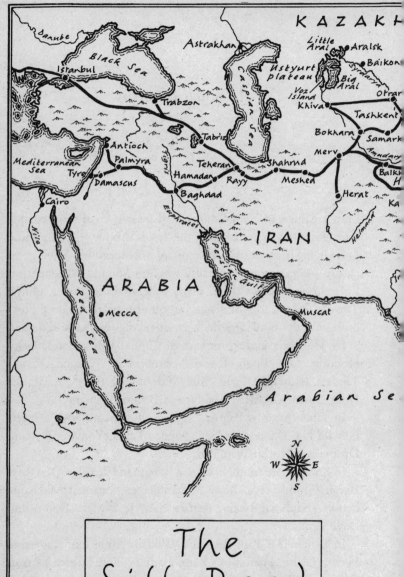

The Silk Road

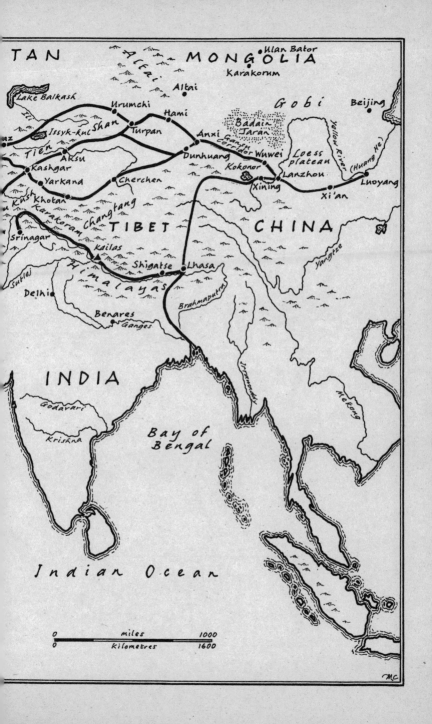

Into the Wilderness of Silk

Travelling the Silk Road is the most resonant journey on Earth. It's a thread that links East and West, a network of veins that pumped new lifeblood into mighty empires, a fabled route trodden by innumerable adventurers through the ages. Yet underlying this romantic trail is one of the most extraordinary tracts of land on this planet, a vast region separating China from the Mediterranean that rates as one of the least hospitable on Earth. It's an assortment of hostile deserts and towering mountain ranges, a harsh terrain of howling winds, searing heat and life-sapping cold. These simple facts of physical geography have been a formative influence on two of the world's most distinctive cultures. It was the difficulty of crossing such unforgiving territory that kept East and West apart for so long, allowing them to develop in their own distinct ways.

The raw material of nature and the relationships people have developed with the physical world have always interested me. I am a geographer, and this has long been the focus of my subject; I also believe that eyewitness encounter is the only way to study it. Given that we live in an age still obsessed with communications and the exchange of ideas, it struck me that the world's oldest superhighway might make a good theme for a journey of discovery. In recent years I've been drawn to understand better the challenges of life at the world's maxima and minima – not only going to extremes but surviving them. What better terrain in which to examine this interaction of human and natural forces than a route defined by them?

The story of the tract of land known as the Silk Road is world history writ large, a history dictated in large part by geography. It is a tale of human interaction across space and time, across boundaries of environment and civilization. There are no written records to mark the beginning of what is now called the Silk Road as a route, but trade between Europe and China can be traced back at least two millennia. By the middle of the first century AD, well-to-do Romans had become very taken with silk – although their understanding of how it was made was a bit wide of the mark. The Roman moralist Pliny the Elder stated in his book *Natural History* that it was a substance harvested from forests. The white down was combed off leaves that had been soaked in water, he said. Nevertheless, his countrymen developed an insatiable appetite for luxury goods made of this stuff from China, and Pliny became seriously concerned about the economic effects of their fixation. The name the Romans gave to China was Seres: 'the country of silk'.

However, although these links between East and West stretch back over two thousand years, the term 'Silk Road' is more recent. It was coined by one of the great German geographers of the nineteenth century, Ferdinand Freiherr von Richthofen. Baron von Richthofen spent several years travelling in China, conducting field research, and later, while a professor at the universities of Bonn, Leipzig and Berlin, developing his ideas and writing them up. His expression was a form of shorthand, because the Silk Road, or Seidenstrasse, is more than just one road, and the merchants who used it carried far more than silk. But although technically a misnomer, it was an evocative phrase, so it stuck.

The Silk Road was never a single highway. It was a network of overland routes that wove through the otherwise impenetrable physical barriers of Central Asia. This system of trails carried more than simply items for trade: it was the Internet of its time, a superhighway along which goods, ideas, languages and people thronged. It meant globalization many centuries before anyone came up with the concept. And this flow of life, culture and innovation was not only between China and Europe, but also linked the civilizations of Persia, India and the nomadic peoples who wandered the inhospitable voids dotted across the Asian landmass.

China acquired saddles and stirrups from the steppe nomads to the north and learned how to cultivate cotton probably from India to the south-west, while Chinese jewellers added Baltic amber and red coral from the Mediterranean to their repertoire. Gunpowder, paper and the wheelbarrow are just a few of the innovations that travelled westward from China. The use of passports is traced back to a Mongolian document introduced to ease the passage of official travellers on the roads of the Mongol Empire. Goods such as muslin, pistachios and indigo for dyeing spread from Persia and the countries of the Middle East, while the numerals used in the West today also have their origins in the Arab world. Religions too travelled in all directions: Buddhism from India, Islam from the Middle East and Christianity from the eastern Mediterranean. The spread of these goods and ideas all owe their passage to the legion of pioneering travellers along the Silk Road.

The mission I set myself was straightforward. I wanted to follow in the footsteps of adventurers who had made their names by overcoming the gruelling conditions of the Silk Road: heroic figures in exploration such as Alexander the Great and Marco Polo. I hoped to see how far things have changed since the golden days of travel and exploration, and examine some of the many legacies of this iconic system of highways.

But I wasn't intending to trace the routes in their entirety. Few travellers did. Most trade along the Silk Road took place in incremental fashion, as a series of exchanges through middle-men. Products continually changed hands, finding their way between East and West, North and South by the same means that a relay baton reaches the end of a race. The Silk Road had probably been operating in this manner for more than a thousand years before the first Europeans ventured all the way to 'the country of silk'.

Also, I wasn't sure that this ancient system of freeways should be the main focus of my enquiry. Six years ago I wrote a travel book about the US southern states and a piece of sound advice that I received on the eve of that journey still sticks in my mind. Stay off the Interstate highways, I'd been told, because only by leaving the main thoroughfares would I see the real Deep South. In preparing for my adventures along the Silk Road, I wondered whether that same counsel should apply.

Since putting my Southern exploits down in writing, I'd

looked to more remote spots for inspiration, visiting some of the world's most extreme environments. I had gone to wild, sometimes dangerous places, the journeys fuelled, at least in part, by the simple challenge of reaching little-known parts of a planet that is too easily thought of as small. I was gripped by the lives of people who have relatively little contact with the modern world.

Most of the literature about the Silk Road tends to focus, understandably, on its corridors of cultural, artistic, religious and military might that stretch from the heart of dynastic China to the kingdoms of the Mediterranean and beyond. These studies tell a story of civilizations and their advance, development based on the modernizing influences of this magnificent network of trade routes. The windswept topographies that the Silk Road avoided are often forgotten. Yet their inhabitants played important roles in the development of trade between East and West, often providing the know-how for successful movement, as well as products and ideas that flowed along the system of trails.

Since I hail from an up-to-the-minute culture still besotted with communications, the Silk Road provided a sound thread for a book, but I decided to use it as just that: a thread on which I'd string a series of adventures 'off *piste*'. My focus would be more on the inhospitable landscapes that the Silk Road had to negotiate. I wanted to see what has become of the enduring societies that lived beyond the familiar tracks of the world's oldest superhighway. Above all, I was eager to experience more of the most extreme environments on Earth and learn how people have adapted to them.

THE HIMALAYAS OF SAND

I

The asphalt ceased towards the edge of town and we continued on one of the stony tracks that I'd seen from the helicopter. They radiated out from Altai in all directions into the brown, mountainous wilderness. We hadn't been travelling for more than ten minutes and my jaw was already beginning to freeze.

We were heading into the Gobi, one of the world's great deserts. It's about half a million square miles of dust and gravel, which straddles the border between Mongolia and China. Thanks to its position far from the ocean's moderating effect on climate, it is a place of continental extremes. In summer the temperature can reach a brain-baking 45°C while in winter it can plummet to minus forty. The Gobi is arguably the harshest desert on Earth. Since the beginning of history, it has represented a vast natural barrier between the rolling grasslands to the north and a land of settled agriculture to the south.

My companion and guide, a former paratrooper named Aldaraa, had his head down, concentrating hard on negotiating the bumpy trail. We were coming to the end of a line of rough wooden fences, sectionalized compounds each containing a tent. Altai was typical of rural settlements all over Mongolia: a miserable place with wide, empty roads and a power station that belched thick black smoke from its tall chimney. The roads in the centre of town were lined with faceless apartment blocks, but on its outskirts, where the asphalt ended, the crumbling concrete gave way to these traditional dwellings: round felt-covered tents known in Mongolian as *gers*.

To my mind, nowhere is more iconic in its representation of remoteness than Mongolia, and if Mongolia is still a byword for undiscovered mysteries, then the Gobi remains the jewel in its crown of far-flung seclusion. It's bleak and it's harsh and it's largely empty. But not totally so. The Gobi is for the most part a semi-arid zone, which means that it can support some vegetation, although the clumps of grass and skeletal shrubs are grey, dusty and tired-looking. Where there's vegetation there's an opportunity to graze livestock, which is what Mongolians have done since time immemorial, and the way they do it hasn't changed much in the intervening years. The *gers* on the outskirts of the town looked very much like those described in accounts written during the time of Chingis Khan, 750 years ago.

It was this timeless way of life that I was intent on examining. My plan was to weave my way through the Gobi, starting in Mongolia, then crossing into China, where my ultimate aim was to penetrate a little-known corner of this desert known as the Badain Jaran. The Badain Jaran attracted me not only because it has been rarely visited by outsiders – the Chinese military use it as a testing ground for their missiles – but also because it contains the world's largest dunes, great mountains of sand reputed to be more than three hundred metres high.

But first on my list of Gobi experiences was a night out with a

Mongolian ex-paratrooper. Aldaraa had borrowed a motorcycle and sidecar for the purpose, a mode of transport that has all but disappeared from western Europe but which is still going strong in this part of the world. Mongolians tend to drive them like they ride their horses, in a wild and unfettered way that is totally at odds with the concept of comfort.

We had left the *ger* compounds behind us and were tearing along a track that appeared to be heading towards a distant range of grey hills. It was January, and bright, and patches of snow hugged the clumps of brittle grass. A flock of hefty sheep, their fleeces thick and woolly against the cold, were being driven towards Altai by a figure wrapped in a *del*, a long, flowing robe not unlike a dressing-gown to look at, tied at the waist with a bright silk sash.

The *del* is another element of Mongolian culture that has changed little over the centuries. I was wearing one myself, a winter model lined with sheep's fleece, which was highly effective in keeping my body warm against the wind. My feet were cosy too, in a pair of knee-high Mongolian boots fitted with inner socks made of thick felt. The problem was my face. I'd passed through the painful phase, the wind starting to pummel my features with its sting as soon as we'd set off on our journey. I was now rapidly losing all feeling in my jaw and nose, the biting cold acting like an anaesthetic, which was a worrying sign.

Aldaraa had recommended a visit to the local market in Altai to buy appropriate clothing as soon as I'd arrived on the big orange helicopter from Ulan Bator, Mongolia's capital. I had bought a decent hat as well, a padded silk affair with a brim made from the bushy red tail of a desert fox. A tie at the back was tightened so that it would fit snugly on my head and it immediately outperformed the woollen hat I'd brought from home. But now that I was in the sidecar, it wasn't so successful against a strong wind.

I sensed that my nose and jaw were turning to the colour of white wax, the first sign of frostbite. Placing my gloved hand over my face provided some brief relief, but this action also brought about a different problem. My breath was funnelled up towards my spectacles, coating them with a fine mist of condensation which quickly froze. This meant that I couldn't really see where we were going. Granted, this was not as great a predicament as it might have been had Aldaraa been wearing glasses but, for me, it was a serious issue nonetheless. Being blind to our progress, I had no way of anticipating the humps and bumps of the trail. Consequently I was being jerked and jolted in all directions.

I didn't really want to start complaining so early in our journey, particularly given Aldaraa's former occupation as a man of iron, but the prospect of several hours in this predicament was not an attractive one. I had to do something about the cold, and I had to do it soon or my jaw would have frozen and I wouldn't be able to talk.

Ten minutes later, I asked Aldaraa to stop and informed him of my dilemma. He looked at me sideways. 'You are dressed in traditional way,' he told me. 'Mongolian boots, sheepskin *del*, fox-fur hat. What is the problem?'

I told him my face was in danger of falling off.

'This is because your nose is not Mongolian,' he said.

No it wasn't, I argued. It was because my hat was no good. 'You're not wearing it properly,' he told me, and demonstrated how he'd reversed his so that the tie was under his chin. This adjustment meant his face was enveloped in thick fur down both sides. I made a similar adjustment to mine. Things were much better after that.

The Silk Road didn't go through Mongolia, but beginning my investigation off the beaten track here was appropriate, because this is how the whole system of trans-Asian communications began. Its roots stretch back more than two thousand years to the uneasy relationship between the settled civilizations of China and the wandering hordes that inhabited the lands to the north and west. These nomadic groups, called Xiongnu by the Chinese, occupied the vast Central Asia steppes, an ocean of grass stretching from today's southern Russia across Kazakhstan into Mongolia.

There has been considerable discussion among Western academics about the Xiongnu. The Chinese name comes in two characters which have the literal meaning 'fierce slaves'. The first part is an accurate description, the second more a reflection of wishful thinking. Some suggest they could be equated to Huns; others prefer to think of them as Mongols. It's probable that the Chinese didn't distinguish between the two, using the term vaguely to denote the general rabble of nomadic herders beyond their ken. These people lived in areas that weren't much good for the 'civilized' practice of agriculture and, as far as the Chinese were concerned, they were barbarians of the first order. They had no means of writing and were forever on the move, driven by the need for fresh pastures and water for their livestock. So the Xiongnu had no walled cities or fixed dwellings – further evidence, in Chinese eyes, of their uncouth nature.

But although the Chinese saw them as brutish and uncultivated, these people couldn't simply be ignored. The horsemen of the steppes were great warriors, using their hunting skills to good effect in times of war. These nomadic hordes were perceived as a threat to China's borders, so appropriate actions were taken to keep them at arm's length. Around 400 BC the Chinese had begun to erect an immense barrier to keep them out. It was strengthened and extended over the following centuries, though it wasn't until the Ming dynasty (AD 1368–1644) that the masonry and earth structure we know today as the Great Wall was completed. However, at the same time, the Chinese began to trade with the Xiongnu, exchanging silk and grain for horses and furs. It is thought that this trade was at least in part an attempt by the Chinese to impoverish the nomads: the horsemen of the steppe were very keen on silk, and a chronicler in 81 BC noted that a piece of Chinese silk could be exchanged for articles worth several pieces of gold.

These exchanges were the early stirrings of a system of trade that was to grow and grow. But the history of the Silk Road is documented predominantly by people from urban centres, hence the tendency in written records to cast the nomads in a derogatory light. Settled peoples have long looked down upon their wandering neighbours and, at times, lived in fear of their raids. However, the nomads were pivotal to the development of trans-Asian communications, perhaps even the most important group in the whole process, because it was they who controlled the routes and were masters of the means of transportation.

Not that they traditionally travelled by motorbike and sidecar, of course, but in my mind I could allow this modern aberration, given that so many other aspects of life in the Mongolian Gobi were unchanged. It was to sample one such enduring practice that I had embarked on my journey with Aldaraa.

'Tonight we are going to sleep in Mongolian-outlaw style,' he shouted, after I had adjusted my hat and we had set off again.

This sounded interesting. 'What does that mean?' I shouted back.

'We will sleep on hot rocks,' he replied.

Intriguing, I thought to myself. We were passing through the grey hills, the foothills of the Altai mountains, the track winding its way along a narrow valley. Despite the bright sunshine, the landscape was drab and desolate, painted with a lifeless palette of browns and greys. There was pure white snow on the far mountain tops, giving way to grubbier patches on the lower slopes. It felt odd to be in a desert with a covering of snow.

'How do we make the rocks hot?' I shouted.

'With fire.' Aldaraa changed down a gear to navigate a section of track that had been invaded by tussocks of stubbly grass. 'First we have to find an area with special bushes, the saxaul,' he went on. 'These we use to make the fire.'

Although I considered the prospect of warming up the ground before we slept on it fascinating, I was beginning to have my suspicions.

'Do we have a tent?' I cried casually. We had negotiated the tussocks and Aldaraa gave the engine some revs.

'No need for tent or sleeping-bag,' Aldaraa yelled, with what sounded like glee. 'Hot rocks are enough. You will see.'

I learned later that the hot-rock technique for night-time survival in the Gobi during winter had been pioneered by a group of outlaws whom Aldaraa likened to Robin Hood and his Merry Men. The Men of Good Will, as they were known, made it their business to round up wild camels and horses and hand them over to itinerant herders. I couldn't establish why this made them outlaws, but maybe it was because they weren't above stealing the occasional beast from more prosperous herders, thus doing their bit towards the redistribution of wealth.

Nomads are by definition highly mobile, hence the invention of the *ger*, which can be dismantled and loaded on to the back of a camel within an hour. But the Men of Good Will had forfeited their *gers* in the interest of a speedy getaway. Sleeping under the stars during the summer months was no hardship, but in winter it was a different matter. Hence the hot rocks.

We passed plenty of rocks on our way. The word Gobi means 'waterless place' in Mongolian but its abundance of rocks and stones has given it a more specific meaning to physical geographers, who use it as shorthand for gravel desert. But when, a few hours later, we finally arrived in an area that boasted saxaul bushes, the rocks had become notably absent.

We had all but left behind the Altai mountains and were on a wide, featureless plain. Aldaraa had turned off the track and bumped towards the bushes in question. He stalled the engine and we came to an abrupt halt. Aldaraa dismounted and took in the scene. 'I will gather firewood,' he announced. 'You can collect stones.'

I unfolded myself from the sidecar, threw my arms above and behind my head to stretch my aching bones, then looked around. The saxaul bushes were gnarled and dusty but plentiful, each nestling in its own patch of windblown snow. It wasn't fresh, fluffy snow, but icy and encrusted, indicating that it had fallen some time before, perhaps months ago. Between the snow-patches, the ground was made of clay and there was not a rock to be seen. I scuffed the earth with my boot, generating a small cloud of dust.

Aldaraa was examining the motorcycle's engine.

'We may have a problem, Aldaraa.'

He looked up. 'Why?'

'No rocks.' I scuffed the ground again, creating another puff of dust.

'Yes, there are rocks here. Look over there.' He pointed in a direction that to my eyes didn't look any more promising. I walked towards it, scraping the ground with my boot as I went. There was nothing in the way of rocks, not even small stones. Wherever I scraped, the clay was the consistency of talcum powder.

Aldaraa was still inspecting the motorcycle. 'I tell you what,' I called, 'I'll collect the firewood and you can get the stones.'

The saxaul bushes were brittle and desiccated but I made a point of not pulling up any by the roots because, despite appearances, they were unlikely to be dead. Many desert plants are like that. They play dead for much of the time until a shower of rain comes along and off they go into a rapid cycle of reproduction. Once the water has gone, they revert to inactivity for a year or two, or however long it takes for another shower of rain to appear. At the best of times, which this wasn't, the saxaul is almost leafless, another adaptation to the scarcity of water, but it can grow into a tree up to four metres high. Here none was above my knee, but there were more than enough for a decent fire. Meanwhile, Aldaraa had set about searching for rocks.

After half an hour of scavenging, we had amassed a large pile of saxaul branches and, to my surprise, a sizeable collection of rocks and stones. 'Now we dig,' Aldaraa declared, wandering back over to the motorcycle. From the sidecar he produced a shovel.

He marked out a large rectangle in the dust and looked at me quizzically. 'This is where we sleep,' he said. 'Big enough?' I lay down inside the rectangle. Aldaraa nodded, and began to dig out a hole around ten centimetres deep. Once dug, we piled in the saxaul branches and set them alight. They caught fire immediately and crackled satisfyingly in the failing sunshine. We'd taken it in turns to dig, the physical exercise keeping each of us warm, but now that all we could do was wait for the flames to die down, at which point we'd add the rocks, the fire was a welcome source of heat.

The theory was that once the stones had cooked for a couple of hours, by which time the sun would have disappeared below the horizon, we would cover them with a thin layer of earth and that would be it: underfloor heating in the Gobi. The temperature, which had fallen noticeably over the last hour or two, took a further dramatic drop as soon as the sun had set. The cold was now bitter and biting.

As we spread the earth over the stones, I asked Aldaraa what he thought the temperature was.

'Below zero,' he said.

'How far below zero?'

He thought for a moment. 'Maybe twenty-five.'

It certainly felt it, and as Aldaraa disappeared into the murky darkness to grab a padded tarpaulin from the motorbike to lay over the stones, it crossed my mind that I might freeze to death in the Gobi – and on my very first night.

But when I looked at our prospective sleeping area, I saw a strange sight. Wisps of steam were seeping up through the layer of earth over the stones. It looked as if we'd decided to bed down on the side of an active volcano.

Later, when we'd taken off our boots to use them as pillows, my thoughts returned to the carcass of a dead horse I'd noticed while collecting saxaul – I was trying to forget that I had no bedclothes other than my *del*: it didn't seem enough to keep me from a sub-zero demise.

'Are there wolves in this part of the Gobi?' I asked.

'Yes,' replied Aldaraa. A moment of silence passed.

'What are the chances that they might come to check us out?' I enquired.

'Not very likely. But I can scare them away.' Aldaraa sat up, took a deep breath, then let out a long, haunting whoop that sounded as if it should have echoed all around us, but didn't because we were in the middle of a flat plain. He giggled. 'That should do it,' he said.

'Good,' I replied. 'It was just that I didn't want them to steal the motorbike.'

The Mongolian outlaws' method for sleeping rough in the Gobi in winter was a truly bizarre experience. Initially, I thought we'd wasted our time with the stones because I was getting no warmth from them at all. 'Give it time, you will see,' was all the response I got from Aldaraa, and sure enough, little by little I began to feel the warmth seeping through.

To begin with, the effect was feeble and I wondered whether it really was the hot stones or just my imagination wishing our efforts to produce some results. But bit by bit, the ground we lay on grew warmer. Below me the temperature continued to rise and after fifteen minutes of lying there the ground wasn't warm any more. It was positively hot. I settled down and gazed at the stars, a sultry wave of good-feeling cascading in slow motion through my body. My boot pillow was surprisingly comfortable, and for the first time that day I thought that maybe I would be getting a night's sleep after all.

The temperature of the ground continued to rise. To my surprise, the side I lay on was beginning to feel too hot. I turned over. In what seemed like no time at all, I had to turn again, to lie on my back this time. The ground was still getting hotter. By this time I was sweltering.

I kept turning. As one side grew uncomfortably hot, I'd turn to do the other. I felt as if I was being roasted on a spit. I did the occasional turn on to my back, but this wasn't as satisfactory as being on my side because my nose stuck out through my fur hat and got very cold very quickly. Being on my side was fine in this respect because the fur effectively closed over my nose. But I still had to keep up the regular turns.

This was ridiculous. Here I was in January in the middle of the Gobi desert. It was the middle of the night, at least twenty-five degrees below zero, and I was being baked alive.

Somehow, I drifted off to sleep. At 2 a.m. I was awake again. Now I was cold. I could still feel the heat from the stones, which kept the side I lay on warm enough. The problem was on my upper side. I had been sweating, and the dampness on my exposed side was cooling rapidly. From having to make regular turns because one side was too hot, I now had to do the same because one side was too cold. I looked over at Aldaraa beside me. He was fast asleep.

I kept turning, first one side then the other, but it was no good. Unbeknown to Aldaraa, I had brought along a small tent of my own, and now was definitely the time to use it. Quietly I left the bed of hot stones and was immediately enveloped by the bitter, searing cold.

I put up the tent and crawled inside to put on all my clothes and settle down to try and get some more sleep. But it was still one of the coldest nights I've ever experienced.

II

Aldaraa reckoned the temperature had dropped to below −30°C during the night, a judgement based on the length of time it took to warm up the motorbike the following morning. This he did in unorthodox style, using a blowtorch. I'd witnessed this early-morning ritual of resuscitating a motor vehicle in Siberia, a few years previously. Engine oil freezes at −32°C, and grease, particularly in the axles and wheel hubs, before that. These parts of a vehicle are commonly coaxed back into life with a small bonfire or flaming torch. In particularly cold areas, bonfires are kept going all night beneath the fuel tank of diesel-powered vehicles to prevent the diesel freezing, which it does at −48°C.

But I'd never seen this done on a motorbike. It struck me that on this smaller vehicle, with all its parts closer together, there might be a greater danger of some kind of serious accident. Aldaraa was playing the blowtorch over the engine. 'Aren't you worried it might explode?' I asked.

'No,' he replied. It was clear that he knew what he was doing, but I was glad I'd put up my tent a good ten metres away — at least I could dismantle it at a safe distance from any potential disaster.

We penetrated deeper into the Gobi, driving south-eastwards in the direction of a small town named Biger. I'd thought we'd left the Altai mountains behind, but they closed in again, the snow on their peaks shining in the morning sunlight as if they'd been freshly coated with whitewash.

Aldaraa had made no comment about my tent but I felt the need to explain myself. He nodded and said I'd done all right: moisture seeping up from the ground with the heat from the stones was always a problem, he told me. It had been partly his fault, he added, because he had forgotten to bring a waterproof tarpaulin for us to sleep on.

The landscape was still rugged and inhospitable with few obvious signs of life and fewer patches of snow the further we drove. We passed a herdsman clambering down a steep slope after his sheep and I waved from the sidecar, but he didn't respond as we sped past. Motor vehicles are an unusual sight in the Mongolian countryside. Some hours later we passed our first camels. A small group were tearing at some desiccated clumps of grass and paused to stare at us. Their deep-piled fur made them look more substantial than their single-humped cousins, which I'd seen in African deserts.

We were heading for an area where some friends of Aldaraa's lived, an extended family of herders who kept camels, cattle, sheep, goats and a few horses. In summer they wandered all over the place in search of fresh pastures, Aldaraa told me, but they spent the winter months in a particular spot an hour or so's drive from Biger.

It took us all day to get there, and I was frozen to the core by the time we arrived. We were greeted at the entrance to one of the family *gers* by Sharbaatar, a kindly-looking elderly man who ushered us straight inside for a bowl of hot tea. We were soon joined by his wife, Delgertsogt, who had been milking the camels with one of their daughters, Erdenezul.

Traditionally Mongolians use only one name, although in recent times many have taken to adding the name of their father, often in the form of an initial, as a prefix. This initial is only really used in formal situations, such as on documents or letters, so in everyday circumstances it was just plain Aldaraa, for example. Except, that is, when a name had a familiar shortened form. Sharbaatar, therefore, became Shara, and Delgertsogt was Delger.

As is customary when visitors arrive at a *ger* in the countryside, Aldaraa and I filed in and took up kneeling positions to the left of the entrance, the visitors' side. There's a more or less standard layout to the inside of a *ger*. The first thing you come upon when stepping through the wooden door is the hearth. The metal stove stands roughly in the middle so that its chimney can poke up through a central hole in the roof. This hole was traditionally referred to as a 'sky window', and is the only source of natural light inside the *ger*, but here I noticed that it was complemented by an electric light bulb, dangling from the opening. Shara had a set of solar panels on the outside of his tent, which charged an old car battery that was wired up to the bulb in the evening. Beyond the fire was a low wooden table, and Delger quickly filled it with bowls of nibbles: small hard blocks of curd and wrapped sweets.

Around the sides of the *ger* were the family's beds, and opposite the door sat an extended wooden sideboard painted a bright orange colour with a flowery pattern. On display, attached to the furniture, was a collection of family photographs and a selection of medals. This position, directly facing the door, is also where you might find a small Buddhist altar, in this case reduced to a picture of a Buddhist god cut from a magazine.

Mongolians were discouraged from following Buddhism for most of the twentieth century when they were led by a Communist regime under the watchful eye of their neighbour, the Soviet Union. 'Discouraged' is not really the right word. The Communists destroyed most of the country's monasteries and did away with most of their monks. But in the years after 1990, following the collapse of the USSR and a move towards a Western-style democracy in Mongolia, the Buddhist faith has made a comeback.

Mongolia's special place in Western minds as the epitome of remoteness is partly a function of the country's peculiar status between the establishment of Communist control in 1921 and its breakdown sixty-nine years later. This country approaching the size of western Europe had been sealed off from the outside world and subjected to an ideological experiment in Soviet-style Marxism-Leninism. Not that we knew much about what went on in Mongolia during the century before that, when the Chinese were in charge of the whole place. This was the period during which Europeans adopted the curt distinction between Outer Mongolia, today's country, and Inner Mongolia, still a territory of China that was only marginally less uncouth in their eyes.

I was lucky enough to visit Mongolia in 1987, during the last years of Soviet-inspired Communist rule (not that anyone thought the system was on its last legs at the time). It was a visit of mixed emotions, but the restrictions I faced as a suspicious Westerner were outweighed by the excitement I felt at having been granted entry into this fabled land. One of the frustrations of that trip had been the unwillingness of the authorities to allow me to travel anywhere outside the capital. But what I had seen during that stay had been enough to whet my appetite for Outer Mongolia, and I returned several times in the early 1990s when I was able to explore some of the country outside the confines of Ulan Bator.

Although it was twelve years since my last visit, I still remembered many of the dos and don'ts of *ger* etiquette. I had been careful when entering the thick padded door of Shara's home not to set foot on the threshold: someone had told me that to do so is tantamount to stepping on the owner's neck. Not really polite behaviour. As Aldaraa and I sat sipping our tea, Shara produced a small snuff bottle from a silk pouch at his hip. A tiny spoon was attached to the pink coral stopper, and Shara carefully placed a pinch of the contents on the fold of skin between the base of his thumb and forefinger, raised it to his nose, sniffed, then replaced the stopper and handed the bottle to me. There is a correct way to offer the bottle, with the right hand touched at the elbow with the left. The giver holds the bottle vertically in an open palm, resting on the little finger, and the bottle is taken by the next person with the fingers outstretched in a scraping-like motion, the tips of the fingers brushing as the bottle is taken. I took a snort myself and passed the bottle to Aldaraa.

We spent the inside of a week with Shara and his family,

Aldaraa and I sleeping in a second *ger* that was part of their winter camp. The family had established themselves in a wide, flat valley flanked to east and west by distant snow-topped mountains. The spot was well stocked with clumps of dry, hay-like grass for the animals, and the Biger river, which meandered across the valley floor, provided a ready source of water. Each day, it was someone's job to trudge the few hundred metres to the frozen watercourse and break the ice.

I accompanied Shara to the river the morning after our arrival and saw for myself what a time-consuming operation this was. The ice, which gave off satisfying squeaks beneath the leather soles of our boots, was more than a metre thick and had to be attacked with a long metal spike. We took it in turns to thrust the spear into the slowly deepening hole, a process that took half an hour before we struck water. It gurgled up from below and quickly filled the mini-crevasse we'd excavated, allowing us to fill our buckets. We left a small pool for the shaggy camels and small black cattle that had materialized out of nowhere for a drink.

The camels were Shara's most valuable animals, providing wool that he sold in Biger every spring. This was his sole source of monetary income to support a way of life that was otherwise self-sufficient. I'd seen the lifestyle of a herder elsewhere in Mongolia during previous trips, but I'd never penetrated this far into the Gobi, and here, despite the fact that Shara also kept some cattle, sheep and goats, the camel was king. In addition to being a source of valuable wool, some of which Shara kept to make rope, they were beasts of burden and a regular source of milk. Occasionally, camel meat supplemented the family's diet and they cured the hide to make leather bags and straps. Shara's camels were also walking fuel dispensers: sizeable mounds of their desiccated dung pellets were piled up outside the *gers* ready for use in the fire. Last thing at night, Delger would appear inside the tent to feed the metal stove. She used a large round ladle to shovel the brown pellets, the shape and weight of ping-pong balls, into the stove. They burned slowly and without any odour.

Camels are better adapted to life in the desert than almost any other mammal. Although Shara's beasts had queued at the hole in the ice, they can go without a drink for several months in winter. Bactrian camels are also extremely adept at withstanding wide variations in temperature – from the blistering heat of summer to the bitter cold we experienced in January. They shed their shaggy winter coats, with hairs up to twenty-five centimetres long in their beards and manes, when the air temperature rises. Huge sections peel off, almost as if they have been shorn.

The Bactrian camel was domesticated at least four and a half thousand years ago in Bactria, a province of the ancient Persian empire. Its use as a draft and pack animal spread across Asia into Mongolia and China, where it became the main form of transport on the Silk Road. As pack animals, these beasts are virtually unsurpassed, able to carry up to 250 kilograms, a quarter of a metric ton, up to fifty kilometres a day. Bactrian camels are also said to be good swimmers, but they don't get many opportunities to prove this in the Gobi.

Incidentally, if you've ever had trouble remembering the difference between a Bactrian camel and a dromedary, there is a simple way to commit it to memory: in your mind's eye, rotate the first letter of each name so that it sits flat, and you have the number of humps. When it comes to riding them, the Bactrian's second hump provides a definite advantage. I can say this because I have some experience of riding dromedaries in the Sahara. In West Africa, a Tuareg nomad places his saddle more or less on top of the dromedary's single hump, which makes for a precarious ride. A lengthy time in this hard saddle is also rather distressing for the rider's rear end. Riding a Bactrian camel is, by comparison, much more stable since you're wedged in between the two humps, one providing good support at the back, the other offering abundant deep fur to hang on to. The Bactrian ride was also considerably less painful thanks to a felt saddle, the other purpose of which is as a base on which the stirrups are hung.

Late one afternoon when Shara invited me to accompany him and Aldaraa to round up his grazing camels for milking, I eagerly agreed. Once up on my mount, I was versed in the standard methodologies for riding: sharp taps with a stick to make the animal go, and obvious tugs on the reins for turning and stopping. Then I came upon another difference between the dromedary and the Bactrian, or at least in the way the camels are viewed by their owners in the Sahara and Gobi. I asked Aldaraa whether my camel had a name, thinking that it might help me when encouraging it to do my bidding. Aldaraa looked at me in a way that indicated he thought this was a most extraordinary question. 'It's only an animal,' he told me. 'Why would it have a name?'

We set out at a canter across the arid plain, Aldaraa advising me to give my camel a short rein so that its head was kept well up – the best posture for going in a straight line. I was pleased I could keep up with the others, and held my own until we paused within sight of the grazing herd, a few kilometres from the *gers*. The camels were dotted across the bleak landscape as far as I could see, all widely scattered except for a group of relatively small younger specimens that were more tightly clustered in the near distance.

Apportioning the round-up duties was a rapid affair. Aldaraa told me that he and Shara would deal with the scattered individuals if I would herd the younger beasts back to camp. Shara had two pieces of advice before he and Aldaraa raced off into the distance. First, don't get too close to the small camels for fear of spooking them into a stampede; second, be on the look-out for large males – it was the mating season and they might challenge my mount, a situation that could turn nasty. As I couldn't yet tell a male camel from a female, I condensed my instructions into one: don't get too close.

My mission, to herd the younger camels back towards the *gers*, sounded straightforward enough, but I soon realized that there might be more to it than met the eye. My camel had taken the opportunity of our brief stop to start munching on the sallow clumps of grass at its feet. When I pulled on my reins to raise its head, nothing happened. I tugged harder and my camel simply shook its great head, as if to shrug off a bothersome fly, while it continued tearing tufts of grass to chew. I looked up for assistance but Aldaraa and Shara had already become rapidly diminishing dots in the distance. It was just me and my camel.

I gave it a sharp tap on the rump with my stick and a hefty jerk of the reins. The animal's reaction was surprising. It raised and turned its head in one rapid movement and tried to bite me. The sudden attack also had the effect of nearly throwing me from its back. But at least I had its attention. Hanging on to the thick fur on the front hump, I leaned back so that the rein was tight as the beast tried to lower its head once more for another mouthful of washed-out grass. It gave me a snort of disapproval, and I gave it a dig of my heels to move it forward.

We did so, and I relaxed slightly, which was a mistake. My camel obviously sensed that my guard had been lowered slightly and abruptly stopped once more to lurch for some grass. I hauled on the reins and gave the beast another whack with my stick, which must have been too hard because my camel then decided that this was a sign to start galloping. We charged across the plain, me clinging on for dear life to the front hump until eventually I managed to rein it in to a trot. It was rather like learning to drive a car all over again, with a tankful of 'kangaroo petrol'.

In front of me, the pack of young camels had all looked up from their grazing to stare wide-eyed at me and my mount. One or two nearest me turned and wandered away, but the rest looked dangerously skittish. I slowed my camel to a walk and guided it to one side, aiming to go round the youngsters and drive them gently towards the camp.

The key, it seemed, was to keep moving so that my camel didn't have a chance to think about eating, so I did my best to maintain a steady pace until we reached the far side of the herd of youngsters. As we turned to face the far-off *gers*, I could see in the distance Shara and Aldaraa galloping round stray camels, gradually assembling the adult herd.

I managed to keep my camel walking as we rounded the young herd and gradually closed in on them from the far side. After my false start, things seemed to be going well. I even had the presence of mind to realize that with all this activity my fingers had stopped throbbing with the cold. Slowly but surely I moved in, but things then took a turn for the worse. As I got closer to the animals, instead of being driven gently forward, as I'd expected, they simply ambled to either side to let me pass. A gap opened up in front of me into which my camel was quite happy to stroll. Before I could react, I had successfully split the herd in two, neatly down the middle. If I'd been wanting to do this, I'm sure I'd have failed miserably, since it seemed like a rather advanced manoeuvre.

I turned once more and tried to encircle one half of the animals so that I could reunite the herd, but only succeeded in driving them further away from the other half. This half now seemed happy to walk in front of me, which had been what I'd wanted all along. But I now had only half the herd under my control and I was driving them further away from the camp.

Aldaraa was now within shouting distance, and asked what I was doing. I had to admit that herding camels wasn't as easy as it looked.

Milking them was only slightly less troublesome. Once I'd been rescued and the entire herd was at the *gers* (the rescue was entirely effortless and I still don't have a clue where I went wrong), Delger took over. The older female camels had been herded into a wooden corral while the younger ones just hung around. One by one, Delger brought out a mother whom she hobbled by coaxing up its left front leg and tying a short rope round it so that it was permanently bent at the knee. Once the mother had been disabled, her youngster quickly joined her and set about getting some milk to drink. After a few sucks, Delger's daughter disengaged the young camel from the teat and led it away, at which point Delger had her pail up underneath the camel's hindquarters and was milking energetically. The pail was balanced on Delger's knee, leaving both hands free to pull. As she demonstrated, a sharp pull on a teat was all that was needed for milk to spurt into the bucket, but when I tried most of it shot up my sleeve.

In other more personal ways, however, I felt that I became better adapted to life in the Gobi in winter as my stay with Shara and his family progressed. One tactic I learned quickly was the desirability of limiting the amount of tea I drank in the evenings. It was, in fact, a lesson I only had to learn once. Mongolian *gers* do not come with toilet facilities, and getting up in the middle of the night to relieve myself outside in temperatures below $-30°C$ was not an experience I felt the need to repeat, so I soon put a strict limit on my intake of fluids.

Another policy decision I eventually got the hang of concerned how much clothing to wear during the day. Initially, deciding the number of layers to put on in the morning was a tricky operation. At first, it was fairly obvious to me that I'd need fewer layers when I was engaged in doing something physical rather than just sitting there doing nothing, as I had been in the motorbike's sidecar. But a thermal vest, a thick, wind-proof shirt, a heavy woollen jumper, and a bulky synthetic fleece beneath my sheepskin *del* had not really been enough when travelling in the sidecar. Conversely, I'd worked up quite a sweat beneath these five layers while helping Shara hack away at the ice of the river.

In other circumstances, the principle of wearing multiple layers in the cold is a sensible one. If you feel that you're beginning to work up a fug, you simply shed a layer. But with a *del* as the outermost garment, this is a time-consuming business. The silk tie around the middle is an incredible nine metres long and it takes quite a time to unravel. Winding it round the waist is also an art. It was only after several days of trying that I was able to do it for myself. For the first few mornings, I'd stand in the middle of vast swathes of bright yellow silk and get hopelessly tangled within seconds. Aldaraa got bored of helping me on the second day, but Delger and her grandchildren thought that dressing the foreigner was a highly amusing distraction from their daily routine. They all looked quite disappointed when I emerged one morning having succeeded in tying it myself.

'Why do you need nine metres of the stuff?' I asked Aldaraa, when we bought it in Altai market.

'It is necessary,' he replied simply. 'Mine is only seven metres and it is not enough.' After finally mastering the art of tying a nine-metre sash, I can only agree with him. Anything shorter would be insufficient.

On my final afternoon Shara and Delger's three sons turned up to say goodbye. They'd been tending the sheep and goats in the foothills on one side of the valley, and brought along a goat for dinner.

I've seen sheep and goats dispatched in Mongolia before. Further north, in the Khangai mountains, they kill them by laying the animal on its back, held down by a person at each end, and slitting its chest just below the ribs. A man then plunges his hand into the animal's chest and squeezes its heart until it stops beating. I was told that when killed like this the animal's whole system stops abruptly and there is no bleeding, making its meat more gamey than that from an animal drained of its blood.

The three brothers didn't slaughter their goat like this because they were intending to cook it in a special way that involved another ingenious use of hot stones. They dispatched the creature very simply, using a hammer to give it a sharp whack on the head between its horns. While they proceeded to skin the goat, Aldaraa and I were asked to make our contribution to the preparation of dinner, which involved the familiar activity of collecting stones and firewood. As the rocks were being heated in our bonfire, the technique for cooking the goat became clear to me. The hide had been skilfully peeled off in a single piece with just two holes, one at either end. One brother was securing the hole in the rear end of the skin with wire, leaving the neck end open, while the other two were butchering the skinned carcass.

'They will return the meat to the skin,' Aldaraa explained, 'along with the hot rocks. This way it will cook from the inside.' The only addition would be a few onions and some salt, bowls of which Delger had just brought to the scene.

Refilling the skin was a chaotic affair, conducted in billowing clouds of hot steam that whirled up from the inside of the goat every time a hot stone, precariously picked from the embers with a pair of metal tongs, was popped in to accompany a layer of meat. The smell of instantly roasting dinner was totally delicious, but we had a considerable wait before the goat was ready to eat because, once filled and the neck end secured, the bulbous goatskin had to have its fur removed. Nobody could tell me exactly why; this was just the way it was done. Some of the thick white hair could be pulled off in tufts, but Aldaraa produced his blowtorch to finish the job and we took it in turns playing the flame over what remained of the fleece.

An hour later we were all sitting round the low wooden table inside the main *ger* salivating at the sight of the goat beside the hearth. Blackened by the flame of the blowtorch, it had been so tightly packed with hot rocks and meat that it looked bloated, resembling an inflatable toy with its four legs splayed. Shara did the rounds with his snuff as Delger handed out bowls filled not with tea but a colourless liquid. This was *arkhi* – Mongolian vodka – distilled on the premises that afternoon by Delger herself, using a complicated series of metal bowls and tubes arranged on the stove. It was made from fermented camel's milk and consequently had a curious combination of flavours: the oily tang of hard liquor followed by a sour aftertaste of rancid milk.

Shara raised his bowl and dipped the third finger of his left hand into the alcohol. 'First, a toast to the spirits,' he declared. 'For the sky,' he flicked his finger into the air, 'the earth,' another flick towards the ground, 'and for our good health.'

This final tribute saw him touch his finger to his forehead before downing the clear liquid in one. We all followed suit with the three finger flicks and sank our camel's-milk vodka.

When we finally got to grips with dinner, it was mouth-wateringly good. Delger opened the clean-shaven goatskin with a knife down its belly, gave us all an appetizing waft of cooked meat and handed round some of the hot rocks to warm our hands on. 'This is good for health,' Aldaraa explained as we each juggled a hot, greasy stone from palm to palm. Delger piled a metal plate high with meat and we all tucked in using our hands.

Like desert nomads the world over, Mongolians don't have much in the way of vegetable matter in their diet. They seldom stay in one place long enough to cultivate the soil, and vegetables are virtually impossible to grow anyway. The onions in the goat had, I suspect, been bought in the nearby town of Biger, although in other parts of the country they do grow wild. Besides, eating large amounts of animal protein is really the only sensible way to fuel the human body during the long, hard winter.

Shara and Delger made use of every piece of any animal they slaughtered. The goat's head would be cooked later, they told me, its horns turned into knife handles, and the hooves boiled up to make glue. 'We use all parts of an animal,' Delger said, 'everything but the breath.'

As I'd expected from previous trips to the Mongolian countryside, the lifestyle of this family was seemingly little different from that led by generations of Mongolian herders before them. As Shara explained, he'd learned how to raise livestock at his father's side, as his father had before him, and so on back through the ages. The sale of camel wool enabled the family to purchase the few modern additions to their ancient way of life, such as solar panels and the occasional light bulb. Otherwise, it was much as it's ever been for Gobi desert nomads, even down to the ingenious use of hot stones.

Later that evening, after we'd shared a bowl of rich broth scooped from the inside of the goat, I outlined the rest of my journey through the Gobi to Shara and Delger. When I told them about the Badain Jaran, I asked Shara if he could give me any advice for when I got to the world's largest sand dunes. 'Eat lots of meat,' he told me.

III

Chingis Khan has had a bad press in recent times. Ask anyone to tell you what they know about the greatest Mongolian ever to ride out of the steppes and I bet they mention atrocities at some point. Certainly there are some horrific stories of the death and destruction wrought by Chingis – or Ghengis, as older translations have him – and his hordes of nomadic horse-men, but his more positive achievements tend to be subsumed beneath these tales of carnage. Let's face it, conquering the largest empire the world has ever known was probably quite difficult to do in the thirteenth century without employing a few bloodthirsty tactics.

But after Chingis had ridden roughshod over an area that stretched from the Black Sea to the Pacific Ocean, the fact that most of Eurasia was under his control must have been good for trade. Well, maybe. Opinion among the experts is divided on whether travel along the Silk Road was easier for the average merchant during the so-called Pax Mongolica. Those in favour point out that the first direct contacts between Europe and China occurred during the Mongol period. This was also the time when cobalt from Persia first arrived in China, an import that transformed Chinese ceramics. The use of cobalt-blue pigment produced an intensity of colour never seen before. The blue and white porcelain of the Ming dynasty in the fourteenth and fifteenth centuries is widely acknowledged to be the pinnacle of human achievement in ceramics.

Those who doubt the importance of Mongol unity to transcontinental trade relations highlight other factors. The Mongols were good at fighting among themselves, so the Pax Mongolica was not quite as peaceful as it sounds. There was also the little matter of a whole string of trading posts along the Silk Road having been razed to the ground in the Khan's wake.

As one biographer of Chingis Khan has suggested, in the early years of their rise to power under the great man, the Mongols didn't really understand what a town was for. All they knew was to ransack and destroy it, and massacre its inhabitants. But one thing the men from the steppes did appreciate was the importance of communications, and in this respect Chingis set about organizing his empire with outstanding proficiency. A good communications system was of vital importance in the successful administration of such a vast territory, so one was quickly set up, for both the rapid dispersal of commands and the speedy reception of news of impending trouble. An official who travelled on the imperial roads of the Mongol Empire was issued with a *paiza*, a document that detailed who he was and what rank he held. This certificate, which entitled the traveller to accommodation and assistance according to his status, was the forerunner of today's passport.

Among those holding *paizas* were members of the system established to keep Chingis Khan in touch with developments in the far-flung corners of his empire: a mounted courier service known as *yam*. Staging posts were established along the *yam* routes where riders could obtain fresh horses, food and rest. For particularly urgent messages, riders announced their arrival by ringing a bell, so that a new mount could be made ready quickly. In this way, they could cover three hundred kilometres in a day and some couriers would ride an incredible two thousand kilometres with only short pauses for rest. To do this they wrapped themselves tightly in strips of silk to prevent their internal organs shaking, which might otherwise have resulted in their death. This meant, however, that these elite riders could not eat en route.

To what extent the *yam* facilitated trade remains a moot point, but its effectiveness as a means of communication is unquestionable. To give an idea of how efficient it was, I remember comparing the length of time it took for a postcard sent by a fellow student, of Hungarian origin, with whom I spent most of my time in Ulan Bator in 1987, to arrive at his grandmother's flat in Budapest – the comparison was apt, given that Hungary was effectively part of the Soviet Empire at the time. The distance between Ulan Bator and Budapest is about eight thousand kilometres. Riding at three hundred a day, Chingis Khan's elite *yam* couriers could have delivered the message in twenty-seven days, just short of four weeks. The postcard, we later discovered, had taken six weeks to arrive by airmail.

I repeated the exercise on this trip: I asked my mother in England to note the date she received a postcard I sent her from Ulan Bator. This time it took four weeks. If the *yam* had stretched that far, some eleven thousand kilometres, it would have been delivered in just over five weeks. It has taken humanity nearly eight hundred years to improve on the system set up by Chingis Khan.

The lynchpin of this exceptional feat of organization was, of course, the horse. Mongolians are inextricably linked with horses. The time I spent with Shara in the Gobi had shown me that the camel is a better all-round bet in a desert but, given the choice, all Mongolians would prefer a horse. It was their mastery of the horse, the supreme animal of the nomads, that enabled them to take control of their enormous empire. Equestrian hunting skills learned from the very earliest age were turned to devastating advantage to create a rampaging cavalry.

Marco Polo, whose Silk Road journey took him to the court of Kublai Khan, Chingis' grandson, was very taken with the Mongolians' skill on horseback, pointing out that, when necessary, they could even shoot arrows backwards while in full flight. Men were so attuned to life with their mounts that they could survive for a month on mare's milk. During campaigns, they might not dismount for two days, sleeping in the saddle while their horses grazed. It was this amazing expertise, combined with exceptional endurance, Polo rightly surmised, that enabled them to subdue virtually the entire known world at the time.

Horse-riding is still a basic skill for virtually all Mongolians, and horse-racing remains one of the most popular national sports. The horse is central to the national identity, and it was the search for a particularly special type of horse that provided the impetus for the next leg of my Gobi journey.

I was heading south towards a nature reserve called the Great Gobi Strictly Protected Area. This reserve is, in fact, divided into two separate parts, cleverly named Gobi A and Gobi B, both on the border with China. It was the more remote of the two, Gobi B situated in the area known as Dzungaria, that I was travelling towards and, as ever, I was doing so in Aldaraa's sidecar.

I was off to see the *takhi*, or Przewalski's horse, the last wild relative of the domestic animal found today across the globe. The story of the *takhi* is a sad one with a potentially happy ending. It was first discovered scientifically in the spring of 1879 by a Russian soldier and explorer named Nikolai Przewalski, who was shown it by some local hunters. But it was Przewalski, a former geography teacher who had become a seasoned Asian traveller, who realized its significance as possibly one of the few wild strains of horse left on the planet.

Despite the excitement generated at the time by Przewalski's find, the *takhi* declined steadily in numbers throughout the twentieth century, driven into ever more remote regions by increasing human populations. From once being widespread across the steppe and forest regions of Central Asia and Eastern Europe, the last sightings of *takhi* in the wild were made in the 1960s in the Dzungarian Gobi. That might have been it, but for the efforts of a few conservationists who have in recent times been trying to reintroduce the *takhi* to its natural habitat using animals kept in zoos and private parks around the world.

Two reintroduction programmes operate in Mongolia, but

the one I had chosen to visit was located in the very area where this species' last free individual was seen alive nearly forty years before. They began air-freighting *takhi* from zoos in Europe to Gobi B for reintroduction in 1992, while the project's current director was still at school. Ganbaatar, a sturdy young man who had studied biology at university in Ulan Bator, installed Aldaraa and me in one of the project's *gers* and gave us a brief tour of the operation at Takhin Tal, the Plain of Przewalski's Horse.

Captive horses had been brought to Takhin Tal almost every year since 1992, Ganbaatar explained. They started off in a large corral where they were fed hay, checked by a vet, and kept under observation until it was thought they could cope on their own. Transforming a creature born and raised in a zoo into a wild animal was a lengthy process, he continued. We were standing beside a huge haystack on the edge of the corral, looking through the fence. A horse might stay in this enclosure for several years before being released, Ganbaatar told me. It was a big corral, but it wasn't the vast open spaces of the Gobi.

I was straining to spot one of these fabled beasts through the wire mesh; the corral extended so far into the distance that I couldn't see any outlying stretches of fence. The enclosed space was a huge area of typical Gobi: a dry, dusty plain with a few tufts of grass and a liberal covering of stones. Other than this, I could see nothing.

Ganbaatar raised the binoculars he wore round his neck and scanned the arid landscape in front of us. 'There,' he said eventually. He handed them to me, and I could just make out a small group of horses, so far off that they were little more than specks.

'And once you release them, is that it,' I asked, still trying to discern some detail in the group we'd spotted, 'or do you continue to monitor their progress?'

'We maintain observations,' Ganbaatar replied. 'Often at the start they keep returning here because they know they can find food by the corral, so we have to drive them away. Even when they no longer return, we do regular surveys to assess their adaptation to the wild.'

Deciding just when a captive-bred population can truly be said to be wild is, in part, a matter of expert opinion. But reintroduced *takhi* had successfully bred here in the Gobi too, and many of the sixty-odd free-ranging animals that Ganbaatar kept an eye on had been born and raised in the wilds of the Gobi B nature reserve.

Reproducing in the wild sounded like a significant step to me. 'Yes,' said Ganbaatar, 'but even so, sometimes if I see some *takhi* who aren't doing well – in a bad winter, for example, when food is short – I take a bale of hay to them to help them through.'

This sort of assistance, though vital for the continued well-being of the released animals, still meant some reliance, however small, on human help. So were there any *takhi* in the Gobi that he considered to be truly wild, I wondered?

'There is one stallion, Pas we call him, who is the best adapted to life in the wild. He has his harem and he is very good at protecting his foals from attack by wolves. Pas is the closest we have to a truly wild *takhi*.'

'And what are the chances of my seeing Pas and his group?' I asked, finally giving up trying to glean any more details from the specks on the horizon.

Ganbaatar pondered. 'We can try,' he said. 'Last time I saw him he was very far from here. That was about ten days ago. He moves over a very wide area, but we can try.'

The following morning we set off in search of Pas in an old Russian Uaz jeep. Ganbaatar had his telescope with him and one of the park rangers was nursing a telemetry device on his lap. Some of the *takhi* are routinely fitted with radio collars to help Ganbaatar and his colleagues find them when they need to. Other *takhi* have satellite tracking devices, but ironically these can only be monitored from the project's head-quarters in Germany. Sometimes, Ganbaatar told me, he had to email his German colleagues to ask them where the horses were.

We bumped along a rough trail for half an hour before coming to a ridge where a couple of *gers* had been pitched to overlook the surrounding plain. A few herders are allowed to graze their sheep in the Gobi B reserve, and their presence provided Ganbaatar with extra pairs of eyes to help him track the *takhi*.

We pulled up in front of the *gers* and all jumped out as a man emerged from one of them. Behind the *gers* was a small stone-wall enclosure where three tiny lambs were skipping about in the sunshine. A docile dog looked on. Hanging from a stick stuck in the ropes lashed to the side of the nearest *ger* were the skins of three foxes, their bushy tails nearly touching the stony ground. These were future fur hats, drying in the desert wind. As the ranger walked further up the slope with his portable aerial to check for a signal, Ganbaatar asked the man at the *ger* whether he had seen any *takhi* in the area recently.

Neither attempt to gain information was successful. After another hour of rough driving, we came upon another *ger*, also perched on a slope, splendid in its total isolation looking out across the endless desert plain. Here Ganbaatar spoke to a woman whose husband was out with his herd. Although I couldn't understand the conversation, I looked into the distance as the lady of the *ger* pointed in the direction we'd been following. Ganbaatar motioned me to accompany him as he walked up the slope to mount his telescope on its tripod.

'This woman says she saw a *takhi* herd over there a few days ago,' Ganbaatar murmured, as he scanned the horizon through the telescope. 'But I see nothing now.' The ranger had again failed to pick up a signal on his aerial, so we climbed back into the jeep and drove on.

'Anyway, the herd she saw was not Pas,' Ganbaatar said. I asked him how he could tell. 'From what she said it was too small. Pas has sixteen in his herd.'

Vantage-points like the ridges where the *gers* had been were few and far between in a landscape that was otherwise magnificently level. This was the Gobi in all its austere splendour, immense stretches of stony plain fading into a bleak horizon. In places, the rocks and stones were dotted with clumps of wispy feathergrass and stunted saxaul bushes, useful fodder for the *takhi* in winter. Elsewhere, it was just a flat desert full of stones.

The areas with vegetation were fed by springs that brought water from distant mountain ranges. Many of these springs carried surface water all year round, Ganbaatar told me, providing water as well as food for the free-ranging *takhi*. Much of the grassy area we were now careering past in the jeep also came with a blanket of snow. It wasn't deep, as far as I could see, but it provided almost total ground cover. The current winter had been relatively good from this point of view, he said. A bad winter, when the snow cover was thick, meant the horses faced difficulties in finding enough food.

It is the general scarcity of fodder and the extreme temperatures that represent the biggest challenges to *takhi* brought to the Gobi for the first time. These horses, shipped in from the relatively moderate climatic conditions of Europe, must wonder what's going on when they arrive in a place that has such a huge swing in temperature between summer and winter. The Gobi is also subject to vicious dust storms, another unfamiliar element the *takhi* must learn to cope with.

More than ten years of importing the horses to the unforgiving territory of Gobi B has shown the scientists in charge of the project that individuals over three years old have particular difficulty in adapting. They're just too set in their ways. In the first six years of reintroductions, about half of the horses that arrived when over the age of three didn't make it, while the younger horses had a much higher survival rate. Now they bring in only the younger animals.

Pas was three when he arrived at Takhin Tal. He spent four years in the enclosure, getting used to his new home, before being released into the wild. That was seven years ago, Ganbaatar told me. He'd obviously settled in pretty well. It made me wonder whether I'd ever get to see him.

We stopped on the summit of another minor ridge for Ganbaatar to set up his telescope and the ranger to brandish his aerial. A bank of hazy cloud had settled in across the sky and a stiff breeze had started to blow. I felt its icy fingers clawing at my fur hat as I stared out across the horizontal wilderness through Ganbaatar's binoculars. A few camels were quietly grazing in a cluster of what looked like saxaul bushes in the middle distance, but there was no sign of any *takhi*.

It was now some hours since we'd seen the last *ger*, and the sense of penetrating the very heart of the great desert was palpable. I once read that the Gobi is the least populated environment outside the polar ice caps. Until this point, that notion had seemed faintly ridiculous given the number of herders I'd come across in my travels. But now even these solitary, single families in their padded tents had vanished, leaving nothing but an endless sea of stones.

I'd almost given up hope by the time we spotted them. We had driven up a smooth rise studded with pebbles that glistened in the late-afternoon sunshine. I think Ganbaatar was losing hope too because he'd taken the binoculars from my lap for an initial scan when he first got out of the vehicle. 'I think he's there,' he said quietly, as he returned to the jeep for his telescope. Now I was looking through the binoculars in the direction he indicated. It took me a while before I could make out the distant specks because they were hardly moving. They were just standing in the snow, acting like tiny models of horses from a bygone age.

Ganbaatar was counting aloud as he clutched the top of the tripod, peering through his telescope. 'Yes,' he said firmly, 'sixteen *takhi*. This is Pas. I think we should get closer.'

An almost tangible atmosphere of excitement materialized in the jeep as we drove down the stony rise and entered the plain. Being level with the *takhi* meant they disappeared from view for twenty minutes, obscured by slight undulations in the plain, and I found myself anxiously hoping that they wouldn't get wind of our approach and move away. If they did that, my quest would probably be over, since following them would doubtless be construed as a chase and the whole point of these *takhi* being here was to minimize human contact.

The driver slowed. The terrain had become particularly bumpy. Ganbaatar, leaning across me to peer out of my side window, ordered a stop. He got out of the vehicle, stepped forward to the bonnet, and leaned on it to steady his binoculars. Pas and his herd were standing some three or four hundred metres away, apparently knee-deep in snow.

I joined Ganbaatar and we took turns in staring at the horses through his binoculars. They were small, stocky creatures, their coats russet and golden brown. I wanted to know which was Pas. 'The one off to the far right,' Ganbaatar whispered. I slowly swept the binoculars that way and spotted him, slightly removed from the main body of the herd, standing guard over his harem. 'Probably we can go a bit closer,' Ganbaatar told me, so we left the vehicle and walked slowly towards the primitive herd.

The going was uneven, the *takhi* having taken up position in a setting punctuated by mounds of clay sporting long, thick tufts of pallid feathergrass. Between the mounds the snow was more than ten centimetres deep. The clay sparkled in the light of the setting sun but somehow the sparkle didn't look like ice so I bent to see what caused this glittering terrain. Licking my finger, I brushed it over the soil and tasted the residue. It was very salty.

We were perhaps two hundred metres from the herd, which remained undisturbed. The horses continued just standing there, the tableau broken occasionally as one bent its head to nibble some grass. Ganbaatar and I stopped in the lee of one of the salt mounds and watched.

The *takhi* had large heads with small, almost delicate ears, and a mane that seemed to be bristly, standing erect like a donkey's. They looked like horses but at the same time they didn't: they were horse-like creatures. Compared to the horses I knew, they didn't seem quite right – in the way that a zebra is not quite shaped like a domestic horse. These beasts looked like prehistoric cave paintings of horses.

Among the feathergrass the air was still, not even the suspicion of a breeze. Up above, the bright blue sky offered just the hint of a cloud bank on the mountainous horizon. As the sun continued its descent, its rays lit up the grass so that it shone like brilliant yellow straw. And throughout the time we watched, Pas stood a little off to one side of the herd. He was erect and alert, like a soldier on sentry duty, the world's wildest horse, back in the Gobi where he belonged.

IV

Turpan is set in a large depression renowned throughout China and beyond as the purveyor of the finest grapes and raisins. They come with and without seeds in dozens of different hues. Turpan has green ones and black ones, pink ones and white ones; chubby and slight varieties, elongated 'mare's nipples' and seedless 'green pearls of China'. They say they have literally hundreds of different types.

And it doesn't end there because although famed above all for its grapes, the lush oasis teems with all sorts of other produce. It's a green island in a stony wilderness, a luxuriant haven in an otherwise aching void. They have mulberry trees and peach trees, apricots and apples, pomegranates and pears, figs and walnuts, not to mention melons galore. In summer it's the 'orchard of a hundred fruits'; in spring it's the 'garden of a hundred flowers'.

They enjoy making statements like that in China, but arrive in February and it's not quite so idyllic. The trees have shed their leaves, the vines have been buried to protect them from the frost and the whole place is pervaded by a feeling of wintry slumber. But it's still a thriving oasis and the contrast with what I'd seen on my trip so far was stark.

In the Mongolian Gobi, I'd grown accustomed to a nomadic population spread so thinly across the desert scene that you could travel for hours and not see a soul. The vagaries of the climate meant that only the mobile could survive because resources were so sparse. Cultivation was impossible, so tending hardy livestock was the only viable way of life, and when the animals needed new pasture you had to dismantle your house and move to keep up with them. But here in the Turpan Depression was an oasis teeming with people all engaged in settled agriculture and living in solid, mud-brick dwellings.

The one factor that made this alternative existence possible was water. Most of the Gobi forces people to adapt to its harsh physical geography, but here the inhabitants had taken the opposing view: they had adapted nature to make it do their bidding. They'd done this by bringing water from the surrounding mountains and all the evidence suggested they'd made a pretty good fist of it.

I was walking across a dusty gravel plain outside the city. It looked like all the other dusty gravel plains I'd seen so far, but with one exception. It was peppered with mounds of earth. Dozens of them. Among the rocks and the dust and the piles of dirt there was not a blade of grass to be seen. On the surface, it was as arid a stretch of desert as any you might hope to see. But down below it was a different story. I was about to get first-hand experience of how Turpan came into being.

The earth mounds that marched in lines across the plain were surface echoes of underground channels that carried water from the foothills of the nearby Flaming mountains to farmland lower down in the Turpan Depression. I could trace the route of each subterranean passageway, known as a *karez*, on the ground surface because at regular intervals along its length vertical shafts had been sunk to allow access for cleaning and maintenance. The entrances to the shafts were readily visible because they were surrounded by mounds of excavated earth.

I was trudging towards a mound with my interpreter, a young woman named Amina. Although her home town of Turpan is only about four hundred kilometres from the spot where I'd finally laid eyes on Pas and his harem, it had taken me the best part of a week to travel there. For political reasons, my route had not been a direct one. You may only cross between Mongolia and China overland, if you're a foreigner, at a few designated border posts, none of which is anywhere near the Gobi B nature reserve. Having considered my options, I soon came to the conclusion that the most efficient route between the two places was to return to Ulan Bator, fly to Beijing and then take an internal flight to Xinjiang, the autonomous region of north-western China. So, instead of a four hundred kilometre drive, I was forced to take a near-five thousand kilometre detour.

I'd hooked up with Amina through a quirk of Chinese bureaucracy. I'd been advised to arrange my trip to China through official channels (given the restricted status of Badain Jaran, my ultimate destination) and had been assigned an interpreter who usually worked for a company that built high-ways. I suspect that Amina had been appointed to the job because someone along the chain of command had seen mention of the Silk Road on my application.

We had come here to see some *karez* cleaners in action and we clambered up the side of a mound to the top where it sank a little in the middle like a mini-crater. Two men were scraping away earth with shovels to reveal three large concrete slabs laid side by side.

'Stop falling in,' Amina announced. I wasn't sure what she was getting at. 'Cover to stop things falling in,' she explained, pointing at the slabs.

With considerable effort, the two men manhandled one of them to one side to reveal a dark opening. They proceeded to remove the other two slabs, along with the thick tree-trunks they'd been resting on, to leave a large hole in the ground a metre or so in diameter.

I stepped closer to the hole to look down into it; the man nearest me took my arm to steady me. He was small and smiling, dressed in an old blazer and pink woollen scarf – the only splash of colour in the grey landscape. Peering carefully into the hole, I could see that after just a few metres, the opening was swallowed by darkness. I tried to listen for the tell-tale sound of flowing water, but could hear nothing. It was impossible to tell how much further down the hole continued into the darkness before reaching water.

'How deep is it?' I asked.

'Fifty metres.'

The small man with the pink scarf grabbed a stone, stretched his hand out over the middle of the hole, and let the stone drop. We all held still and waited. It seemed like a long time before I heard a very distant plop.

'Fifty metres,' Amina said again.

Karez have been bringing water down into the Turpan Depression for at least two thousand years. Meltwater from the mountains runs off the solid rock and accumulates inside great fans of sediment that spew forth to link the foothills with the surrounding plain. A *karez* taps the water in these aquifers and conveys it through the underground passageway to lower-elevation farmland. Being virtually all underground, it reduces the amount of water lost to evaporation. The flow of water through the gently-sloping *karez* tunnel occurs entirely thanks to the force of gravity, so there is no need for pumps.

Nobody is entirely sure how the technology developed in the Turpan area, but written records dating back to the seventh century BC leave little doubt that the technique originated in Persia, where the underground channels are known as *qanat*. It seems most likely therefore that the technology moved north and east from Persia along the Silk Road to Turpan.

This easternmost limit of underground water-carriers was also marked by an ethnic divide. In leaving Mongolia and entering this region of China I had stepped into the world of the Uighurs; I had left an outpost of Buddhism and arrived in the land of Islam. The faces of the man in the pink scarf and his colleague, and indeed that of Amina herself, all suggested that their roots lay somewhere in the Middle East. They could even have passed for Turks or Romanians.

The use of this Persian technology here in northwestern China had established a string of oases that enabled travellers along the Silk Road to cross the barren desert, from one lush stopping point to the next. Indeed, the Silk Road owed its existence to the chain of oases like this one. I had, however, been a little thrown when Amina blithely stated that her company had built the Silk Road. The comment had stopped me in my tracks for a moment, conjuring up visions of a centuries-old concern, until further questioning led to Amina's disclosure that it had recently resurfaced the road between Turpan and nearby Urumchi, a modern highway that follows the course of a branch of the old Silk Road into Kazakhstan.

I looked up at the distant mountains. They were rugged and grey and deeply incised, their gullies the result of hundreds of centuries of water flowing down into their hidden aquifers. In one sense, the mountains of Central Asia, like the deserts, are obstacles on the Silk Road. They are great physical barriers that enforce laborious detours round their lofty peaks. But in another, equally real sense they are a source of life. Mountains provide water and without water there can be no fertile oases.

The *karez* cleaners were becoming animated and Amina was doing her best to translate. 'He says you go deep and try,' she told me.

At first I didn't understand. 'Yes, yes,' Amina insisted. She looked at me as if I was behaving like a particularly stupid child. Pink-scarf man was smiling and nodding and gesturing vigorously into the hole. His colleague was doing the same. 'Everyone wants you go down,' Amina said.

My bowels felt suddenly unsafe. 'Down there? Inside the *karez*?'

All three nodded enthusiastically and did some more pointing. Evidently they thought it was an excellent idea.

I didn't. I don't like heights and this fifty-metre hole was a great height in reverse. I didn't want to go underground either.

'I'd like to watch these guys do their work, but I don't need to go down there myself. I can imagine what it's like.'

My concerns were totally lost on Amina. 'OK, good, you go down now with this man.' She gestured to the man without the pink scarf. He was still smiling at me from beneath a flat cap. 'His name Ruper.'

Ruper held out his hand. I knew that if I shook it, I would be agreeing to the descent, but I couldn't refuse. Pink-scarf man slapped me on the back. Both of them seemed delighted to have an apprentice for the day.

'Tractor coming now,' Amina declared, 'put you down.' She had turned towards the distant sound of an engine, and I saw a small tractor trundling across the plain towards us. As it drew nearer I could see that it was pulling a trailer on which was mounted a strange metal contraption.

This was dragged into place over the shaft's opening and fitted with a pulley over which a rope was fed to dangle above the hole. It had a length of wood tied to the end on which the *karez* cleaner sits; the other end being attached to the tractor. When all was in order, the tractor would drive slowly towards the hole, feeding the rope and cleaner – and in this case, me – into the *karez*.

Ruper and I had each been handed a pair of waders by the tractor driver. It suddenly struck me that I had no idea how much water there was in the underground passageway. I didn't know whether it was a small stream or like the Grand Canal.

'How deep is the water?' I asked, as I struggled reluctantly into the legs of the waders.

'Water only,' Amina assured me.

'Yes, but how deep is it?'

Amina's brow furrowed. She was thinking. I assumed she was trying to remember the appropriate English word. 'Pardon?' She asked eventually.

'The water in the *karez*,' I said slowly, 'how *deep* is it?'

'Oh!' she cried. 'Yes, yes.' Then she paused. 'Not deep,' she said shaking her head without much conviction. I wasn't convinced that Amina knew what she was talking about, so I asked her to consult Ruper or one of his colleagues. She seemed baffled by my insistence, but turned to ask him. After a lengthy exchange, she turned back to me. 'Not deep,' she said again.

It was obviously the only answer I was going to get.

Still against my better judgement, I was led to the rope dangling over the large hole and sat on the piece of wood tied to its end. There had been a disturbing frenzy of activity when the tractor first arrived, but I'd been impressed by the length of time everyone had taken to check the rope.

Ruper was giving me some last-minute instructions. 'Hold tight here,' Amina translated, as his hands closed over mine on the rope. 'Cross your legs, so not falling. And don't touch sides of hole. Are you ready, Nick?' she asked finally. I supposed I was. Someone called to the tractor driver, who was sitting at the controls of his machine. To me, he seemed a very long way away, and that was how far I was about to descend.

'Be careful,' Amina called, rather more urgently than I liked, as I was slowly lowered into the bowels of the earth.

The first thing I registered was that the rocks strewn across the arid plain continued down through the soil, yet this was but a passing thought before my glasses misted up. After descending just a few metres, the air in the hole felt warm, which surprised me. It was also becoming increasingly fuggy. This really was like being winched down into purgatory.

The rope was spinning gently as I sank lower into the ground, which wasn't a particularly pleasant sensation. My foot struck the side of the hole, sending a shower of earth and pebbles down into the abyss. I heard the debris cascading below me, followed by the distant sprinkling sound of its fall on water.

The sunshine above had all but gone and I was comforted by the light from a head torch – not that I could see much, thanks to the condensation. Mind you, peering over the top of my glasses just confirmed that there wasn't a great deal to see. Just a wall of dirt slowly slipping past me.

I suppose anyone who goes underground and can see that ground all around must consider the possibility of collapse. The thought crossed my mind as I watched all this earth pass me by. It was an unnerving prospect.

The sound of the tractor had all but disappeared too, leaving just the noise of my thumping heart to keep me company, which didn't do a lot to calm my nerves. Then I realized that there was another sound: the unmistakable trickle of water.

I stopped descending. Far above me there was a cry. It was Amina, and I think she was asking if I was OK. I shouted, 'Yes,' which my beleaguered self-esteem persuaded me was a justifiable lie. I looked down. Just below my feet was a small river.

I put my foot against the earth wall and managed to pull the piece of wood from between my legs, enabling me to step down into the water. It was warm and came up to my knees.

I was standing in a passageway. The simple fact that I was able to stand upright was a sort of surprise for a start. The roof of the cavern was well above my head, and its width was greater than my arm span.

There was another call from above: they wanted to know whether they could retract the rope, so I shouted up that they should. As it disappeared, I moved away from my position beneath the shaft. Another surprise was how fast the water was flowing. Underneath the shaft, I'd been standing in a pool, but as soon as I waded into the passageway proper, where the channel narrowed, the water swirled round my legs with some force. And as I stood there, in that ancient subterranean public works, I realized that I no longer felt so anxious. It was dark and dank, but the passage wasn't nearly as constraining as I'd feared. There was still the little matter of a few thousand tons of earth right over my head, but considering how long ago these passageways had been dug, I persuaded myself that they were unlikely to collapse right now.

Behind me, as I stared into the darkness, I heard a gentle fall of earth announcing Ruper's arrival. He nodded in greeting and gave me his big moustachioed grin. The rope disappeared again, soon to reappear with two wicker baskets and a shovel. Ruper untied the equipment and we set to.

In cross-section, the *karez* was shaped like a giant keyhole, with the water flowing along the narrow section at the bottom. Our cleaning activities were focused on the banks where, particularly below the shaft, fallen rocks and loose material were perched precariously. As we shovelled this debris into the baskets, Ruper made clear to me that we should not stand immediately below the shaft in case of further rockfalls.

When he had cleaned the area, dispatched the full baskets to the surface and received them back empty, Ruper led the way along one of the channels. I could see by the light of my head torch that for the most part it was clear of fallen material. The gently sloping clay banks were smooth, perhaps worn so by the passage of water at some previous peak time. I could make out a groove in the passage walls, suggesting that at one time the *karez* had been filled to the height of my shoulders.

We waded upstream for perhaps thirty metres before the passageway opened out again and Ruper pointed upward. The beam of my torch picked out another service shaft, only this one was closed off at the top. Lying on the bank to my left was a large concrete slab, like the ones I'd seen Ruper and Pink Scarf remove at the top of the shaft we'd descended. It must have fallen in and I hoped there hadn't been a *karez* cleaner down here at the time because it would easily have killed him. Ruper started clearing dirt from the banks and filling one of our baskets.

We shovelled dirt and rocks like this below three shafts and after perhaps an hour Ruper indicated that our task was complete. Then came a moment I'd put off thinking about. While pulling on our waders, Amina had suggested I might like to follow the entire course of the *karez* to where it emerged lower down in the Turpan Depression. Ruper was now indicating that I should trudge off down the tunnel while he exited via the shaft.

I paused. Ruper was wedging the wood between his legs,

preparing to leave. Did I really want to do this? He hollered up the shaft for them to winch him up. Unable to decide, I just stood and watched as he disappeared. My inaction seemed to indicate that I'd reached a decision, so I turned away from the tiny patch of light and began to make my way downstream.

Exactly why was unclear even to me. Since embarking on the series of journeys that has taken me to numerous extreme parts of the planet, I've found myself in several similar potentially dangerous situations. I'd jumped naked into a hole in an icy river in Siberia in winter and taken part in a kind of football match in Ethiopia where the other players had turned up carrying Kalashnikovs and very long knives. In New Guinea I'd climbed to a treehouse thirty-five metres high, despite my acute fear of heights. In each case, after the event I've been very glad to have done these things, but beforehand I've been uncertain as to the wisdom of the idea. Some might suggest that it's all due to a primordial desire to prove my manliness, but I'm not so sure. I think it's more to do with my realization of the importance of first-hand experience. Geography, as a subject in school and university, emphasizes the value of getting out and seeing things in the flesh. Reading about *karez* in books can never be as informative as seeing one for real, and even talking to a *karez* cleaner like Ruper was second-best to actually helping the guy shovel dirt fifty metres below ground.

So here I was, attempting to push the worries to the back of my mind, about to walk the entire length of one of these underground waterways. When I'd asked Amina how long a walk it might be, she'd said about 30 minutes. I'd insisted on her asking Ruper's opinion on this matter, and he'd confirmed the time. It would be half an hour before I saw daylight again.

There are around a thousand *karez* in the Turpan area, with a total length of about five thousand kilometres. Each tunnel varies in length from two or three kilometres to twenty. I assumed that half an hour meant I was in one of the shorter versions.

To start with, the tunnel was fairly wide but it narrowed progressively before opening up again beneath the next shaft. I felt a sort of thrill at being alone in the darkness, and there was something comforting about the incessant sound of running water. As I waded I marvelled at this extraordinary feat of engineering, five thousand kilometres of underground tunnels all dug by hand.

Beyond the shaft, the *karez* narrowed again and I found myself having to walk sideways, my bottom brushing against the damp clay bank. I came to a bend, the first I'd encountered. It ended in a sharp turn, which unnerved me. I stopped just beyond it and shone my torch ahead. The *karez* appeared to narrow further and for a terrible moment I thought I wouldn't get through it. I took another few steps forward, the water rushing past my legs. I thought I could probably just squeeze through, but I also reckoned that this was probably a key moment. Was it too late to turn back? I tried to work out how long I'd already been wading. Stupidly, I hadn't checked my wristwatch when Ruper left me so I could only guess. Would Amina and the others have closed the shaft I'd come down?

Something inside me told me to run, but wedged between the two clay walls meant this wasn't an option. In either direction. I took some more steps forward and my torch indicated that the squeeze would not last long. Just beyond, I saw the tunnel widening once more. Sideways, I felt the walls press in against me as I edged forward, and a wave of relief washed over me as I thrust myself out of the constriction. The feeling of relief was temporary because almost immediately something much worse happened.

A loud splash exploded in front of me and water splattered my face. My torch beam indicated that I was approaching the bottom of another shaft, which was closed off, as expected. A split second before the splash I'd heard the faint sound of disturbed mud, but I had no idea where the debris had come from. All I understood was the shock of an unexpected splash, and it was obviously a sizeable one because I felt droplets of water splatter my face.

The trauma of the moment froze me. I played my torch beam over the roof above to see if the *karez* had any more bombshells in store. I saw nothing unusual. I couldn't even make out where this fall had come from. But I was well and truly spooked. After one final quick check I plunged on through the water to cross the splash point and put it well behind me. All of a sudden I really didn't want to be there.

Running was impossible in all this water, but I waded as fast as I could, eager to leave the confines of the tunnel. It crossed my mind that paddling in a *karez* was not really what you wanted to be doing during an earthquake. Didn't they have earthquakes in this part of China, I wondered. I couldn't remember for sure.

I had to stoop along one section where the roof was decidedly low, but I wasn't thinking about getting stuck now. I just wanted to get out as quickly as possible. I slipped, and nearly fell headlong, plunging my hand into the water to steady myself. I've never had those nightmares about running away from something terrible through treacle, but I imagined that this was what it would be like. I wasn't panicking, I assured myself, but I was pretty close. All I needed to do was keep going. Wade hard and keep going. It couldn't be that far now.

I came to the end of a bend and saw a distant light. I told myself not to get excited. Maybe this was the end of the tunnel, but then again maybe it wasn't. I sensed that the air had cooled somewhat. This was consistent with the scrap of light potentially being the tunnel's opening, and that was growing bigger all the time.

There were desiccated chunks of fallen mud on the banks now, but I didn't concentrate on them. I just kept my eye on the light ahead of me. Then I stopped. There was something peculiar about the light. It was a dreary grey, but it had an unexpected texture. I waded on, not looking where I was putting my feet, my eyes fixed on the emergent grey patch. I felt a curious sensation take over my face: I was smiling. I'd realized what was odd about the light. It wasn't just light. I could see trees.

Amina, Ruper and the man with the pink scarf met me near the *karez* exit. I'd emerged into hazy sunlight and walked some distance along a stream thick with small poplar trees before I found a place where I could scramble up the steep bank.

The world here was still grey and dusty, but I'd arrived in a scene of intensive farming on its winter break. Lines of trellises marched away in every direction along neat ridges of earth where the grapevines were buried to protect them from the frost. Standing nearby in clusters were square single-storey buildings constructed from rough bricks. The bricks did not make solid walls. Every other one had been left out to give the buildings a honeycomb appearance. They were ventilated barns where bunches of grapes are hung to dry on wooden frames during the harvest. Raisins are best dried in the shade, but the gaps between the bricks allow the hot, desiccating winds that sweep through the Turpan Depression in summer to do their work.

We retired to Ruper's house for dinner. When we arrived his wife was washing carrots in a stream that ran through the courtyard, a *karez* branch that brought water right up to the doorstep. We ate cross-legged, sitting on silk drapes laid on a raised platform that took up most of a room behind a metal stove. The walls were hung with thick red carpets.

Sitting on the floor is typical throughout much of Asia and the chair is one of the more surprising imports to have passed along the Silk Road. It is thought to have arrived in the East from areas beyond Persia and Arabia, where they preferred cushions and divans, probably the Roman or Byzantine empires. In China people traditionally sat on mats, a custom still reflected in the language. The Chinese characters for Mao Zhuxi, usually translated as Chairman Mao, literally mean 'Chief Mat Person Mao', denoting his usual position on the most important mat.

Cleaning of the *karez* ran through Ruper's veins. He told me that his father and grandfather had done the job before him and his son was carrying on the family tradition. It was hard work, he agreed, as we tucked into bowls of steaming mutton and noodles, but not as hazardous as I'd thought. Ruper could remember only one incident of danger in which a colleague had fallen down a shaft and broken his legs when the rope lowering him had snapped. He couldn't remember ever having heard of a tunnel collapse.

The mutton was accompanied by hot tea and mulberry wine, and followed by bowls of dried fruit: garish strips of candied melon, figs, plums, three varieties of apricot and several types of Turpan's famous raisins. Sweet and delectable, all depended on the water brought from the mountains by the *karez*. I asked Ruper what life here would be like without this ancient technology. He paused with a wrinkled green raisin to his lips and smiled. 'Nothing,' he replied, with a slow shake of his head. 'Without the *karez*, none of this would exist.'

V

The driver stamped on the brake, turned off the ignition, and was out of the door before the jeep had rolled to a halt. 'What now?' I wondered aloud to Bruno, who sat beside me in the back of the vehicle.

He shrugged. 'Drivers are always like this in China.' We'd been going for less than half an hour since the previous stop, when the driver had jumped out to let down the tyres as we'd entered the soft sand of the dunes. 'You hire him but you mustn't think you're in charge,' Bruno went on. 'He is. He stops when he feels like it and no explanation is necessary.'

The driver had now opened the back of the jeep and Bruno leaned over to ask him what was up. The reply was curt. 'Tea break,' said Bruno.

I opened my door and got out. The delay was frustrating, but it was clearly beyond our control. Bruno was as eager as I was to get in among the world's largest sand dunes. I was back in the land of the Mongols – Inner Mongolia, as the Chinese still like to call it – and heading into the Badain Jaran. For Bruno, our trip was a return to the scene of an earlier expedition, a solo crossing of this sand desert a few years previously that had nearly ended prematurely in disaster. Having run out of water deep in the arid wilderness, Bruno had struggled to the top of a dune crest to be met by an extraordinary sight. In front of him, nestling in a depression surrounded by walls of sand, was a house. Bruno had made it to the house, inhabited by a man named Lao Gao and his family. Lao Gao had saved his life.

The driver carried a plastic bag a few steps away from the vehicle and sat down on the sand. He pulled out a parcel of newspaper, carefully unwrapped it and began to chew on a long mutton bone.

Earlier in the day, Bruno had shown me the pair of binoculars he'd brought as a present for his saviour. Lao Gao had moved to the Badain Jaran in the 1950s with his family. He was getting on in years and he found it increasingly difficult to see his camels at round-up time. The binoculars would help. It wasn't much, Bruno said, but how else do you thank someone for saving your life?

On meeting Bruno my initial reaction had been one of relief. He was an Austrian and, given his solo trek across this unforgiving region, I'd been expecting a hardy, humourless type. But although he exuded restless energy, he wasn't a masochist. When I'd asked tentatively how he thought we should make our journey into the dunes to see Lao Gao, he'd immediately suggested hiring a jeep. 'I've walked across that desert once,' he told me, 'I don't need to do it again.'

My relief on hearing this was all the more profound because it would have been well-nigh impossible for me to venture into this region without him. His importance to this leg of the trip was two-fold. He knew the sand dunes intimately and, almost as vital, he had taken care of the bureaucratic minefield that needed to be negotiated before entering them.

Bruno was still in the jeep. The dunes here on the edge of the Badain Jaran were hardly dunes at all. The terrain was made up of gently undulating sand broken by a few brittle bushes and clumps of wispy grass. On the horizon I could see larger dunes, but as yet nothing even close to the three hundred-metre giants the area was reputed to hold. We still had some way to go.

For me, this journey was the realization of a long-held dream. I first became aware of the Badain Jaran when I was a university student in the early 1980s. I was directed to read a survey of global sand deserts based on information from satellite imagery. This was back in the days when the satellite was a new tool for geographers, enabling the rapid study of landscape features across the globe. Satellites also gave researchers an insight into regions that were difficult to reach in person for political reasons. I remember leafing through the hefty tome, marvelling at the detailed maps of vast dunefields. It was like poring over an atlas of remoteness.

When I came upon the section that included the Badain Jaran, I was amazed. Here was a huge region of sand dunes covering nearly fifty thousand square kilometres at the heart of the otherwise sandless Gobi Desert. The commentary suggested that these dunes were big, some of them measured more than three hundred metres in height. This made them the biggest dunes on the planet – 'Megadunes', they called them. They were sand giants. All the rest were peanuts. And I'd never even heard of the place.

I looked above the horizon. The sun was pale and watery this morning. I'd become well acquainted with its failure to raise the temperature to anywhere near freezing, but until now it had always bathed the desert in a vivid brightness. Today it was just an insipid orange ball, its rays struggling to penetrate the haze that had taken possession of the heavens.

The sky was concealed beneath a veil of dust. Fine material like this is constantly excavated by the fierce winds of the Gobi and blown south-eastwards across China. Thousands of centuries of this wind action has laid down a thick layer of the stuff, hundreds of metres deep, in a region known as the Loess Plateau. It makes rich, fertile soil. The plateau is dubbed the Rice Bowl of China. This is another aspect of deserts that satellites have allowed us to study more easily. Immense plumes of dust from the Gobi have been tracked by satellites far beyond China, driven out over Japan and Korea and across the Pacific Ocean. Some even reaches Alaska.

Studying deserts by proxy like this is all very convenient, but it can never replace the thrill of first-hand experience. And here I was, more than twenty years after I'd first read about the Badain Jaran, standing on the perimeter of the real thing.

The driver had finished his snack. Trotting back to the jeep, he leaped into his seat, slammed the door and turned the key in the ignition all in one fluid movement. The vehicle coughed into life, and I had to hurry back as he rammed it into gear and we took off again.

The rutted track we'd been following soon petered out and we wove our way through the dunes as they slowly became larger and larger. Driving on soft sand is difficult. Knowing when to accelerate and when to take it steadily, when to change down a gear and when to employ the four-wheel drive is no easy task. Choosing a route through dunes that rise gently to a sharp crest and then suddenly plunge down at an acute angle is also a matter of skill and experience, but our driver was good. He talked himself through it, muttering the odds as we bounced along, occasionally slamming on the brakes and diving out of the door to dash up a nearby dune and survey the options in front of him.

I dozed off, despite the rough ride, and awoke some time later to see that the dunes around us had grown. We were careering across a sandscape of modest, rolling dunes, with megadunes towering above us on three sides. They were colossal. As if in celebration, the haze had cleared and the sun was shining brilliantly. I looked at Bruno. He smiled, raised his hand and gestured out of the window. 'I call them the "Himalayas of Sand",' he said.

But it wasn't until I saw the first lake that I could properly appreciate the dunes' true scale. More than a hundred and forty lakes nestle among the dunes of the Badain Jaran and they've given the desert its name. *Badain* is a Mongolian word meaning 'mysterious' or 'from the heaven', and *jaran* means 'lake'. As bodies of water, the lakes themselves are not spectacular. They tend to be shallow and not more than a few hundred metres across. But their situation, each located in a depression at the foot of a sheer precipice of sand that soars up to a megadune peak, lends them an extravagant beauty. This lake appeared from nowhere, popping up from behind a knife-sharp dune crest like a glimmering pearl. It was one of the most dramatic sights I've ever laid eyes on.

'Alashan Miao,' Bruno announced. 'At the far end of that lake, there's a small monastery, the only one in this desert. You can't see it yet, but that's where we should sleep tonight.' It would be another day or two before we reached Lao Gao's house, he added.

Although the lake was visible, getting to it wasn't easy. From our vantage point we drove down a long, steep slipface into an elongated corridor running at right angles to the direction of the lake. Directly in front of us now the dunes rose up to challenge us, a chaotic wall of sand that twisted and turned in every direction. To me, it looked too steep to drive up head-on, but that was just what the driver tried to do. He revved the engine and sped up the corridor, leaning over his steering wheel to scrutinize what lay ahead. Having picked his spot, he turned the wheel to approach the gradient in a gentle arc. Then he put his foot down and we shot up the hill.

We nearly made it. As we approached the crest, the jeep gradually slowed. The engine was screaming, and our driver crunched the gears as we came close to stopping, urging the vehicle forward and upward through the treacherous sand. Eventually, with the engine still screeching, we slowed to a stop a dozen metres from the crest. The driver kept his foot down, trying to coax a little more from his vehicle, but we just sat there, the wheels spinning in the sand, but going nowhere, until he muttered something dark and broody and took his foot off the accelerator. He flung open the door, leaned out to look at the wheels, and let the jeep roll slowly backwards down the hill.

He tried and tried again, each time at a different section along the confusion of dunes. He turned round and drove back up the opposite ridge, away from the lake, and swept round to park and stare at the sand barrier.

We all studied the obstacle, now riven with tyre marks, each set ending in a gouged mess just short of the summit. From here, I could now see that there were no obvious alternative routes. The chaotic ridge of dunes we'd been trying to scale, which peaked at no more than eighty metres above the corridor, continued up to our left towards a vast megadune. To the right, it degenerated into a more haphazard series of even steeper ridges.

'I guess we'll have to go the long way round,' I murmured, as much to myself as anyone. Bruno spoke with the driver who was transfixed by our predicament. He didn't look round, and almost shouted in response. 'He says the dunes are even worse on all the other sides of this depression where the lake is,' Bruno translated. 'This is the only way in.'

The driver kept trying. On a couple of occasions, we all jumped out to dig when our wheels buried themselves in the sand, each time agonizingly close to the summit of the ridge. After the second time, Bruno and I stayed out and trudged up to the summit to watch the vehicle, now slightly lighter, descend, circle and try again.

It was late in the afternoon when we finally gave up, unloaded what we could carry and walked the rest of the way to the Alashan Miao monastery on the edge of the lake.

★

Alashan Miao had five Buddhist monks, not all of them full-time, and only two were in residence. They were standing outside the whitewashed walls of their monastery when we arrived and didn't seem the least bit surprised to see us. The driver was the first to greet them, pulling from his trouser pocket a short sky-blue silk scarf that had previously been hanging above the rear-view mirror in his jeep. He held it stretched out in front of him in both hands, his head slightly bowed. The monks produced identical scarves and returned the gesture.

To my considerable satisfaction, I was able to go through the same procedure. I'd bought myself a similar silk scarf, only in yellow, in Mongolia, primarily to keep my neck warm, but also because it was an appropriate emblem to carry on my Silk Road journey. I'd been aware of its religious significance, but had never seen one used in Mongolia. Bruno told me later that offering the *kata*, as it's called, in greeting lends a positive note to the start of any enterprise or relationship and indicates the good intentions of the person presenting it.

The monks grinned when we outlined our predicament. They knew Lao Gao and obviously found it amusing that we'd thought we'd drive to his house. The older man said that a camel was a more reliable form of transport across the dunes, a comment that triggered the flicker of a scowl from our driver. The monk's son was a camel-herder, he told us, and could take us.

The following day we set off early from Alashan Miao with Ha Su, the herder, and three of his camels. As we skirted the lake, back the way we'd walked the previous afternoon from the stranded jeep, Ha Su told us that the monastery had been here for more than two hundred and fifty years. It had been built by a lama named Mani on his return from a trip to Tibet. The spot was auspicious, Ha Su said. Behind the monastery, a sickle-shaped curve in the crest of the great sand dune resembled the moon, while the sun rose every morning above the dunes opposite. The lake was salty, but beside the monastery a well had been sunk to reach sweet water.

It was a full day's camel ride from Alashan Miao to the edge of the sands, but Lao Gao's house was still more remote. It would take another two days to reach it. I was having trouble getting my head round the fact that people lived in this world of sand. The monks I could understand. They valued the serenity of location and lived mainly on the products of Ha Su's camels. Also they were only a day's ride from the nearest town where they could buy any extras they needed. But I still wondered why Lao Gao was living at least three days from anywhere. 'You must ask him,' was the only help I got from Bruno.

After my time with Shara and his family in Mongolia, I could recognize a healthy camel when I saw it, and Ha Su's animals were in fine fettle. Their humps were plump and erect: a telltale sign. If forage is scarce, the humps tend to sag and lean to one side. But despite their good condition, we weren't riding the camels.

We maintained a stately pace, the three of us leading the small caravan with Bruno in front. From his rucksack he had produced a pair of metal walking-sticks, rather like ski poles, which helped in the soft sand. We spent most of the morning in a continual, hard-going ascent. Within twenty minutes of starting, I could feel trickles of sweat running down my back.

I had left my *del* and fox-fur hat in Mongolia and purchased replacements on arrival in China. I was pleased with my decision because here in Inner Mongolia no one wore the traditional *del*, but my padded military-style coat was far too hot and unwieldy for this walk. I wanted to shed my synthetic fur hat too, since it was like wearing a plastic bag on my head. But having begun to swelter, I'd left it too late. Removing my hat would have been suicidal in the cold breeze. When we stopped for a breather, I slipped it off and instantly felt my skull start to freeze.

We ate lunch in a wide col high among the dunes. If we'd been in the midst of real mountains, it would have been a high-altitude pasture. It was long and relatively flat and actually fairly well covered with scrub and clumps of grass. The breeze had strengthened so we found shelter in the lee of a dune. Bruno and I helped Ha Su unload the camels and they wandered off to graze on the pallid vegetation.

The afternoon's trek was more of the same. We trudged on, up and down small dunes, the sand soft and yielding to each plod of my boot. I became jealous of Bruno, who seemed to be walking easily thanks to his sticks. Without such support, I was finding it hard work on my knees. Ha Su's gait was almost a shuffle so I tried mimicking that for a while, but found it even more exhausting.

When the wind freshened it was biting cold. It had been some time after my arrival in north-east Asia that I'd eventually adjusted my mindset to the strange combination of brilliant sunshine and severe sub-zero temperatures. The snow too had been a curiosity elsewhere in the Gobi, but here in the Badain

Jaran there was none. It was just sand. Endless, smooth, sifting sand that was torturous to walk on.

But just as I'd reach a low point, and my thoughts would turn to asking Ha Su if I could ride one of his camels, I'd stagger to the top of a dune where the sand became mysteriously firm. The wind dropped, leaving me to walk tall in the sunshine along the razor-sharp crest. I gazed with awe at my surroundings, the largest sand dunes on the planet, and felt as if I was walking on the top of the world.

We slept in the dunes that night, setting up camp on the edge of a small hollow scattered with scrawny, bone-dry shrubs that burned well in our fire. Bruno had brought two tents but Ha Su preferred to sleep outside wrapped in his coat and a heavy padded quilt. So we pitched just one, which Bruno and I shared. The wind blew harder still as the sun went down, blasting the nylon walls with flurries of sand.

It was still strong the following morning, but at least we weren't walking into it. The blast came from our left, whipping the sand against my legs and forcing me to lower the ear-flaps on my hat. The sky had disappeared again above a dusty haze. Ha Su announced that we should make it all the way to Lao Gao's house today if we kept up a steady pace.

I was surprised not to be stiff after the previous day's trek, but it was still tough going. We weren't walking particularly fast, but the tempo was relentless. Anyone could call for a brief rest – though it was usually me – yet our stops were short-lived because the loaded camels couldn't stand still for long. If we paused for more than five minutes, Ha Su had to unload them, which was a time-consuming process. My body was beginning to tire. I felt like a clockwork toy, rhythmically marching through this sea of sand. Up ahead, I could see that Bruno's sticks were his secret weapon. Four legs, it seemed, were certainly better than two.

I tried to take my mind off the monotony of my mechanical movement with some positive thinking. How pleasant it was, I told myself, to have left behind the Gobi's stones. I'd seen a lot of rocks since leaving the town of Altai in Mongolia, and I'd been intrigued to discover how useful they were when heated in a bonfire. But I'd grown bored of the featureless plains. How much better it was to be trekking among the fluid curves of the dunes. But my appreciation of this landscape was fleeting. I could feel it sapping my strength. All my energy was seeping out through my legs into the soft sand.

That afternoon was mostly uphill. When we were confronted with the largest dunes yet, two giant monoliths that blocked our way, Bruno and Ha Su paused to consider our route. 'Now we are coming to the hardest bit,' Bruno told me. 'They are very tight now, the mountains. You don't find a passage so easily.' Slowly we climbed a steep rise, keeping to a snaking sand ridge that swept up precipitously towards a col between the two peaks. Partway up, my legs had had enough. I asked Ha Su if I could ride for a bit. But he shook his head, smiled and said he was sorry. The going was too steep for his camels to carry passengers. I trudged on.

We paused again on reaching the col. The megadunes rose up to either side of us and my yearning to reach the summit of one of these monsters had waned. Bruno read my mind. 'I think to climb such a one it's quite tough, eh?'

Aldaraa, ex-paratrooper and specialist in sleeping on hot stones

The small town of Biger nestling at the foot of the Altai Mountains

Above: Shara dismantling a *ger*, the abode of the Mongolian nomad. The process takes less than half an hour

Left: The author ready to lend a hand rounding up the camels for milking

Below: Delger contemplating a dinner of goat stuffed with hot stones

Above: The contraption by which *karez* cleaners are lowered into the shaft

Right: Ruper's wife and a friend washing vegetables in a *karez* branch that brings water to the doorstep of their home in Turpan

The small monastery at Alashan Miao, a day's camel ride into the Badain Jaran

One of the Badain Jaran's many lakes nestling among the dunes

Ha Su leading his camels down into the depression where Lao Gao didn't live
Top inset: Bruno at the summit of a sand dune that was higher than the Eiffel Tower
Bottom inset: Lao Gao drawing sweet water from his well

Above: Pilgrims prostrating themselves in front of the Jokhang, Tibet's most revered Buddhist temple

Above right: Trainees participating in a question and answer session at Sera, a monastery once famous for its fighting monks

Right: Working the prayer wheels at the foot of the Potala Palace in Lhasa

Patients waiting for a consultation with the *amchi* or Tibetan doctor

The Changtang, one of the world's highest, most remote and least known regions

It certainly wasn't a mission for today. We traversed the col, the wind spraying great trails of sand from the dune crests above us, and came upon an extraordinary sight. Laid out below us in the haze, hemmed in by dramatic walls of sand, was a deep depression. In its centre was a broad ashen patch, a dried-out salt lake surrounded by what looked like hummocks of grass. A great white spiral of salt and dust corkscrewed into the air from the dry lake as Bruno stopped and pulled off his woollen mittens. He leaned on his stick and took in the view. 'Nick, this is the final countdown,' he called, against the wind. 'We don't have to go up any more, we only have to go down.' He pointed with his stick down into the distance. 'Lao Gao's house, you see it?' I couldn't make it out in the haze, but I didn't care – I was just pleased not to be going uphill any more.

We plunged down the steep incline, a good two hundred metres of sheer sand, and marched off into the depression. Bruno hurried ahead, eager to see the man who'd once saved his life. After the exhilaration of the descent, my energy levels subsided again and I was bringing up the rear when I noticed that Bruno and Ha Su had stopped, well short of Lao Gao's abode.

Bruno turned to me as I approached. 'Sorry,' he called, the word nearly carried away on the wind. I didn't know what he was talking about. 'It's not Lao Gao.' A slither of disappointment ran down my spine. 'I was so excited I thought that was it,' Bruno went on. I just stood there with my mouth open. I'd left my sense of humour some distance away, back in the dunes. Then it crossed my mind that maybe Bruno's reassurance up on the col had been a ploy to keep me going. 'You're not playing some kind of psychological game with me, I hope, Bruno.'

'No, no, you can really rely on that,' he told me, 'but for sure it is over the next hill – one hundred per cent.' It could only be another couple of kilometres, he reckoned, although for me his credibility had lost some of its shine. But however far it was, there was little alternative but to continue.

Needless to say, the next hill was more than just a hill. It turned into a series of ridges that conspired to keep us walking. Each one offered the possibility of being the last, the rim of another depression, the one where Lao Gao really lived. But every time we ascended, we were met with another undulating corridor of sand stretching into the distance. The light was failing and the temperature was falling. Bruno hurried on ahead, leaving Ha Su and me to follow in his wake.

When at long last Bruno stopped, far in front of us, and turned to wave, I didn't allow myself to get excited. We'd been walking for two days and I was both profoundly tired and past caring. 'Yes,' he shouted, punching the air. 'This time we are really here.'

Ha Su and I caught him up and looked down on another deep basin surrounded by sand. 'That must be the view of heaven,' Bruno cried, 'Lao Gao!'

The depression looked similar to the one that had just failed us, and it was very murky down there. 'Are you sure this time?' I asked Bruno. I could pick out a few skeletal trees, but I couldn't see a building of any kind.

'Definitely,' he replied.

By the time we finally reached Lao Gao's house it was dark.

Bruno started shouting as we approached, and a figure emerged from the shadowy building to peer into the gloom, trying to see who was coming. I caught a flicker of recognition on Lao Gao's face as Bruno enveloped him in his arms. It was an emotional meeting. I was just glad the guy existed.

I never received a totally satisfactory explanation of why the family had settled in the middle of nowhere. Lao Gao had arrived there as a little boy with his parents in 1957; they'd come from the province of Gansu some distance to the south. There was an irony here. Gansu is a province plastered by loess, the fertile farmland created by dust from the Gobi laid down over time. But Lao Gao and his family had made the opposite journey. They had left the productive corridor and headed for the desert itself. It didn't make sense to me. I suspected that the long arm of Chinese politics might be involved. A programme to settle the desert, perhaps, or maybe Lao Gao's parents had been exiled for some misdemeanour.

When I asked Lao Gao through Bruno why his family had moved to the Badain Jaran I was told that this was a good place to settle. 'Why?' I wondered.

'He says it's good here,' Bruno translated.

'Yes, but why here particularly?' I persisted. 'It's three or four days' walk from anywhere.' I had trouble imagining a whole Chinese family volunteering to traipse for days across this vast sand sea and suddenly deciding to stop in this spot.

'The water,' Bruno cried. 'It is good water, a very special quality, sweet water.' Even then I wasn't totally convinced, but Lao Gao was still talking. 'And also because things were bad in

Gansu province,' Bruno added finally. It struck me that things must have been pretty hard if this sandy basin had seemed like a better option.

But I'd had a tour of Lao Gao's set-up and it was impressive. He kept camels and goats which grazed the clumps of vegetation spread out across the depression as well as the grasses and shrubs that clung to the dunes, and had a sizeable patch of land on which he cultivated fruit and vegetables. There wasn't much to see in winter, but Lao Gao proudly walked us across the neat plots in his garden indicating what was grown where. There were dusty spots for cucumbers, tomatoes, melons, onions and aubergines. He even had an apple tree. The well of sweet water was on the edge of the garden. Each morning he or his daughter would fill two metal buckets and carry them back to the mud-brick house on each end of a pole balanced across the shoulders.

Lao Gao showed me proof of his green fingers in a hole in the ground between the garden and the house. He removed an old padded quilt and some slabs of rock to reveal a subterranean storehouse stuffed with last year's vegetables.

The family house was large, forming three sides of a long, walled courtyard. Just outside the wall, a set of solar panels was mounted on a stand that could be turned to follow the sun, and provided enough electricity to power light bulbs in all the rooms. Bruno told me it was easy to identify a Chinese house in Inner Mongolia because they were built with a wall like this. A Mongolian, by contrast, would never enclose his home in this way. And it was the fact that Lao Gao was a Han Chinese that made his presence here in the Badain Jaran all the more remarkable. Certainly he kept animals, like a Mongolian herder, but he had transformed his remote basin into a self-sufficient farm, producing all manner of crops from the sandy soil.

Ha Su, Bruno and I stayed for several days. One of Lao Gao's daughters and her three children, who lived in the town of Alashanyouqi outside the dunes, were visiting too, so the house was bustling. We helped out where we could, in the evening gathering around the table in the kitchen to make small dough parcels filled with minced lamb and chopped onions for dinner. I'd eaten similar fare in Mongolia, where the parcels are known as *buudz*. When a batch was ready, Lao Gao's wife ladled them into a big bowl of boiling water on the stove.

It is popularly believed that Marco Polo introduced pasta into Italy from China following his adventures along the Silk Road in the thirteenth century. But *Larousse Gastronomique* suggests otherwise, advising that the first known reference to pasta can be traced to Sicily in the Middle Ages. About a hundred years before Marco Polo was born, an Arab geographer named Al-Idrisi was commissioned to write a survey of world geography for King Roger II of Sicily. In this compendium, known as the *Book of Roger* after its sponsor, Al-Idrisi mentions that the inhabitants of the Sicilian town of Trabia made a form of pasta from hard wheat that was manufactured in large quantities for export to other regions. Whatever their true origins, the steaming parcels we ate with chopsticks out of china bowls looked very similar to ravioli.

One evening I asked Lao Gao if he ever climbed the dunes that surrounded him. He said he did when he was looking for his camels, but when I wanted to know whether he'd climbed to the very top of any of them, he smiled and shook his head.

He obviously thought this a curious question. 'I don't have to climb to the top to get a good view,' he told me. Bruno and I had been plotting an ascent of a dune from the morning after our arrival. The three we could see from Lao Gao's house were as big as any Bruno had passed on his solo trek across the Badain Jaran, but it was tricky deciding which of the three was the highest.

One afternoon, we stood on the flat roof of Lao Gao's house and surveyed the options. The nearest peak soared straight up from the depression, its towering flat slipface orientated towards the south-east. On the other side of the basin, which was perhaps a kilometre across, two further megadunes rose to scrape the more distant skies. Deciding which of these three monsters was the highest was difficult from where we stood, but eventually we plumped for the nearest dune. The two furthest might be easier to ascend, we thought, given that the slopes up to their crests would be gentler from our starting point, but the fact that climbing the nearest dune would mean going more or less straight up the slipface gave us an added impetus.

We set out to conquer the peak one afternoon, ambling across the salty terrain to the foot of the slope where we checked our altitude with a Global Positioning System. It was 1,237 metres above sea level. Then we started to climb.

The slipface is the steepest slope on a sand dune and it is aligned with the dominant wind direction. These slopes are remarkably constant in their angle all over the world, almost always between 33° and 35° to the horizontal. This is the angle of rest of individual sand grains, which cover a narrow band of particle sizes. Any larger and they are classed as gravel; if smaller, they are known as clay or dust. But the slipface that Bruno and I were intent on climbing appeared to defy the laws of physics. It was steeper.

We soon realized that going straight up a slope of at least 40° was impractical. A foot set into the sand simply resulted in a gentle cascade that brought you right back to where you had started. Even with his sticks, Bruno found it impossible, so we altered our plan to follow a sinuous ridge that snaked its way up just to one side of the enormous slipface.

The reason for the over-steep slipface is probably related to how the Badain Jaran's megadunes are thought to have grown so large. The theory is that they have reached their exceptional height due to alternating periods of relatively wet and dry climate over tens of thousands of years. During wetter phases, vegetation helps to stabilize the shifting sands, a process reinforced by the formation of crusts on the dune surface. Calcium blown on to the dunes from the area's numerous lakes mixes with rainwater to develop a hard cement. This combination of vegetation and cementation fixes the dunes, which are then covered with loose sand once more during a drier period, like the climate of today, hence gaining height. I had seen the hard crusts a few times on our walk to Lao Gao's house, exposed in places by the shifting sands. These rigid patches of cemented sand made for occasional light relief during our long trek, but on the slipface of the dune we were climbing they were nowhere to be seen, covered by soft mobile material that swallowed our legs up to the shins.

Mounting the snake ridge entailed only marginally less effort than attempting the slipface head-on, but at least it was possible. We ascended slowly, Bruno leading the way with his sticks. I found the going slightly less tiring if I placed my feet in his footprints where his feet had compacted the sand, but it was still strenuous work.

We stopped after a while to catch our breath and look out over the basin. Far below, a wisp of smoke escaped from the chimney of Lao Gao's house. Bruno checked our altitude on the GPS. It was 1,352 metres above sea level. We had passed the 100-metre mark in our climb, but when I looked up I figured we weren't even close to halfway. This was a serious megadune.

The snake ridge was getting steeper and I had to stop more frequently to get my breathing under control. The sand seemed to be getting softer too and the strain on my knees was close to unbearable. Looking up and down, it was difficult to say whether we'd passed halfway, but we were now on a level with the sand ridge on the opposite side of Lao Gao's depression. On we went. I was a clockwork toy again, plodding up a gargantuan pile of sand. I was losing strength fast and within reach of the summit crest I collapsed, gasping for breath. Bruno stopped, leaned on his sticks, and checked the GPS. We'd covered three hundred vertical metres, nearly a thousand feet. It seemed like a very significant achievement to me.

'I can see the final ridge,' Bruno puffed, shading his eyes from the sun, 'but I have to warn you it's a long way and this is the hardest part.'

The sand was the softest so far. Each step, even when I placed my feet in Bruno's footprints, resulted in a mini-avalanche. I tried Ha Su's shuffling technique, but it made no difference. Each time I moved I generated a cascade of grains and I soon discovered that I had to keep moving or I lost height. After another five minutes of incredibly hard work, I fell flat on my face and started to crawl. On all fours, progress was more manageable, but I'd been reduced to the status of a four-legged animal and I still had to stop about every ten metres to rest.

Panting hard, I began to wonder if I had the stamina to make it. I could understand why mountaineers say they got to within twenty-five metres of the summit and gave up. But now Bruno was standing on the crest and I wasn't going to let him make it alone. I delved deep and crawled another few metres, as if I were swimming the doggy paddle to the top of this bloody sand dune. I collapsed, my heart racing, and waited before edging a little closer.

As my head emerged over the crest, a blast of wind filled my eyes and mouth with sand, but I didn't care. I'd made it. Bruno was standing, still catching his breath. 'Almost there,' he called. I looked up to where he stood, gazing off towards the slightly higher peak. The crest we were on curled away to our right, climbing another few metres to the summit. Bruno started walking and I regained my feet to join him.

We tottered along the narrow crest in single file, battling against the furious wind. It sent torrents of sand streaming into the ether. It was so strong I was seriously concerned that I might lose my balance, and plunge back down the slope I'd just crawled up, but we both managed the last few metres and sank down on our haunches at the summit.

Bruno checked the GPS. Laid out all around us was the

world of sand, a mountain range of megadunes that stretched far into the distance. It took a few minutes to locate the satellites that would give us our final altitude. At last, he said '1,582 metres.' In our exhausted state, it took a little while to do the mental calculation.

'345 metres high,' I said eventually, 'about twelve hundred feet.' We'd just climbed a sand dune that was higher than the Eiffel Tower.

We made our way back along the sharp crest to stand and stare at the slipface that dropped below us. I looked at Bruno. 'I think this is probably the quickest way down.'

He grinned. 'Yes, I think so too.'

I took one last look at the peak we'd conquered and stepped into the void. Gravity grabbed me and yanked me down. My legs instantly became a blur, as I sprinted at an impossible speed just to stop myself nose-diving. I was running faster than I'd ever run before. Somewhere to my right I saw Bruno flying slightly sideways across the slipface, but I was going straight down. My heart was bursting, but I couldn't stop. It had taken us nearly four hours to climb the megadune. Our descent was closer to four minutes.

THE NAVEL OF THE UNIVERSE

I

Of all the topographical barriers to transAsian communications, Tibet is the largest. Look at a map of the continent's physical geography and it sticks out like a big purple birthmark. My focus on the benighted terrains that the Silk Road avoided meant that a visit was obvious, but I admit I was nervous about the prospect. It was the altitude that concerned me. I don't like heights, but this wasn't the source of my unease: I thought that unless I was hanging off the side of a mountain, which I wasn't intending to do, I wouldn't have much visual evidence that I'd be walking around some kilometres above sea level (an accurate prediction, as it turned out). My apprehension was based on fears of how my body might react to the thin air and lack of oxygen.

Everyone knows that Tibet is high, hence its sobriquet as 'the roof of the world'. The Tibetan plateau covers an area of nearly 2.5 million square kilometres, or about a million square miles, and averages out at around four kilometres above sea level (roughly thirteen thousand feet). At this altitude the composition of the air remains the same as at sea level, it's just that it gets thinner. In other words, the relative amounts of gases are constant (nitrogen 78 per cent, oxygen 21 per cent etc.) but there's less of everything. Oxygen is the key concern because we use the oxygen we breathe to help burn food and liberate energy to keep our bodies going.

At 3,500 metres above sea level, the oxygen content of the air is some 35 per cent lower than at sea level. As you pass 5,000 metres, the oxygen content is halved. My body, accustomed to loafing around in low-lying Britain, was starting this trip in Tibet's capital, Lhasa, which lies at about 3,600 metres. My itinerary dictated that I'd be spending a month at this height and above, peaking at 5,600 metres. Given these particulars, I knew that trouble might lie ahead.

Some years before, I'd spent a few days at high altitude in the Andes in Chile, topping out at 4,500 metres, and survived to tell the tale. I'd suffered from occasional headaches, lost my appetite and had some trouble getting to sleep at night – all classic symptoms of acute mountain sickness, or AMS as the professionals call it – but nothing really debilitating. I'd avoided some of the more unpleasant effects, such as dizziness, nausea and vomiting.

This was a good sign, or so I thought until I started reading around the issue and discovered that having been previously unaffected, or at least little affected in my case, was no guarantee for future visits to high places. Worse news came with the realization that there didn't appear to be anything much I could do in preparation.

Why one person goes down with AMS and the next doesn't is a mystery. It doesn't make an appreciable difference if you smoke, or have coronary artery disease, are pregnant, have diabetes or hypertension. Some studies suggest that those over sixty may have slightly less AMS incidence, but this wasn't much help to me. Fitness is no protection either. In fact, it may actually be a risk factor if the athletic type forges on ahead and overdoes it, since physical exertion soon after arrival at altitude may increase AMS. All I could do, it seemed, was take my chances.

Dissatisfied with this conclusion, I made an appointment to see a specialist in high-altitude illnesses in London. Dr Paul Richards was very matter-of-fact about the whole thing. He gave me a PowerPoint presentation, interweaving pretty pictures of mountains with unemotional flowcharts showing the sort of physical signs and symptoms I should look out for. All the familiar AMS symptoms were in the first flowchart, along with recommended courses of action such as painkillers, rest and stopping further ascent. Since this information was well-known to me, I didn't find it too troublesome. But when Dr Richards got to flowcharts two and three I became seriously unnerved. Unbeknown to me, routine AMS is thought to be the benign end of a spectrum that ends in something called high-altitude cerebral oedema, or HACE, a condition involving the swelling of your brain. AMS can also precede another dangerous condition, namely high-altitude pulmonary oedema, or HAPE, which appeared to result in the lungs slowly filling with fluid.

The flowcharts for HACE and HAPE looked similar to that for AMS, but with a significant difference. At the bottom of the two charts for these ailments were two boxes that had not appeared on the AMS chart. The first new box was labelled 'coma', and it came with an arrow leading to the second box, labelled 'death'.

In his summing up, Dr Richards stressed the importance of being on constant alert for the warning signs and emphasized that both HACE and HAPE were severe and potentially fatal. The only course of action open to someone who develops either of these high-altitude illnesses, he told me, is immediate descent. That would, in all likelihood, mean the end of my trip. On making my appointment to see Dr Richards, I'd been guided by the maxim that 'forewarned is forearmed'. As I left his clinic, with visions of the flowcharts' coma and death boxes still flying though my mind, I thought that perhaps I should have opted for 'ignorance is bliss'.

Dr Richards did not recommend flying straight into Lhasa but, because of time constraints, that's what I did. I teach at Oxford University and squeeze in trips such as this between terms. With a limited number of weeks at my disposal, I'd decided to take the risk. In consequence, I was expecting to be hit by the effects of acute mountain sickness and I was, so I spent the first couple of days on the roof of the world wandering the streets of Lhasa feeling groggy and a bit sorry for myself. These sentiments were exacerbated by the fact that wherever I went I was accompanied by a small gang of manual labourers making structural alterations to the inside of my head.

These men were hard at work the morning I ambled down to Barkhor Square, in the centre of the old Tibetan part of town, where I had arranged to meet Gylsang, a young physics lecturer at the Tibetan University in Lhasa who I'd been put in touch with by a friend of a friend. Gylsang had kindly agreed to show me round and had suggested I meet her in the square for an early-morning pilgrimage circuit. I'd been slightly concerned by this plan, wondering if Gylsang thought I was religious, which I'm not, but she'd just laughed on the telephone and told me not to worry. 'Anyone can do the *kora*,' she said, 'I'm not religious either.' She also said that the circuit wasn't long, 'maybe twenty minutes.' I thought I could just about manage that in my current state.

There was a bitter chill in the air as I made my way along the streets leading to the square. Most of the shops were still closed and I wasn't expecting much as I entered the wide-open plaza, but as I neared the Jokhang temple at the far end of Barkhor Square, I was met by a sea of humanity striding across my field of view from right to left. Gylsang was waiting for me beside a large incense burner, a bulbous whitewashed structure that exhaled a steady waft of fragrant vapour. 'Let's go,' she said almost immediately, and we joined the throng streaming past the temple.

The pilgrims were an extraordinary mix, sporting a variety of headgear: thick woolly hats and trilbies, skullcaps with earflap wings and bright red turbans. Most people looked as if they'd come straight from the countryside, dressed in long sheepskin coats encrusted with many years' worth of dirt. 'Some of these people travel great distances to this spot,' Gylsang said as we were carried along in the flow. 'They come here from all over Tibet.'

There were men and women, boys and girls, the old and infirm, the young and sprightly. Gnarled, elderly men ambled along on stout walking sticks, some sporting dark goggles in anticipation of the glaring sun that was yet to make an appearance above the rooftops. Young women, their silky black hair adorned with hefty jewellery – chunks of turquoise shining among pink coral, amber beads and silver filigree – walked in groups, some carrying babies strapped to their backs. These pilgrims, who looked as if they'd strolled out of the Middle Ages, were mixed with city types wearing suits, taking a quick turn round the Jokhang before going to the office, Gylsang told me. Other city-dwellers appeared to be doubling up their religious duties with walking the dog. Virtually everyone carried a small prayer wheel, a metal cylinder on a stick, that they kept constantly spinning as they walked. The perpetual parade was marked by a constant hum generated by the muttering of mantras.

I'd been happy when Gylsang had suggested we meet in Barkhor Square because I'd been keen to witness pilgrims walking the *kora* round the spiritual heart of the holy city. It made a sensible starting point for several things I wanted to do while in Tibet. In my effort to examine how life is lived on the roof of the world, I was intending to spend some time with the nomads who roam the plateau, people living at altitudes as high or higher than any other humans in the world, before joining a pilgrimage round a sacred mountain in the south-west of the country.

My idea of visiting Mount Kailas came in two connected parts. First, was its peculiar geographical status as the fountainhead of four great South Asian rivers. The second lay in the mountain's pivotal position as an object of worship for adherents to four major religions. Buddhists, Hindus, Jains and followers of the Bön religion (Tibet's ancient faith, which hasn't been totally supplanted by Buddhism) all make pilgrimages to Mount Kailas. I was attracted by the irony that while commercial travellers actively avoid such topographical obstacles, pious explorers seek it out. The Mount Kailas *kora* was 52 kilometres in length, most of it at 5,000 metres and above, so the Barkhor circuit, which is less than a kilometre, would be a gentle introduction to the art of devotional exercise.

It was, and watching Lhasa office-workers mingling with pilgrims from the countryside was not the only surprise the Barkhor *kora* had to offer. I was also rather taken aback by the curious blend of religious zeal and everyday commerce. All along the route that took us through the back streets encircling the Jokhang, the most revered Buddhist temple in Tibet, small shops and stalls selling merchandise, religious and otherwise, were opening for business. Pilgrims would break their purposeful stride to linger over brightly-coloured silk prayer scarves or a display of gleaming daggers. They stepped aside from the flow of humanity to finger the goods, some obviously just browsing, others clearly intent on making a purchase. Their prayer wheels were kept constantly whirling, but I was still surprised at how effortlessly the devout could switch between their religious commitments and the opportunity to conduct a commercial transaction.

Gylsang and I had been ambling so that I could take in the crowd, and I paused beside a man who was setting up his stall, laying out strings of multi-coloured prayer flags on a small wooden table. The strips of cloth were printed with Buddhist scriptures. I'd already seen them fluttering in the breeze, releasing their prayers to the heavens, strung between the flat roofs of buildings all over the Tibetan part of town – they were mostly absent from the larger Chinese sectors. The colours were symbolic, Gylsang said. 'Red represents fire, green is wood, yellow the earth, blue is water, and white is metal.' She paused. 'A particular metal,' she added as her brow furrowed in thought. 'Iron,' she said finally.

A tall man wearing pink coral earrings stopped beside the stall and engaged its proprietor in brief conversation. The pilgrim's jet-black hair was wound round his head and kept in place by a length of bright red cloth like an open turban. He passed the prayer wheel he was spinning from his right hand to his left so that he could thrust his right hand into the front of his coat. He brought out a wad of grubby banknotes, peeled off a couple with his thumb and handed them to the stall-holder, who folded up a length of prayer flags and popped them into a plastic bag. The pilgrim took the bag, slipped it inside the front of his coat and walked off, snapping back into *kora* mode.

By the time we returned to Barkhor Square, the sun had finally shown its face above the city's skyline, casting a golden glow over a further extraordinary sight at the entrance to the Jokhang. Gylsang took me aside from the stream of pilgrims to point out a group practising another powerful act of devotion. Beneath the towering stone walls, scores of people were prostrating themselves in front of the temple.

Prostration follows a sequence that we watched a young woman perform. She had segments of cardboard attached to the palms of her hands and she was wearing kneepads. Holding her lagged hands together in a prayer-like gesture, she touched her forehead, throat and chest in turn before kneeling down on the end of an old foam mattress. She lay face-down, sweeping her hands forward along the flagstones until her arms were stretched out in front of her. The movement of the cardboard along the ground made a soothing swishing sound. She held this pose for a few seconds before pushing herself up to stand at the foot of the mattress and repeat the exercise. The process looked like a cross between a press-up and a squat thrust, I suggested to Gylsang. She laughed and agreed. 'Very good for stomach muscles.'

We watched the young woman continue her devotions, chanting quietly as she did so. She had placed her shoes neatly at the foot of the mattress she was reclining on. The mattress itself had seen a lot of use and had been compressed into a permanent body-shaped hollow with deeper indents for the knees. Each time she lowered her face, her long pigtails dragged in the dust.

I asked Gylsang how many times she thought this woman would prostrate herself. 'She is young, so probably a thousand times a day. For older people, five hundred times may be enough.' I said nothing because I couldn't think of anything to say.

Beyond the woman we were watching – who, judging from her clothes, looked as if she had come from the countryside – dozens of other pilgrims were similarly ensconced in their own private prostrating worlds. My headache had cleared during our walk in the fresh air, but all this mesmeric bobbing up and down in front of me set it off again. The workmen inside my head resumed their banging and crashing, synchronizing with the pilgrims, all of whom were slightly out of step with each other.

'I wonder how far she's come to get here,' I said, and immediately wished I hadn't because Gylsang asked her. I was interested to know, but hadn't wanted to pry, and I was concerned that my interruption would offend religious etiquette. But the young woman didn't seem upset by the intrusion. She paused to answer Gylsang while standing at the foot of her mattress.

'It is a village about a hundred and fifty kilometres away,' Gylsang translated. 'This is her first visit to Lhasa.'

The young woman was still talking. 'The journey took her fifty-seven days,' Gylsang went on.

I did a double take, thinking maybe Gylsang's English had failed her. 'How long?'

'Fifty-seven days,' Gylsang repeated.

'That sounds like an awfully long time,' I said, still trying to work out how her journey could have been so protracted.

'Yes, prostration is a slow way to travel,' Gylsang told me.

I opened my mouth, but no words came out. Here in Barkhor Square, each time the woman prostrated herself she did so on the stationary mattress. Travelling in this way meant that after each prostration the next one began where the outstretched hands had touched the ground. This woman had covered a hundred and fifty kilometres caterpillar style: it was like dolly steps, only ten thousand times more tiring. Never mind being on the roof of the world, I now realized I had entered a completely different universe.

★

Westerners like me usually turn up in Tibet equipped with romantic notions about the place and its inhabitants. Mere mention of its name is enough to set the exotic juices flowing. Tibet is one of those instantly captivating locations, in the same league as Zanzibar and Timbuktu, that has long cast a magic spell over the Western mind. Tibetans are thought to be simple people who live in a spiritual and peace-loving Shangri-la, enjoying blissful, snow-clad isolation from the rest of the mortal world.

Like many romantic notions, this image is not entirely correct, as I had begun to realize while researching for the trip. For a start, it's not actually that cold or snow-covered. Tibet's high altitude means that temperatures do sink low, particularly at night, but most of the population lives in the south-east around Lhasa, which is on about the same latitude as Kuwait and Cairo and has one of the sunniest climates on the planet. On average, the sun shines for about 3,400 hours a year, which helps to melt the snow that does fall, which isn't much, because most of the atmospheric moisture brought from the Indian Ocean tends to fall over the Himalayas. In consequence, much of the countryside is semi-desert.

Tibet's reputation as the epitome of seclusion dates back about two hundred years to when the Chinese Qing Empire attempted to seal off the country from contact with the West. But delve back further into the region's past and you see that historically Tibetans ruled over a vast dominion that stretched across great swathes of Central Asia. In the seventh and eighth centuries Tibet governed all of today's Nepal and Bhutan, most of Bangladesh and Pakistan, a good deal of northern India, and large chunks of Burma and China (Turpan, for example, was under Tibetan rule until the Uighurs took over in about 840). During this period, the Silk Road trade routes that wound their way across Eurasia were controlled by Tibetans.

Such control was enforced by Tibetan armies, which is inconsistent with the territory's peace-loving image of today. But those were the days before Buddhism became firmly established. Buddhism first took hold in Tibet at the height of Tibetan expansion, but faded somewhat for a hundred and fifty years after the collapse of the Tibetan state in the mid-800s. Since the resurgence of Buddhism, Tibet has never again controlled so much territory. But that's not to say that Buddhism can be equated with non-violence per se. Buddhist monasteries throughout the country, the largest of which were effectively self-contained city states, maintained their own armies of fighting monks. They were fully trained in the martial arts and usually tooled up with concealed weapons to keep the peace inside the huge monastic establishments. And this wasn't just a brief hangover from pre-Buddhist times. Fighting monks operated in the monasteries well into the twentieth century.

Outside the monasteries, Tibetans also continued to defend their country whenever necessary, as numerous Europeans intent on penetrating the forbidden territory in the nineteenth century found to their cost. Nikolai Przewalski, the Russian accredited with discovering the *takhi*, was one of those who made a series of attempts to reach Lhasa in the late 1800s. He wanted to become the first European to write a scholarly account of Tibet's capital, but all his efforts were rebuffed by Tibetan forces. And the Tibetans' fighting skills weren't only employed in defence. Also in the nineteenth century, the Goloks and Khampas from central-eastern parts of Tibet earned a reputation for banditry, preying on those who travelled through their homelands. In the eyes of many outsiders, these people still have a rather fearsome reputation today.

Sitting in my study at home in Oxford, I had already started to wonder about the form of Buddhism practised in Tibet. Having now witnessed the stamina and physical strength of the woman prostrating herself outside the Jokhang in Barkhor Square, I began to speculate on the religion's importance to life at high altitude. At a superficial level its significance was unquestionable, as evidenced by the pilgrims on the Barkhor *kora*, but my thoughts turned to examine the issue on a different plane. Could it be that adhering to this faith was actually a necessity for life on the roof of the world?

This proposition was based along the following lines of thought. Tibet is without doubt a harsh environment. Its semi-arid climate and high altitude mean that most of it is only good for herding tough animals, like goats and the supremely well-adapted yak. Planting crops isn't an option; the growing season is too short and the weather too unpredictable. In the western parts of the Tibetan plateau, where I was heading, the average temperature is below freezing on more than two hundred days a year. The temperature can drop below zero at night even in the summer, when during the daytime the mercury hits 38°C (100°F). In this part of Tibet in winter, the thermometer regularly dips below −40°C at night. Abundant sunshine there may be, but even this has its downside: the inhabitants of Tibet have eye problems. The prevalence of cataracts is thought to be one of the highest in the world, a statistic that is very likely linked to the intense ultraviolet radiation received on the plateau. There are also strong winds that constantly sweep these highlands, along with intermittent violent hailstorms. And on top of all this, in a way literally as well as metaphorically, I couldn't forget the altitude factor which was still causing me discomfort. There simply isn't a lot of oxygen to keep you going in Tibet. All in all, however you look at it, the Tibetan plateau is one of the most extreme environments on Earth.

So how do people cope? Physical hardiness was obviously crucial, but was it enough in itself, I wondered. A few years ago, on my only other visit to high altitude, in Chile, I'd joined a group of commandos on a two-day desert survival course. The exercise involved a lot of marching, both at night and during the day, on meagre rations. We were allowed one meal and just a litre of water to drink each day.

I didn't finish the course. Physically, I think I could have kept going, but after about thirty hours my psyche was telling me otherwise. I realized then the importance of mental strength as well as physical stamina in surviving environmental extremes. What I'd seen and read so far about religion in Tibet suggested that a steadfast belief in Buddhism might be the key to unlocking the necessary mental energy.

One afternoon, I put this proposition to a lama at the Sera monastery on the outskirts of Lhasa. It was my third day in Tibet and the first on which I'd woken without a headache. The previous twenty-four hours had been a write-off after I'd worn myself out seeing the sights with Gylsang. We'd moved on from the Barkhor *kora* to scale the heights of the Potala

Palace, the empty winter residence of the exiled Dalai Lama. It looked majestic and timeless as it loomed above the city like an organic architectural growth on its hillside, but I'd under-estimated the amount of puff it would take to climb its winding steps. I was gasping for breath by the time we reached the roof, and the views over the city were rather lost on me.

But after a day of rest, I felt a lot better. Sera, erected in 1419, was one of the country's largest monasteries in its heyday, and had at one time been famous for its fighting monks. I'd come across a book about one who had fled his homeland after 1959, when Chinese troops occupied Tibet. He'd lived the rest of his life in exile, finally settling in the British Isles where he died on the Isle of Man in 1986. Sera has not been the same since 1959, although it still houses some eight hundred residents. I'd timed my arrival to coincide with the debates that take place every afternoon in an open-air courtyard, thinking it would be apt to encounter the monks in talkative mood. What I hadn't expected was a multiple shouting match.

There were several dozen monks gathered in groups of two or three. Hemmed in by a low stone wall, they filled the courtyard. It was designed in the way you might make over your garden if you adopted a minimalist, low-maintenance approach. The ground was covered with a layer of bright white stone chips dotted with a few trees. One of them had some white silk prayer scarves tied to its branches, but otherwise there was nothing else at all. As a setting for the monks, all of whom were dressed in burgundy robes, it was serene, if slightly surreal. Or at least it would have been without the noise. It sounded like pandemonium.

Gylsang had given me the name of a senior lama whom I found standing at the side of the proceedings watching his younger protégés in action. 'It is question-and-answer session,' he told me, when I asked him what was going on. I only heard this on the second time of asking, because the hubbub was so loud. Each group of monks consisted of one man who stood and addressed his seated companions in a thunderous voice. Those who sat cross-legged had looks of intense concentration on their faces, occasionally broken by a wry smile. An orator's speech was punctuated by questions, the lama told me. These queries were highly animated. The man would stand and wave his hands in the air as he built up to his question, and then deliver it to his colleagues with an exaggerated skip towards them and a clap of his hands right in someone's face.

I had to shout to make myself heard. What exactly were the monks talking about, I wanted to know. 'It is revision,' the lama said. He didn't turn towards me to answer and was speaking quietly, the only monk in the courtyard who was, so I had to lean closer to catch what he was saying. 'They discuss what they learned this morning,' he added.

I could see that my lama was taking mental notes. I suppose he was a little like a football manager who stands on the sidelines with his arms folded watching his team. But the lama didn't shout advice or interrupt the discussions he was observing. He simply stood with a look of supreme composure on his face, watching over his apprentices.

His not looking at me was off-putting. It made me feel like the stupid foreigner that I was, but I pressed on to ask him about the importance of religion to Tibetans. Life was difficult in Tibet, the lama said after a short delay. He paused again, and I followed his line of vision to look at an orator who had completed his pronouncements and was sitting on the ground cross-legged. One of those previously seated unfolded himself and took up position for his turn.

'We are Buddhists, but we eat meat,' the lama said eventually, still studying the new monk. 'This is because of the altitude,' he went on slowly. 'We must eat meat to survive.'

The monk who had just stood up folded the long sleeves of his robe around his forearms and launched into his monologue. The lama was still watching carefully but, since he had just delivered his longest sentence yet, I put to him my theory on the importance of Buddhism as the basis for mental strength.

There was another long pause. The monk we were watching was getting highly animated. Still facing his listeners, he took a large step backwards, threw his hands up in the air, and bounded back towards his seated companions. He lunged at one of them and smacked his hands together about an inch in front of his nose.

The lama slowly turned his head to face me. His eyes were brown and kindly. 'Yes,' he said, 'in a way what you say is true.' Then he gave me an almost imperceptible nod and turned his head back to continue observing the question-and-answer session. I waited for some time to see if the lama would say anything more, but this was obviously going to be his only comment on the matter.

II

Tibet is the highest and largest plateau in the world, but it didn't get where it is today without a bit of help from one of its neighbours. Around fifty million years ago, the landmass we now know as India crashed into Asia. The Earth's surface is made up of vast plates that tend to move around, and India had previously broken off from a supercontinent called Pangaea. The collision between India and the rest of Asia caused a huge pile-up. The rocks in the crunch zone got compressed and condensed, developed fissures and faults, and were buckled and folded to create a vast mountain range: the Himalayas. As India continued to drive northwards, it pushed the deeper part of the Indian plate beneath Tibet, thickening the crust it sits on and thrusting it towards the heavens in one great slab to produce the plateau.

This literally earth-shattering event has helped form the land-scape across an extraordinarily wide area of Asia. Along with the Himalayas, up popped the Karakorams and the Hindu Kush. A sort of ripple effect created the mountains of the Tien Shan in north-western China and the Altai mountains in Mongolia. Faults appeared in the Earth's crust as far away as Siberia, where Lake Baikal opened up.

The impact zone has created the world's greatest collection of mountains. This planet has just seventeen peaks that stand at 8,000 metres or higher and they're all in the Himalaya-Karakoram-Hindu Kush ranges. The region remains active. As India continues to push, the Himalayas continue to rise, at about four millimetres a year, though this growth is offset, at least in part, as the mountains are worn away by weathering and erosion.

Given that the Tibetan plateau is a great slab of high land surrounded by mountainous walls, and therefore constitutes one of Central Asia's huge physical barriers, it is easy to understand why it was an area best avoided by traders along the Silk Road. But there was a long-established route from what is now north-west China, on the edge of the Gobi desert, that skirted the plateau southwards to Lhasa, and on down to the mouth of the Ganges. From Lhasa, another highway led westwards along Tibet's southern edge into Kashmir, following the course of the Yarlung Tsangpo, the local name for the Brahmaputra river. It's a route that is still travelled today, and it led me towards my rendezvous with some high-altitude nomads.

I had teamed up with another geographer, a German named Daniel who had been working in Tibet for many years, and had agreed to let me accompany him on this trip up on to the plateau. We'd hired a car with a driver who was very formal and introduced himself as Tsetan, which sounded like Satan when he said it. 'I am most proud to have you in my vehicle,' he told us.

A procession of poplar trees followed us as we drove out of Lhasa along a wide valley lined with arid hills, but the trees dwindled away to reveal grey fields and sheep grazing on the hillsides. One of the fields was being ploughed by a man walking behind two hulking yaks. Barley was the main crop here, Daniel told me, but we wouldn't be seeing any more cultivation when we climbed up on to the plateau. 'Too high to grow anything,' he said, as we sped through a small village where all the walls were garnished with neat patterns of round yak dungpats stuck there to dry in the sunshine. As in the Gobi, dung is the most important source of fuel in Tibet since wood is scarce. Many of the valleys around Lhasa had once been enveloped by juniper forests, Daniel told me, but there were precious few such trees left now. They'd all been cleared for firewood and for ritual purposes. 'Juniper branches are used commonly as incense,' he said.

I received a more interesting take on local produce when we passed some large plastic greenhouses a little further on. 'What do they grow in those?' I asked Tsetan.

'Vegetarians, sir,' he replied.

'Vegetables?'

'Yes, sir. Vegetarians and salad.'

After an hour or so, the road became a dirt track and we met the Yarlung Tsangpo. Most rivers flow more or less directly down to the sea, but the Yarlung Tsangpo is an exception. It is one of the four rivers that rise on the flanks of Mount Kailas, my ultimate destination, and for much of its length it is trapped behind the impenetrable Himalayas, tracking the great mountain chain eastwards before it slips down into India and Bangladesh. Between Lhasa and Shigatse, where we would stop for the first night of our three-day journey, its course was dramatic. The trail we were on, which didn't live up to the affable name the Chinese have given it – the Northern Friendship Highway – hugged the slopes of a deep, plunging canyon. Snow-capped mountains peeped over the valley sides where evidence of vast rock slides was strewn down the precipitous slopes. Between the landslips, the inclines were riven by razor-sharp gullies. Down below, the icy blue river flowed round boulders as large as houses as it swept through the gorge.

It was physical geography on a grand scale and a colossal challenge for the highway engineers who were intent on widening the road, a main route to Nepal and India, Tsetan told us. In less than a month the work would begin in earnest, for which the road would be closed and wouldn't be reopened for two years.

The job had already begun and, incredibly, much of it was being carried out by hand. We passed gangs of labourers toiling along the roadside, wearing grubby facemasks against the dust. Most were armed with shovels and wheelbarrows. I gazed in astonishment as we approached an outsized handcart being loaded with large rocks. Three men were using all their strength to lift a boulder on to the back of a colleague who was crouching down on his haunches to receive the load. As we slowed to pass, the man, bent double, tottered up a wooden plank and let the rock crash into the cart.

We left the course of the Yarlung Tsangpo with its medieval road-widening programme at Shigatse, and continued westwards on our second day through more moderate terrain. We'd be gaining altitude slowly throughout our journey, and Shigatse was about three hundred metres higher than Lhasa. Dr Richards had informed me that above 3,000 metres, the altitude at which you sleep should not be incremented by more than 300 metres per day, so Shigatse was textbook perfect as a location to spend our first night.

I felt that I was acclimatizing. The headaches were all but gone and I was sleeping more peacefully but, as if to counter these improvements, I was developing a heavy cold. This was, I think, almost entirely my fault. After consulting the lama at the Sera monastery on the importance of Buddhism to life at high altitude, I'd become increasingly uneasy at my lack of preparation for this trip. I was convinced that mental as well as physical strength was required for the Kailas *kora*, and I was deficient in the former department. Worse still, I could see no obvious way out of my predicament. I wasn't particularly religious and I certainly wasn't a Buddhist. After some consideration, I reached a decision. Since an emergency course in Buddhism wasn't really an option, I thought that I should concentrate on self-help. I would invest time in training myself to think positively, and since my dilemma was based on the link between the mental and the physical, I reckoned that if I changed my physical appearance in some way, it might just help. Having recently visited Sera and seen all the monks shouting at each other, I decided to have my head shaved.

It had taken me some time to communicate this to the woman in the barbershop in Lhasa. There was a poster on the wall in her salon depicting a wide range of styles, but none of them as straightforward as baldness. Eventually I conveyed my need to her with the aid of the inside of my forearm and some pantomime actions to indicate that that was how I'd like it on the top of my head. She sat me down in the operating chair, adjusted her facemask, plugged the shaver into a Bakelite cable extension, and set to. As I watched my hair being removed, my eyes flicked back and forth between this scene and a postcard of a yak that was stuck in the corner of the mirror. I noticed that outside it had started to snow.

The flakes were fluttering down from the heavens in considerable numbers. It looked very pretty, but for me it spelled disaster. By the time I made it back to the hotel, my head felt as if it had just spent a week in the deep-freeze.

Daniel clocked my hairlessness the moment we met. 'You must be going native,' he quipped, but I resisted the temptation to pass judgement on his hair. It was decidedly unkempt, most of it hanging down his back in a straggly ponytail. By the look of it, he hadn't visited a barber since the late 1970s.

Our second night on the road, spent in a basic but comfortable guest house at just over 4,000 metres, was my worst yet. My cold had now kicked in with a vengeance, blocking my sinuses and making my new-style head feel heavy and unwieldy. This was particularly unfair, I thought, given that I'd only just recovered from my initial bout of altitude sickness. I'd also been sticking to a regime that Gylsang had recommended when she assured me I'd get used to being up high.

'What you should do is rest when necessary and drink lots,' she'd told me, 'but not alcohol.' So far, I'd been conscientiously avoiding the large tempting green bottles of Lhasa beer that Daniel had been draining each evening with his dinner.

But now sleeping was easier said than done. Breathing through my nose was impossible, and my mouth dried out very quickly in the dry upland air, a drawback that woke me up a couple of times soon after I eventually fell asleep. The last look at my wristwatch told me that was after 2 a.m.

However, worse was to come. I'd been warned that, when sleeping at high altitude, I was likely to wake up spontaneously gasping for breath due to a lack of oxygen. In all the excitement, I'd forgotten about this particular high-altitude hazard.

Until now. From being deep in slumberland, I was suddenly and rudely wide awake and gasping for breath. It was like being jolted out of a terrible dream, only worse. Much worse, because this wasn't a dream. It was the stark reality of my body desperately struggling for oxygen.

It was obviously a situation so urgent that my unconscious physiology couldn't cope on its own. My body had been carrying out its usual routine functions, but for reasons that weren't immediately clear to my befuddled and frankly terrified brain, the standard procedures that had worked on every other day of my life tonight proved inadequate.

I guess the automatic functions gradually slow down, working on less and less fuel until they drop below the minimum required. At that point, the alarm bells ring and an adrenalin-fuelled instinct kicks in. An emergency electrical impulse must have surged through my body, sparking motor reflexes that shocked my consciousness back into action.

My body jerked bolt upright and my eyes snapped open. I knew instinctively that I was in the epicentre of a personal crisis, but it wasn't immediately clear to me where the danger was coming from. Confused by the abrupt return to reality, and the absence of obvious causes – no bad dream, no hand on my shoulder – it took me a little while to make sense of the situation.

My heart was thumping loudly in my chest, almost as if it wanted to get out, but it too had clearly been startled by the rude awakening. Within milliseconds, the surprise had been subsumed by the stark realization that I'd just been brought back from the brink of drowning in a lack of oxygen. I knew this because my mouth and lungs were literally gasping for life itself.

A rather lengthy period passed before I got back to sleep again.

Daniel laughed when I told him about my near-death experience. 'Welcome to Tibet,' he said.

Tsetan was more sympathetic. 'You must take your cold to see doctor, sir.' And he said he knew one en route who we'd pass later that day.

We had left the Northern Friendship Highway where it dropped down to the border with Nepal, and were continuing westwards along the rim of the plateau. I hadn't seen a tree for a couple of days, and plots of cultivated land had become fewer and further between, leaving just herds of livestock to graze the dry rolling pastures. There was very little snow on the ground and the sunshine was bright and glaring. Whenever we stopped for a toilet break by the side of the trail, I felt its rays warming my skull, reminding me to anoint it with sunscreen. I could do without sunstroke to add to my catalogue of woes.

We passed through occasional villages strung out along the highway, comprising sturdy square dwellings, usually single-storey, made of baked mud-bricks, typically with a coating of whitewash. Strings of red, green, yellow, blue and white prayer flags were stretched across the rooftops, or wrapped haphazardly around sprays of sticks that sprouted from the corners of the buildings. The flat roofs were topped with neatly stacked lines of dry dungpats.

In a number of villages I had seen some strange metal contraptions with kettles on top, and spotting one as we slowed to negotiate a brook flowing across the main street, I asked Tsetan to stop so that I could look at it more closely. A gaggle of small children soon gathered round as Daniel and I inspected the device. It was made of a sheet of gleaming, curved metal, a little less than my outstretched arms in width, propped just above the ground, with a couple of stanchions that met above it to form an open ring on which you could stand a kettle. The purpose of the device was to focus the sun's rays on the bottom of the kettle, thus boiling the water inside.

'A clever invention,' Daniel remarked. 'You go into any Tibetan home, and they offer you tea immediately. Always there is a kettle on the boil. These things save a lot of firewood, of course.'

A boy who had appeared through the door in the nearest house and had soon disappeared, now emerged carrying a teapot and three small cups. He had a flop of black hair and his shirt was hanging out underneath a green pullover. He picked up the kettle and emptied the hot water into his teapot. Then he poured us each a cup of black tea. We thanked him and drank. The tea was salty, which was a bit startling, even though I'd read that Tibetans add salt to their cuppa in the same way that people at home like sugar.

I asked the boy if he had any more water and he nodded, ducking back into his house to fetch a bucketful. I poured some of it into the kettle and got back to my tea which was refreshing despite the salt.

I wanted to conduct an experiment. I'd brought a thermometer along in my bag and was interested to measure the temperature at which the water boiled. Every child at school in Britain learns that water boils at 100°C, which it does, but not everywhere. This is the boiling point of water at sea level. At higher altitudes, water boils at lower temperatures.

The reason for this is linked to the gradual thinning of the atmosphere as you rise above sea level. The atmosphere exerts pressure on everything below it, and since the air becomes thinner, or less dense, with altitude it consequently exerts less pressure. We boil water by introducing energy (heat) that agitates the water molecules until they break loose from the surrounding liquid and rise as steam. Since higher altitude means less air pressure, it takes less energy to agitate the molecules enough for them to boil off. Less energy means less heat is needed, so the temperature required to boil the water is lower.

That's the theory anyway, and I wanted to see if it worked. I had brought along a special wristwatch that measured altitude, which also worked on the pressure principle. While I waited for the water to boil, I noted down the height of the village above sea level. It was 3,890 metres.

When the water in the kettle started to boil, I took my cooking thermometer – designed for tasks like jam-making and thus able to cope with temperatures well over 100°C – and held it in the water. The red liquid rose, slowing down as it passed 70°C. Steam was still gently billowing out of the kettle as the thermometer reading crept past 76°C, 78°C, and finally stopped rising bang on 80°C. I held the thermometer in place for a little longer, just to make sure, but it was clearly not going any higher.

Even I was surprised by how low the temperature was, but I was very happy with the result. The phenomenon is one that Marco Polo indirectly noted when crossing the high mountains of Central Asia in the thirteenth century. He observed that his food didn't cook as well at high elevations as it did in lower situations, which is precisely because water boils at a lower temperature, hence taking a longer time to cook things. Marco Polo didn't record what he was eating, but whether he was boiling rice or a goat, the effect would be the same. In order to have cooked it properly, he'd have had to leave it over the heat longer. The result is probably similar if you don't brew your tea for longer than at sea level, but I can't comment since the tea tasted peculiar anyway thanks to the salt.

We drove on, turning off our east–west route to travel north-wards and climb up on to the plateau. We stopped in the late afternoon to look at a geyser, evidence, if evidence were needed, of continued subterranean goings-on as India ploughs into the rest of Asia.

We stopped for the night at Mendong, a curious hybrid of a place with a modern Chinese centre surrounded by miserable-looking Tibetan houses. The Chinese part was just one street and it looked as if it had been built the day before. On closer inspection it was not quite finished. The shiny blue public telephone boxes that lined the road were yet to have telephones installed and many of the shopfronts were just that. No one had moved in to sell anything yet.

We'd arrived too late for me to see the doctor, so after another disturbed night, I went along to find him first thing the next morning. He operated from the local monastery. Tsetan led Daniel and me into a mud-walled courtyard where a couple of other people sat minding their own business in the dust. They told Tsetan they were waiting for a consultation, so we squatted beside them to join the queue. There was a solitary golden prayer wheel in a wooden frame with a silver top-piece that looked like a mini-pagoda, but the man and woman waiting had brought their own handheld versions which they kept in constant motion while they waited.

After a few minutes, just for something to say as much as anything, I asked Tsetan whether we should have made an appointment. He looked confused. Then he said, 'Don't worry, sir. He is *amchi*, good Tibetan doctor.' Tsetan nodded his head and smiled encouragingly. 'He give you good grass for your bad cold.'

Now I was confused. 'I'm not sure that I want grass, Tsetan.'

'He means he's a herbalist,' Daniel said, 'a traditional Tibetan doctor.'

A quarter of an hour later, I was ushered into the doctor's surgery and introduced to Lama Rinzin Namgyal. He had short spiky hair, buck teeth and a pencil-thin moustache that didn't meet in the middle. A necklace of white beads hung at the V-neck of his thick orange pullover, and a silver dagger dangled at his hip from a canvas belt. He gestured for me to sit on a divan in the window where he joined me. Daniel took up position on a chair opposite to translate the explanation of my head cold.

Lama Namgyal nodded as he listened to the details of my symptoms, took hold of my wrist and placed his fingers lightly on the suicide zone to take my pulse. Paintings of Buddhist gods adorned the walls above a long sideboard cluttered with small silver bowls and a copper teapot. An ancient radio with two very long aerials stood beside an arrangement of peacock feathers in a tiny vase. The sideboard itself was painted intricately in bright colours. I noticed a depiction of the Tibetan Wheel of Law flanked by two sitting deer, symbols I'd seen in gleaming copper on the roof of the Jokhang temple in Lhasa.

Once he'd felt one wrist, the lama took the other one and did the same. 'You only have a cold,' he declared at last, 'and it is not a serious one.' He removed his fingers from my wrist and told me that this was the most common complaint he saw in his patients. There were three types of cold, he went on, very serious, serious and not serious. Mine was in the not serious category.

'I will make you up some herbal tea,' he told me. 'Drink it in the morning and at night, and your cold will soon pass.'

When I told him I was aiming to walk the *kora* around Mount Kailas the lama's face lit up. 'Oh, that is a very beautiful place,' he said. 'You will enjoy it.' Did he think I'd be fit enough, I wanted to know. 'Yes, yes. You will be all right if you eat well, take lots of exercise, drink my tea and plenty of hot water.'

III

Tibet was the source of several products traded all along the Silk Road throughout its long history. Salt and wool from the plateau were carried across the Himalayas to India on the routes that also brought Buddhism to Tibet in return. Other, more coveted, merchandise was exported in all directions – including rhubarb and yaks' tails.

Tibet produced abundant supplies of rhubarb which was sold to combat constipation, indigestion, dysentery and certain skin diseases. Rhubarb's medicinal properties have been recognized in China for more than four thousand years, and for centuries it was one of the most important Central Asian exports to Europe. I asked Lama Namgyal if he used it but he said not. His medicines were based on herbs he collected himself in the countryside around Mendong. Rhubarb grew only in eastern Tibet, he told me. I learned later that on these parts of the plateau the plant can grow to the height of a small tree. Scientists still speculate that rhubarb's medical properties are reliant on its growth at high altitude.

In Europe, rhubarb was a very valuable commodity for many centuries. Marco Polo left a bag of it in his will, and in the

1500s the price of rhubarb in the markets of France was ten times that of cinnamon, and four times more expensive than saffron. By the nineteenth century, the trade in rhubarb to Europe was so great that when wicked British merchants flooded China with opium, a Chinese imperial commissioner wrote to Queen Victoria threatening to ban the export of the laxative, condemning Britons to eternal constipation. This was around the time that Baron von Richthofen first coined the term 'Silk Road'. He could just as easily have called it the Rhubarb Road.

Another popular export from Tibet was the yak tail, which was used along the Silk Road from the earliest times. The tails were set into handles and used as fly-whisks everywhere from ancient Rome to India. The Chinese sewed them into their hats or fashioned the hair into wigs and fake beards to be used in Chinese opera. Yak-tail beards have also been popular further afield in more modern times. In the early twentieth century, white yak tails were imported into the USA for use as Father Christmas beards – some American theatrical suppliers still sell genuine yak's-hair Santa beards and wigs over the Internet.

Yaks are the highest-living large mammals in the world and therefore the mainstay of the high-altitude nomad's herd. Northern Tibet is the area generally accepted as that in which yak were originally domesticated from the wild some 4,500 years ago. Tibetans use the word *yak* for the male of the species. *Dri* is the female, while *nor* is the common name, but I never got used to this so just continued calling them yaks. *Nor* means treasure. Tibetans call this mighty beast 'the treasure of the plateau'.

But the yaks were nowhere to be seen when we arrived at the homestead of the nomads we'd come to visit. We had climbed, almost imperceptibly, on to the Changtang, the name for the northern part of the Tibetan plateau, one of the most remote and least known regions of the world, as well as being one of the highest. Remote and unknown to outsiders, that is: the Changtang is also home to about half a million nomadic herders, or *drokba*.

A few filed out of a black tent when we pulled up in Tsetan's car early in the afternoon. They told us that their yaks had been taken further north to the summer pastures. The men who spoke to us, all dressed in hefty, long-sleeved sheepskin robes, were about to drive their sheep and goats in the same direction.

'We can go with them,' Daniel announced, so we agreed with Tsetan a day for him to come and collect us, and bade him farewell.

The walk to the summer pastures wasn't nearly as arduous as I'd thought it might be. The pace was gentle, dictated by the speed of the slowest animals in the flock: lambs and kids that didn't look more than a few weeks old. Daniel and I were assigned to the right flank of the herd and we spent our time heading off the occasional stray.

The terrain all around us didn't look like a plateau in that it wasn't totally flat. Here and there, the landscape did just about manage a more-or-less level plain, but mostly it was made up of gently rolling hills. The hills were swathed in grass, stubbly and drained of colour. The Changtang is so high that for most of the year its sparse vegetation lies dormant. About mid-September, the grasses and sedges stop growing until late April or early May. Even then it's another month or so before the pastures provide anything nutritious for a grazing animal. This short growing season, which usually offers just three or four months of decent green fodder, means that for most of their lives the sheep, goats and yaks feed on the desiccated plants left at the end of the growing season.

Wherever you go on the Changtang, it's the same story of lifeless pasture interrupted by a brief summer opportunity for verdant grazing, so depending on the size of your flock you don't have to move very far. Daniel told me the average annual movement for a *drokba*'s herds was probably not more than about sixty kilometres. This is in stark contrast to nomadic pastoralists in south-west Asia who typically move hundreds of kilometres in winter to lower regions where fresh pastures are growing.

We were in the second week of May and there wasn't much evidence of the grass becoming greener as we progressed north-wards. I had visions of incipient lushness in the area we were heading towards, but after just a few hours, when Daniel pointed out a black tent in the distance, I realized I was wrong. The grass was just as grey and comatose here too.

The heavy tent, which was made of woven yak hair, was pitched at the top of a gentle slope leading down to a shallow stream. Next to it were a couple of corrals built with mud-bricks where we penned the sheep and goats. Adults went in one corral, lambs and kids in the other. This place was known as Ravu, Daniel told me as I checked my wristwatch. The altitude was 4,720 metres, which for me was a personal best. Better still was the fact that I didn't even have a headache.

Almost immediately, Daniel and I were dispatched with one of the *drokba*, a man named Lobsang, to bring in the yaks. He pointed to a far hillside speckled with black dots. 'There,' he said, and off we went.

The yak is one of the world's most remarkable domestic animals since it thrives in the extremely harsh conditions of the Changtang and in doing so provides a livelihood for the *drokba*. It is related to the ox and our own domestic cow, but with a few key modifications. Its ability to live in conditions that other bovines have trouble surviving in is based on a number of specially adapted characteristics. One way in which a yak copes with the relative lack of oxygen is through its development of larger internal organs than other cattle. It's blessed with a larger chest capacity, bigger lungs and an outsize heart, all of which help it to achieve adequate intake and circulation of oxygen in conditions where the supply is low. The yak's trachea is also particularly voluminous to allow a high rate of air intake. Further, its red blood cells enable it to absorb and retain enough of the oxygen it receives. However, not all experts agree on how the animal's red blood cells are special. Some suggest the yak has larger red cells with a greater surface area and a higher capacity for the retention of oxygen. Others imply just the opposite, that yak have very small red cells in relation to sea-level cattle but have vastly more cells per unit volume of blood. Whatever the details, yak's blood is very good at using the oxygen it can get.

Human inhabitants of high altitudes have, like the *drokba*, adapted physiologically to the thin air, enhancing their ability to convey oxygen from air to body tissues. The main way their bodies do this is through an increased amount of haemoglobin in the blood, which enhances its capacity to obtain oxygen from the air in their lungs.

We were approaching the yaks now, and one or two of the lumbering beasts looked up from their grazing to size us up and amble slowly away. Lobsang sent Daniel and me to one side of the herd, while he walked to the other, giving the animals a wide berth. There were perhaps twenty yaks in total, shaggy, yet rhinoceros-solid, their compact bodies an adaptation to the extreme winter temperatures that characterize the Changtang. A yak has a short neck and limbs, and its skin is particularly thick with few functioning sweat glands, all attributes that help to minimize the loss of body heat. Warmth is also conserved by the thick fleece that covers the whole body. Composed of a long-haired outer coat in winter it is supplemented by a dense undercoat of fine down fibres.

When Marco Polo encountered yaks, he likened them to elephants in terms of size, and noted that their hair was softer and more delicate than silk. The yak's down-like undercoat is called *kulu* in Tibetan, the same word used for a goat's soft undercoat. Goat's *kulu* is also known in the West. We call it cashmere, and exports of cashmere have become lucrative for Tibetan herders in recent decades. But since it is only goat's *kulu* that can legally be called cashmere in Western markets, there isn't much of a market for the yak variety.

Once we'd reached the far side of the animals, we moved in towards them, ushering them down the hill towards the distant black tent. The yaks walked at a stately pace, flicking the air behind them with their future fly-whisk tails. I knew that yaks were used as pack animals, as well as for grazing, but I was interested to learn whether the *drokba* ever rode them. 'They can be ridden,' Lobsang told me, 'but they don't like it.'

His yaks didn't enjoy being close to people in general. I tried to get nearer to them, to examine the hulking beasts at close-quarters but, despite having their backs turned, they were always alert to my approach and trotted away to maintain a respectable distance. As we neared the stream beneath the tent, some of the smaller yaks demonstrated a surprising agility. A young one was nuzzled in the bottom by a companion, sending it leaping into the air and skipping across the stream. A couple of the other younger members of the herd took this as a signal that spring was in the air and also started to get frisky. They bounded into the little river and frolicked in the water.

Once we'd managed to get them all into a wire-fenced enclosure for the night, we retired to drink tea in the tent. The woman in charge seemed happy to boil up my special brew, as provided by Lama Namgyal. She inspected it carefully when she unwrapped the old piece of newspaper in which he'd wrapped it, lowered her nose, sniffed it and smiled.

'Do you have a cold?' she asked me with a knowing smile. I nodded. 'This will make it better,' she said.

Her name was Lhamo. She had introduced herself, which was surprising given that the other *drokba* had all been backward in coming forward when we'd first arrived. Rather more surprising was Lhamo's initial greeting: she stuck out her tongue at us.

'Oh, this is a very traditional way of greeting people,' Daniel announced, so I stuck out my tongue in return. Later I heard it suggested that poking your tongue out at a new acquaintance is done to show that you're not a devil. Devils have green tongues, apparently, even when they assume a human form.

When I left to stretch my legs some time later, I saw that another tent had been erected. A wind had also been rising while I'd drunk my tea, worrying the heavy flaps of Lhamo's abode. They say you can experience all four seasons in a day in Tibet because the weather can change so quickly, and by now I could see just how. That morning, as I'd left Lama Namgyal clutching my newspaper package of herbal tea, I'd stepped out of his surgery into bright, spring sunshine. By mid-afternoon, as we'd drawn nearer to the summer pastures at Ravu, the sun's heat had become stifling. I had to shed two layers of clothing to avoid being roasted on our walk with the flock. Our *drokba* hosts had felt it too, helping each other to cool off by pulling their arms out of the long sleeves of their sheepskin coats, leaving the stiff, empty arms to dangle.

Now that the evening winds had picked up, they brought angry clouds scudding across the heavens. The sky had disappeared behind a leaden veil etched by the light of the setting sun. By the time I was ready to turn in, having been allocated a spot beneath a couple of spare sheepskins in the second tent, the wind had increased to a howling gale. When I later went to relieve my bladder, the windstorm was tearing at the stout fabric of the tents. It hurled tiny flakes of snow that stung my face as an accompaniment to the searing cold. Even the sheep and goats in their corrals seemed to be suffering as they huddled together against the icy blast. Down in the yaks' pen, the snowflakes were accumulating on the bushy brows of the occupants, but the treasures of the plateau just continued chewing the cud, seemingly oblivious to it all.

I was put on dung-gathering duty the following morning. Issued with a canvas sack for the purpose, I followed Lhamo as she led the way with her two grandchildren, a small boy named Choksam and his little sister, Yangdzo. Daniel had left earlier with Lobsang to take the yaks out to graze, but I had decided to stay behind because Lhamo seemed likely to be a more lively companion for the day. She was continually laughing and smiling and eager to show me things, although I hadn't expected that this would include collecting excrement.

What became a daily chore started in the yak pen before moving on to the sheep and goat corrals. Lhamo gave me a quick lesson in identifying appropriate specimens – not too fresh seemed to be the key determinant – and we proceeded to fill our sacks with the lightweight fuel. We were above the treeline on the Changtang, so there were no trees or even shrubs, and yet there was always a fire going in both tents. The drokba didn't have a solar-powered kettle-boiling contraption and dung was the only thing they could burn.

A bag of animal droppings was in place beside the fire at all times and Lhamo had already opened my eyes to the properties of different varieties. Once alight, the large cakes of yak dung would smoulder away quite freely without the need for further attention, but they didn't burn with as much heat as the spherical pellets collected from the sheep and goats. The downside of the smaller pellets was that they had to be constantly aerated with leather bellows. It took me a little while to master them much to Lhamo's amusement. They came in the form of a goatskin bag with two sticks attached at the open end, a bit like a shopping bag. The trick was to keep the sticks apart to fill the bag with air and then close them in such a way as to pump the air through a metal tube at the bottom end that fed into the fire.

Earlier, Lhamo had demonstrated the differential heat properties of the dungs by loading two halves of the fire with different fuels and holding her hands over each. She was able to put her hands much closer to the yak dung before whipping them away. It took me a little while to understand the purpose of her pantomime. Initially, I thought she was simply showing me that fire was hot, which set me wondering where she thought I came from. But when it clicked and I nodded furiously, we both fell about laughing. I'd had no idea that the investigation of animal dung could be so much fun.

Gathering sheep and goat droppings was rather more difficult than yak dung because of their size. I joined Lhamo and her grandchildren on all fours in one of the corrals to crawl through the dust, sweeping the pellets into piles with our hands. The procedure was made more difficult by the presence of dozens of lambs and kids, which had not left the corral to go out grazing with their mothers. They mobbed us the moment we entered the corral, bleating incessantly and falling over themselves for a chance to suckle our fingers. Lhamo thought this was a complete hoot, and threw her head back to laugh out loud when she was surrounded by ten small ruminants, one tugging on each digit.

We all crept forward on our hands and knees, besieged by

the infant flock, nuzzling our flanks, climbing on our backs, gently butting our stomachs and desperately trying to suck our fingers. Somehow we extricated ourselves and left the corral with bulging sacks.

The nomads' diet is almost exclusively derived from their animals. Lhamo had been in the middle of making butter when we'd arrived, churning it in a slimy sheep's bladder on her lap in the tent. It was a vital ingredient in the tea that was always standing by in a battered copper teapot on the edge of the fire. The tea itself is imported from China in rock-hard bricks that keep for decades, but the way it's prepared is uniquely Tibetan.

Each day, when our dung-collecting duties were complete, we retired to Lhamo's tent for a cuppa. She chipped some of the encrusted leaves off a brick with her knife and crumbled them into a pot of water on the fire. When it had boiled she poured the deep-brown tea into a tall wooden churn, adding salt and a knob of yellow butter. She passed it to me, showed me the plunger in the top and made plunging movements with her fist. I did as she indicated, churning the mixture up and down for less than a minute before she wanted the whole thing back. She poured the now foaming mixture into the teapot, filled two bowls and passed one to me. She sniffed hers, grinned broadly, and let out a contented sigh.

Tell anyone who's been there that you're off to Tibet and they warn you about the rancid yak butter tea. This was nothing of the sort. Drinking it made for a curious sensation: in consistency it was more like a broth than the tea I know, and it warmed me to the core. The taste wasn't unpleasant either. I guess they only use rancid butter when fresh is not available.

The other staple foodstuff the *drokba* don't produce from their animals is barley. Anthropologists who have measured these things suggest that ground barley, or *tsamba*, provides about half of the nomads' calories. The barley kernels are tossed into a metal bowl of sand as it sits on the fire and almost immediately begin to detonate like popcorn. The exploded kernels are then sieved, to separate out the sand, and ground between two stones. The resulting flour can be mixed with a little tea and kneaded into a doughy paste, or simply poured straight into your mouth where the saliva does the same job. I opted for the latter technique the first time I tried it, but forgot to hold my breath, inhaled some of the flour and spluttered the entire spoonful of *tsamba* across the fire. Cue further hilarity.

The *drokba* have tended their herds on the Changtang for centuries. Like Shara and his family in the Gobi, *drokba*s such as Lhamo continue to flourish in one of the planet's most extreme settings using techniques of animal management that have changed little through the ages. Herding livestock is the only way to survive on the roof of the world, and the yak is perfectly adapted to its high-altitude surroundings. The severe conditions mean that any attempt to till the ground is pointless. It's virtually impossible to grow crops on the Changtang, as it is in the Gobi, so no one even tries.

The timeless way of life followed by both sets of nomadic herders appears to suggest that modernizing influences have seldom penetrated their bleak territories. Unlike Shara, the *drokba*s at Ravu didn't even have solar panels. This is not through lack of contact with outsiders, no matter how remote their homeland, since trade has long been important to *drokba*.

Tsamba has always featured prominently in their diet and barley doesn't grow on the Changtang. *Drokba* communities obtain *tsamba*, and other basics like tea, through commerce, selling the products of their herds such as wool and yak tails.

These nomadic herders have certainly not been immune to outside influence. In the Gobi and the Changtang, both societies have weathered attempts to change their lifestyles by Communist governments in the twentieth century. The crusade to collectivize herders in Mongolia unravelled when its guiding ideology fell to bits in 1990, while the Chinese efforts in Tibet similarly petered out in the mid-1970s following the death of Chairman Mao. In both cases, running the herds is again the responsibility of individual households, and the nomads are once more in control of their daily lives.

Another foreign system of belief, Buddhism, was adopted in both territories at a rather earlier date and has proved more enduring. Buddhism's spread across Central Asia occurred with the movement of people and ideas along the arteries of the Silk Road, and the links between Tibet and Mongolia in this respect are interesting. Mongolians started dabbling with the Tibetan brand of Buddhism in the thirteenth century when emissaries from the high plateau were seen practising their faith in the court of Kublai Khan. A few hundred years later, the religious links between Mongolia and Tibet grew from strength to strength following a gesture made by a Mongolian prince who had been converted to Tibetan Buddhism by a lama captured during one of his campaigns. Altan Khan, a powerful leader who was descended from Chingis, invited another Tibetan lama to visit him and bestowed upon him the rank of Dalai Lama.

Hence it was a Mongolian prince who created this title for the highest official in the Tibetan Buddhist church.

Now that religion has been allowed to reassert itself after the vagaries of Communism, it is once more clear that Buddhism never totally replaced traditional systems of faith in either Tibet or Mongolia, where aspects of shamanic beliefs continue to thrive. Indeed, Buddhism in both countries has been pragmatically adapted to make it more compatible with life in extreme environments. In addition to *tsamba*, *drokba* eat a considerable amount of meat, although I had none during my stay at Ravu. As the lama at the Sera monastery in Lhasa had told me, this departure from normal Buddhist behaviour was necessary because of the harsh conditions at high altitude. But while eating dead animals was one thing, slaughtering them was rather more difficult for Tibetans than it was for their Mongolian counterparts. Killing another living creature was a direct route to bad karma.

In Lhasa, most of the butchers were Moslems, but up here on the Changtang things were different. Daniel told me that there was a special group of 'polluted' *drokba*s who could be hired for the job. Later, I was told that when a contaminated nomad isn't available, some *drokba* aren't above a bit of subterfuge. A herder will stuff the mouth and nostrils of the condemned beast with mud and leave it to suffocate. Passing the spot some time afterwards, he notices a dead yak on the ground and thinks it would be a shame to waste it.

IV

A flawless half-moon floated in a perfect blue sky on the morning we said our goodbyes. Extended banks of cloud like long French loaves glowed pink as the sun emerged to splash the distant mountain tops with a rose-tinted blush. Now that we were leaving Ravu, Lhamo said she wanted to give me a farewell present. One evening I'd told her, through Daniel, that I was heading towards Mount Kailas to complete the *kora*, and she'd said that I ought to get some warmer clothes. After ducking back into her tent, she emerged carrying one of the long-sleeved sheepskin coats that all the men wore. Tsetan sized me up as we clambered into his car. 'Ah, yes,' he declared, '*drokba*, sir.'

We took a short cut to get off the Changtang. Tsetan knew a route that would take us south-west, almost directly towards Mount Kailas. It involved crossing several fairly high mountain passes, he said. 'But no problem, sir,' he assured us, 'if there is no snow.' What was the likelihood of that I asked. 'Not knowing, sir, until we get there.'

From the gently rolling hills of Ravu, the short cut took us across vast open plains with nothing in them except a few gazelles that would look up from nibbling the arid pastures and frown before bounding away into the void. Further on, where the plains became more stony than grassy, a great herd of wild ass came into view. Tsetan told us we were approaching them long before they appeared. '*Kyang*,' he said, pointing towards a far-off pall of dust. When we drew near, I could see the herd galloping en masse, wheeling and turning in tight formation as if they were practising manoeuvres on some predetermined course. Plumes of dust billowed into the crisp, clean air.

As hills started to push up once more from the rocky wilderness, we passed solitary *drokba*s tending their flocks. Sometimes men, sometimes women, these well-wrapped figures would pause and stare at our car, occasionally waving as we passed. When the track took us close to their animals, the sheep would take evasive action, veering away from the speeding vehicle.

We passed nomads' dark tents pitched in splendid isolation, usually with a huge black dog, a Tibetan mastiff, standing guard. These beasts would cock their great big heads when they became aware of our approach and fix us in their sights. As we continued to draw closer, they would explode into action, speeding directly towards us, like a bullet from a gun and nearly as fast.

These shaggy monsters, blacker than the darkest night, usually wore bright red collars and barked furiously with massive jaws. They were completely fearless of our vehicle, shooting straight into our path, causing Tsetan to brake and swerve. The dog would make chase for a hundred metres or so before easing off, having seen us off the property. It wasn't difficult to understand why ferocious Tibetan mastiffs became popular in China's imperial courts as hunting dogs, brought along the Silk Road in ancient times as tribute from Tibet.

By now we could see snow-capped mountains gathering on the horizon. We entered a valley where the river was wide and mostly clogged with ice, brilliant white and glinting in the sunshine. The trail hugged its bank, twisting with the meanders as we gradually gained height and the valley sides closed in.

The turns became sharper and the ride bumpier, Tsetan now in third gear as we continued to climb. The track moved away from the icy river, labouring through steeper slopes that sported big rocks daubed with patches of bright orange lichen. Beneath the rocks, hunks of snow clung on in the near-permanent shade. I felt the pressure building up in my ears, held my nose, snorted and cleared them. We struggled round another tight bend and Tsetan stopped. He had opened his door and jumped out of his seat before I realized what was going on. 'Snow,' said Daniel as he too exited the vehicle, letting in a breath of cold air as he did so.

A swathe of the white stuff lay across the track in front of us, stretching for maybe fifteen metres before it petered out and the dirt trail reappeared. The snow continued on either side of us, smoothing the abrupt bank on the upslope side. The bank was too steep for our vehicle to scale, so there was no way round the snow patch. I joined Daniel as Tsetan stepped on to the encrusted snow and began to slither and slide forward, stamping his foot from time to time to ascertain how sturdy it was. I looked at my wristwatch. We were at 5,210 metres above sea level.

The snow didn't look too deep to me, but the danger wasn't

its depth, Daniel said, so much as its icy top layer. 'If we slip off, the car could turn over,' he suggested, as we saw Tsetan grab handfuls of dirt and fling them across the frozen surface. We both pitched in and, when the snow was spread with soil, Daniel and I stayed out of the vehicle to lighten Tsetan's load. He backed up and drove towards the dirty snow, eased the car on to its icy surface and slowly drove its length without apparent difficulty.

Ten minutes later, we stopped at another blockage. 'Not good, sir,' Tsetan announced as he jumped out again to survey the scene. This time he decided to try and drive round the snow. The slope was steep and studded with major rocks, but somehow Tsetan negotiated them, his four-wheel drive vehicle lurching from one obstacle to the next. In so doing he cut off one of the hairpin bends, regaining the trail further up where the snow had not drifted.

I checked my watch again as we continued to climb in the bright sunshine. We crept past 5,400 metres and my head began to throb horribly. I'd thought that the labourers had left me some days previously, but they were back at work again. I took gulps from my water bottle, which is supposed to help a rapid ascent.

We finally reached the top of the pass at 5,515 metres. It was marked by a large cairn of rocks festooned with white silk scarves and ragged prayer flags. We all took a turn round the cairn, in a clockwise direction as is the tradition, and Tsetan checked the tyres on his vehicle. He stopped at the petrol tank and partially unscrewed the top, which emitted a loud hiss. The lower atmospheric pressure was allowing the fuel to expand. It sounded dangerous to me. 'Maybe, sir,' Tsetan laughed 'but no smoking.'

My headache soon cleared as we careered down the other side of the pass. It was two o'clock by the time we stopped for lunch. We ate hot noodles inside a long canvas tent, part of a workcamp erected beside a dry salt lake. The plateau is pock-marked with salt flats and brackish lakes, vestiges of the Tethys Ocean which bordered Tibet before the great continental colli-sion that lifted it skyward. This one was a hive of activity, men with pickaxes and shovels trudging back and forth in their long sheepskin coats and salt-encrusted boots. All wore sunglasses against the glare as a steady stream of blue trucks emerged from the blindingly white lake laden with piles of salt.

By late afternoon we had reached the small town of Hor, back on the main east–west highway that followed the old trade route from Lhasa to Kashmir. Daniel, who was returning to Lhasa, found a ride in a truck so Tsetan and I bade him farewell outside a tyre-repair shop. We had suffered two punctures in quick succession on the drive down from the salt lake and Tsetan was eager to have them fixed since they left him with no spares. Besides, the second tyre he'd changed had been replaced by one that was as smooth as my bald head.

Hor was a grim, miserable place. There was no vegetation whatsoever, just dust and rocks, liberally scattered with years of accumulated refuse, which was unfortunate given that the town sat on the shore of Lake Manasarovar, Tibet's most venerated stretch of water. Ancient Hindu and Buddhist cosmology pin-points Manasarovar as the source of four great Indian rivers: the Indus, the Ganges, the Sutlej and the Brahmaputra. Actually only the Sutlej flows from the lake, but the headwaters of the others all rise nearby on the flanks of Mount Kailas. We were within striking distance of the great mountain and I was eager to forge ahead.

But I had to wait. Tsetan told me to go and drink some tea in Hor's only café which, like all the other buildings in town, was constructed from badly painted concrete and had three broken windows. The good view of the lake through one of them helped to compensate for the draught.

I was served by a Chinese youth in military uniform who spread the grease around on my table with a filthy rag before bringing me a glass and a thermos of tea. At first I thought I was his only customer, but my eyes followed the soldier as he disappeared into another room which I glimpsed before he slammed the door behind him. Three more uniforms were hunched over a table like mine cluttered with large green bottles of Lhasa beer. They were playing majong in a thick fug of cigarette smoke. Lounging beside them were three skinny, painted Chinese ladies, which seemed rather appropriate in a town named Hor. The young woman nearest the door gave me the once-over before it was closed. She was pretty and svelte but also looked capable of taking care of herself if the bottles started to fly. I turned to my tea, tucked my chair in and the seat came off in my hand.

Half an hour later, Tsetan relieved me from my solitary confinement and we drove past a lot more rocks and rubbish westwards out of town towards Mount Kailas. It felt good to be leaving Hor and I said as much to Tsetan, but he was muttering about how much the tyre repairs had cost. Less than ten minutes outside the town, we had another puncture. It wasn't bad luck. The bald spare had been replaced with one of the newly repaired tyres, which had developed a leak. Tsetan treated me to what I supposed were some Tibetan swearwords. All he said in English was, 'Rate is high; work quality is low.' I could tell he was angry because he didn't call me 'sir'.

The youths at the tyre-repair shop had closed for the evening, but Tsetan found them in the concrete hovel next door and raised his voice just enough to indicate his displeasure. One of the guys traipsed along the front of his premises and knelt down in the dust to fiddle with two lengths of wire, one of which stretched into the scattered refuse; the other through the work-shop window. He called to his mate, who brought him a roll of Sellotape, a length of which the first guy used to fasten the wires together.

With their source of electricity reconnected, the Sellotape-dispenser jacked up the car, removed the heavy wheel and rolled it into the workshop where the other man had persuaded a large piece of machinery to splutter into life. Acrid fumes from the engine began to billow out through the window, much of it via a battered cardboard tube that acted as an exhaust pipe. They needn't have bothered with the tube because, like most of the other windows in Hor, the glass in this one was broken and the frame didn't fit its opening anyway.

I kicked stones outside in the dust and examined the assort-ment of junk strewn all around me. There were old tin cans and shoe soles, pieces of thick wire and pieces of thin wire, oily bits of machinery and grubby scraps of paper blowing in the wind. A few grimy prayer flags flapped on the rusty metal frame of a roadsign, but the sign itself had long gone. Bottles lay everywhere, both plastic and glass, although the glass ones were mostly smashed.

I took a look in to see how the repair was going. The guys were still trying to lever the tyre off the wheel with the aid of a contraption that made sharp piston sounds, a hammer and several thick lengths of wood. But I couldn't linger for long, despite the rapidly falling temperature outside. The rusty sheet-metal door was wide open and puffs of smoke were still being emitted through the cardboard tube but, even so, inside the workshop the atmosphere was thick with fumes. Repairing our tyre had become a race against time to finish the job before everyone in the tiny concrete bunker died of carbon monoxide poisoning.

I wandered round the side of the tyre-repair shop in the fading light to see what garbage was scattered there. It was much the same as in front, the only significant difference being the rows of desiccated human faeces which bore testament to the absence of local toilet facilities. Tibet certainly had prettier towns to be stranded in.

My experience in Hor came as a stark contrast to accounts I'd read of earlier travellers' first encounters with Lake Manasa-rovar. Ekai Kawaguchi, a Japanese monk who had arrived there in 1900, was so moved by the sanctity of the lake that he burst into tears. A couple of years later, the hallowed waters had a similar effect on Sven Hedin, a Swede who wasn't prone to sentimental outbursts. He was a hard man who had studied under Baron von Richthofen in Berlin and become one of the most prodigious Central Asian explorers, but he was so moved by his initial view of the sacred lake that he found himself a small boat and went out for a row in the moonlight.

It was dark by the time we finally left again and after 10.30 p.m. when we drew up outside a guesthouse in Darchen for what turned out to be another troubled night. Kicking around in the open-air rubbish dump that passed for the town of Hor had set off my cold once more, though if truth be told it had never quite disappeared with my herbal tea. One of my nostrils was blocked again and as I lay down to sleep, I wasn't convinced that the other would provide me with sufficient oxygen. My watch told me I was at 4,760 metres. It wasn't much higher than Ravu, and there I'd been gasping for oxygen several times every night. I'd grown accustomed to these nocturnal disturbances by now, but they still scared me.

Tired and hungry, I started breathing through my mouth. After a while, I switched to single-nostril power which seemed to be admitting enough oxygen but, just as I was drifting off, I woke up abruptly. Something was wrong. My chest felt strangely heavy and I sat up, a movement that cleared my nasal passages almost instantly and relieved the feeling in my chest. Curious, I thought.

I lay back down and tried again. Same result. I was on the point of disappearing into the land of nod when something told me not to. It must have been those emergency electrical impulses again, but this was not the same as on previous occasions. This time, I wasn't gasping for breath, I was simply not allowed to go to sleep.

Sitting up once more immediately made me feel better. I could breathe freely and my chest felt fine. But as soon as I lay down, my sinuses filled and my chest was odd. I tried propping myself upright against the wall, but now I couldn't manage to relax enough to drop off. I couldn't put my finger on the reason, but I was afraid to go to sleep. A little voice inside me was saying that if I did I might never wake up again. So I stayed awake all night.

Tsetan took me to the Darchen medical college the following morning. I hadn't seen Darchen yet, having arrived in the middle of the night, and now that I did, I became more depressed. This was the town where the Kailas *kora* began and finished, but it was a long way from the charming little Tibetan settlement that had been nestling in the mountains of my imagination. Tibetan it was, I could see that from the mud-brick buildings, and it wasn't as grim as Hor, but it came close. The main difference was that here the rubbish was in piles dotted along the streets rather than strewn everywhere. There were the mountains, too, of course. They were stretched all along one side of the town, which ran down a fairly steep slope overlooking a vast dusty plain. But I couldn't spot the distinctive peak of Kailas. 'Where is it?' I asked Tsetan.

'Behind those mountains, sir,' he told me. Not being able to see it was disappointing too.

I think it was my sleep-deprived daze that was doing most of the talking that first morning in Darchen. I had finally left my bed at about 5 a.m., fired up my stub of candle and scrabbled through my bags to find the sheaf of notes that Dr Richards had given me in London. Not being able to lie down, combined with the funny feeling in my chest, had led me to wonder whether I might have developed high altitude pulmonary oedema, or

HAPE. This was the unpleasant ailment that resulted in your lungs being filled with fluid. I remembered Dr Richards saying that if you got it you'd know because you wouldn't want to lie down. If you did, your lungs would fill up and you'd drown. I remembered thinking at the time that this would be an odd way to go, Tibet being several kilometres above sea level.

The thought didn't seem so amusing now. I found the notes and leafed through them to the section on HAPE. Being breathless at rest was a cardinal sign, they told me, which I didn't have.

Good.

Coughing was another indication. Again this didn't apply to me.

Better.

The cough would develop, my notes said, from being initially dry to having bloodstained sputum. Nothing even close to that in my case.

Much better.

But I still didn't know what was wrong with me. I flicked on through my papers and came across a sheet I'd forgotten about. It was headed 'Scoring of Mountain Sickness' and detailed a number of tests that anyone could do on themselves to discover whether they were suffering from acute mountain sickness.

It comprised a self-report questionnaire in which you scored your answers to five questions about symptoms like headaches (no headache: 0; mild headache: 1; moderate headache: 2; severe incapacitating headache: 3). You added up your individual scores and if you had a total of 3, you had it. I scored 5.

Over the page was a clinical self-assessment, so I did that too. A total score of five or more, when added to the questionnaire, gave indisputable proof that the respondent had acute mountain sickness. I knew I was in trouble because I was starting from five. In total, I scored eleven.

The scariest test was that for ataxia. It's the same procedure as that once used by the police to assess drunk-driving suspects: walking heel to toe along a straight line. I tried it twice, once with my hands behind my back, walking along a crack in the concrete floor and, having failed miserably at that, again with my arms outstretched like a trapeze artist. I was still all over the place. I simply couldn't walk straight.

The medical college at Darchen was new and looked like a monastery from the outside with a very solid door that led into a large courtyard. We found the consulting room which was dark and cold and occupied by a Tibetan doctor who wore none of the paraphernalia that I'd been expecting. No white coat, he looked like any other Tibetan with a thick pullover and a woolly hat. When I explained my sleepless symptoms and my sudden aversion to lying down, he shot me a few questions while feeling the veins in my wrist.

'It's a cold,' he said finally through Tsetan. 'A cold and the effects of altitude. I'll give you something for it.'

I asked him if he thought I'd recover enough to be able to do the *kora*. 'Oh yes,' he said, 'you'll be fine.'

I walked out of the medical college clutching a brown envelope stuffed with fifteen screws of paper. I had a five-day course of Tibetan medicine which I started right away. I opened an after-breakfast package and found it contained a brown powder that I had to take with hot water. It tasted just like cinnamon. The contents of the lunchtime and bedtime packages were less obviously identifiable. Both contained small, spherical brown pellets. They looked suspiciously like sheep dung, but of course I took them. That night, after my first full day's course, I slept very soundly. Like a log, not a dead man.

Once he saw that I was going to live Tsetan left me, to return to Lhasa. As a Buddhist, he told me, he knew that it didn't really matter if I passed away, but he thought it would be bad for business.

Darchen didn't look so horrible after a good night's sleep. It was still dusty, partially derelict and punctuated by heaps of rubble and refuse, but the sun shone brilliantly in a clear blue sky and the outlook across the plain to the south gave me a vision of the Himalayas, commanded by a huge, snow-capped mountain, Gurla Mandhata, with just a wisp of cloud suspended over its summit.

The town had a couple of rudimentary general stores selling Chinese cigarettes, soap and other basic provisions, as well as the usual strings of prayer flags. In front of one, men gathered in the afternoon for a game of pool, the battered table looking supremely incongruous in the open air, while nearby women washed their long hair in the icy water of a narrow brook that babbled down past my guesthouse. Darchen felt relaxed and unhurried but, for me, it came with a significant drawback. There were no pilgrims.

I'd been told that at the height of the pilgrimage season, the town was bustling with visitors. Many brought their own accommodation, enlarging the settlement round its edges as they set up their tents which spilled down on to the plain. I'd timed my arrival for the beginning of the season, but it seemed I was too early.

One afternoon I sat pondering my options over a glass of tea in Darchen's only café. After little consideration, I concluded they were severely limited. Clearly I hadn't made much progress with my self-help programme on positive thinking.

In my defence, it hadn't been easy with all my sleeping difficulties, but however I looked at it, I could only wait. The pilgrimage trail was well-trodden, but I didn't fancy doing it alone. The *kora* was seasonal because parts of the route were liable to blockage by snow. I had no idea whether or not the snow had cleared, but I wasn't encouraged by the chunks of dirty ice that still clung to the banks of Darchen's brook. Since Tsetan had left, I hadn't come across anyone in Darchen with enough English to answer even this most basic question.

Until, that is, I met Norbu. The café was small, dark and cavernous, with a long metal stove that ran down the middle. The walls and ceiling were wreathed in sheets of multi-coloured plastic, of the striped variety – broad blue, red and white – that is made into stout, voluminous shopping bags sold all over China, and in many other countries of Asia as well as Europe. As such, plastic must rate as one of China's most successful exports along the Silk Road today.

The café had a single window beside which I'd taken up position so that I could see the pages of my notebook. I'd also brought a novel with me to help pass the time.

Norbu saw my book when he came in and asked with a

gesture if he could sit opposite me at my rickety table. 'You English?' he enquired, after he'd ordered tea. I told him I was, and we struck up a conversation.

I didn't think he was from those parts because he was wearing a wind-cheater and metal-rimmed spectacles of a Western style. He was Tibetan, he told me, but worked in Beijing at the Chinese Academy of Social Sciences, in the Institute of Ethnic Literature. I assumed he was on some sort of fieldwork.

'Yes and no,' he said. 'I have come to do the *kora*.' My heart jumped. Norbu had been writing academic papers about the Kailas *kora* and its importance in various works of Buddhist literature for many years, he told me, but he had never actually done it himself.

When the time came for me to tell him what brought me to Darchen, his eyes lit up. 'We could be a team,' he said excitedly. 'Two academics who have escaped from the library.' Perhaps my positive-thinking strategy was working after all.

My initial relief at meeting Norbu, who was also staying in the guesthouse, was tempered by the realization that he was almost as ill-equipped as I was for the pilgrimage. He kept telling me how fat he was and how hard it was going to be. 'Very high up,' he kept reminding me, 'so tiresome to walk.' He wasn't really a practising Buddhist, it transpired, but he had enthusiasm and he was, of course, Tibetan.

Although I'd originally envisaged making the trek in the company of devout believers, on reflection I decided that perhaps Norbu would turn out to be the ideal companion. He suggested we hire some yaks to carry our luggage, which I interpreted as a good sign, and he had no intention of prostrating himself all round the mountain. 'Not possible,' he cried, collapsing across the table in hysterical laughter. It wasn't his style, and anyway his tummy was too big.

V

Norbu made enquiries about yak rental. The woman who ran the café knew a man whose friend herded yaks but the animals in question were currently grazing on some far-off hillside. The man duly set off to find him. He would be a couple of days, we were told.

Meanwhile, we purchased supplies. The *kora* was a fifty-two-kilometre trek. Some people completed it in a single day, Norbu told me, rising in the small hours of the morning and usually making it back to Darchen before nightfall. He had a serious look on his face when he said this, but it didn't last. 'Don't worry, Nick,' he said, giving way to a fit of giggles. 'This is not possible for us.' He thought we could manage it in three days. We bought *tsamba*, sugar and prayer flags in one of the general stores and dried yak meat from a woman who had a large number of cuts hanging from a rope in her outhouse.

With time still to kill before our beasts of burden arrived, Norbu suggested an outing to a nearby monastery. It was an important one, he told me. The residents of Guru Gyem followed the Bön faith, Tibet's original religion, and its location, tucked beneath the sheer cliffs of an arid gorge, was right below a bluff where Bön originated.

Bön is similar to shamanism in many ways, a religion that harbours gods in mountains, rivers and the air, but Tibet's indigenous faith has been heavily influenced by Buddhism over the centuries, and vice versa, so that to the untrained eye the two appear very similar. Like the Buddhist monasteries I'd seen throughout my travels, the walls of Guru Gyem's compound were studded with gleaming prayer-wheels and bedecked with coloured prayer flags fluttering in the breeze. The Wheel of Law, flanked by two sitting deer, also appeared on the roof of the main temple. But here the strings of prayer flags stretched from the monastery walls to the biscuit-coloured cliffs behind, where an annexe had been constructed in the sheer rock face.

At the top of what looked like a vertical, whitewashed wall I could see more prayer-wheels, and behind them dark recesses. 'Caves,' Norbu announced as we drew closer. 'That is where the lamas go to meditate.'

We ran into a monk dressed in burgundy robes as he was leaving through the gates of the monastery compound. He had a deep woollen bag slung over his shoulder with a leg of mutton poking out of the top. Norbu asked him where we might find the senior lama we had come to see, a man named Tenzin Wangdak. The monk cast his eyes towards the caves. 'Up there,' he said. He showed us the path leading up some steep stone steps.

Norbu paused to examine one of the prayer flags we had to duck under as we climbed. Lines of angular text were printed on the strip of thin material and I asked him what they said. 'I don't know,' he murmured, 'this isn't Tibetan. The writing looks similar, but it's Sanskrit.'

The steps disappeared into the cliff and emerged through a wooden door on to a narrow platform. We followed the rough stone wall, which was lined with more flags and looked over the gorge, to a few more steps that led into a cave. Norbu called out and the voice of an old man echoed from within.

Tenzin Wangdak sat cross-legged just inside his cave wearing a white skullcap and dark red robe. He gestured for us to enter his den with a kindly smile. Norbu and I introduced ourselves and took up position in front of him. As Norbu and the lama talked, I took in the contents of the small cavern. It didn't look like a cave at all. Crammed with an astonishing array of treasures, the centrepiece was an altar piled high with statuettes of religious figures. They were all sitting in the lotus position in front of a line of flickering yak-butter lamps surrounded by metal cymbals, small drums and a few handheld prayer-wheels. Thin strips of what looked like bread sticks, but twisted to form the endless Tibetan knot of eternity, jostled for position between small caskets and inlaid boxes.

Hanging from above the altar on a length of cord were bangles and bracelets, strings of coral beads and silver pendants studded with turquoise. At each end was a yellow silk scarf like the one I'd bought in Mongolia as an emblem of my Silk Road journey. I was still wearing it. The near wall of the cavern was completely taken up by holy books, their pages not bound but kept loose and wrapped in a length of embroidered silk. The wall was a set of pigeonholes, each containing one or two volumes. Wherever I looked I saw more dangling jewellery and glittering trinkets. There were old and new silk wall hangings, horns and goblets and shimmering peacock feathers sprouting from behind large conch shells. The grotto was a riot of colour, a hoard of cherished objects wrapped in an aura of mystery. It could not have been in greater contrast to the bleak gorge outside or the colourless hills of the Changtang. The only reminder that this was a cave was its ceiling of bare rock.

Norbu turned to me. 'The lama wants to know if you have any questions for him.'

Caught somewhat on the hop, I paused and then thought I'd try my theory about the importance of mental as well as physical strength to life in Tibet.

'Yes, physical fitness is only half the battle,' Norbu translated, 'your mind must be prepared too.' The lama smiled. 'You are going to make the *kora*,' he said. I nodded. 'There are two *koras*,' the old man continued, 'the outer one and the inner one. The outer is physical. It is not difficult if your body is fit.' He was sizing me up with his kindly eyes. 'How old are you?'

I told him.

'Forty-four, still young. I am eighty-four. I have done the Kailas *kora* ten times, once by prostration. At your age, you should have no difficulty.'

He paused before continuing. 'The inner *kora* is different. Nowadays, the world is very colourful, but for the believer this is not useful. You must banish all thoughts of your family, your office and your car. The inner *kora* takes place inside your heart.'

★

The sunshine was dazzling by the time I first laid eyes on Mount Kailas. We'd set out westwards to walk clockwise round the mountain, following a well-worn path along a ridge that ran out of Darchen past the walled compound of the medical college. The yak-herder, Tashiduntub, had turned up the previous evening with his animals and we'd agreed to hire three for the journey. He had brought along a sidekick, named Tsetan as it happened, so our party consisted of three yaks and four men.

All morning Norbu had been regaling me with stories of gods and goddesses on the magical mountain. Legends across the East tell of a great peak that sits at the centre of the world, in the navel of the universe. A summit of cosmic proportions, this is the holiest of all holy mountains, revered by millions of Buddhists, Hindus, Jains and followers of the Bön religion. To Buddhists it is the home of the four-faced demon Demchog, and to Hindus it is the domain of Lord Shiva, the destroyer and transformer. Jains venerate Kailas as the place where the first of their saints was emancipated, while the Bön faithful know it as the spot chosen by Shenrab, the founder of their religion, to alight from heaven.

As the trail slowly climbed over the end of the ridge we'd been following, I could see it snaking down into a valley ahead, but Norbu had stopped. We were both tired. Although we hadn't gained much height, the high-altitude trail had still been hard going. I'd been glad of my *drokba* fleece coat when we'd left Darchen in the early morning chill, but as the sun had slowly risen the heavy hide had become increasingly cumbersome and sweaty.

I turned and saw Norbu staring into the distance. For the

first time we had a view over the ridge, and Norbu's eyes were fixed on the wedge-shaped mountaintop. The peak was like a pyramid, with one sheer, triangular face looking down on us from on high. Its snowy summit was twinkling in the sunlight.

'Kailas,' Norbu said quietly, 'at last we meet.'

A few steps further on there was a huge, sprawling pile of stones festooned with prayer flags where we slumped down to marvel some more at the distant mountaintop. It was this southern face, Norbu explained, that gave rise to the mountain's name in the Bön religion: the 'nine-storey swastika mountain'. Kailas had been the scene of a famous duel between representatives of Buddhism and Bön for possession of the holy peak. The contest was won by the faith with the more powerful magic, finally determined by the representative who reached the summit of the mountain first at dawn one morning. Naro-Bonchung, the Bön champion, flew up towards the peak on his shaman's drum while yogi Milarepa, the Buddhist contestant, was still deep in meditation. But at the very last moment, Milarepa soared into the air, overtook Naro-Bonchung, and claimed the summit for Buddhism. The vertical gash down the southern face, interpreted as the magical swastika symbol, is said to have been gouged by Naro-Bonchung's drum which he dropped in amazement on seeing the yogi flash past him.

Kailas disappeared from view again as we descended into the deep gorge that ran up its western flank, so beginning a succession of appearances and disappearances that punctuated our three-day *kora*. Like a magician playing tricks before our eyes, the mountain would emerge from behind a solid rock wall to beckon us forward, and then vanish to leave us alone in its giant landscape.

Lunch was an al fresco test of my teeth on the desiccated yak flesh. Both Norbu and I felt exhausted, sprawled out in the sunshine methodically tearing at our meat. We'd stopped on a gentle fold in the valley floor near a solitary flagstaff. It was wreathed in tattered flags like a maypole in the wilderness and surrounded by piles of *mani* stones, offerings carved with Tibetan letters, sometimes picked out in white on a painted russet background. More prayer flags were splayed out on a web of extended cords running up to the flagstaff like strings of Spanish moss. They continued across the *mani* stones in quivering tangles of bunting.

The flagpole was erected afresh each year, Norbu told me, during the festival of Saga Dawa, on the full-moon day of the fourth month in the Tibetan calendar. If the pole stands vertically, this is a good omen, but if it leans towards the holy mountain it is a worrying sign. If the pole leans away from Kailas, the outlook is even more ominous. I'd become dizzy trying to establish whether it stood at a slant while Norbu and the yak-herders prostrated themselves in front of the *mani* stones.

Leaving Norbu to rest after lunch, I clambered up to a ridge that overlooked the flagstaff. It was a miniature plateau jutting out into the valley, no more than a hundred and fifty metres above where we'd eaten, but the rise was steep and I had to stop four times to catch my breath during the climb. I was panting hard when I reached the mini-plateau, a sky-burial site strewn with rock cairns and the cast-off clothing of the deceased. Most Tibetans prefer a sky funeral, presided over by specially trained monks: it is the only way to ensure a proper rebirth. The monks dissect the body and grind up the bones, mixing them with the flesh to be eaten by vultures.

I had to bend double, my hands on my knees, to take in great gulps of the diluted air before I could continue. Then, as I wandered across the burial site, two great raptors materialized, floating high above me on the thermals. I followed a path that wound its way between the small mounds of stones and the scraps of clothing. Plimsolls, boots, torn shirts and tattered hats were buffeted by the wind. A larger cairn was marked by two poles, almost lost in their garland of ragged prayer flags. Overlooking it all from a respectful distance, the summit of Kailas came once more into view, its triangular peak glimmering in the sun's brilliant glare.

We walked for a few more hours up the valley, before the yak-herders called a halt for the day. Tashiduntub and Tsetan tethered the animals within reach of patches of dry, stubbly grass while Norbu and I cleared the larger rocks from an area where we would sleep. Here, the gorge had become deeper, its rugged cliffs casting a great shadow across the canyon long before the sun gave way to night.

As the gloom gathered, the plunging valley walls seemed to grow in immensity, and lying beneath my *drokba* coat the rocks in front of my nose swelled until they were the size of boulders. I felt as if I was disappearing into the enormous landscape, receding further and further until I became smaller than a dot of dust on the arid valley floor before finally vanishing altogether into the velvet darkness of the universe.

★

The second day's walk was more uphill than the first. The trail continued to follow the valley and we started off beside the river, still predominantly choked with snow and ice, but with the telltale trickle of water audible beneath its wintry façade. The track left the stream to climb the snout of a vast apron of scree and it was mid-morning before the sun managed to emerge above the towering canyon walls to splash its golden light across the parched topography.

Ascending the scree was surprisingly hard work. For the most part, the gradients were not steep, but I soon realized that any rise in the path, no matter how gentle, involved significantly greater effort and rapid fatigue. The difference an ascending slope made was quite extraordinary. Walking on the level, or downhill, was no trouble. I could stroll along quite happily, with time to admire the stark geography. The spiky tufts of grass were becoming more scarce, and here and there the rocks were splashed with orange lichen. It felt good to be alive and I sensed that my body had become accustomed to its new exist-ence at high altitude. But as soon as the trail rose, I became keenly aware that I was working on a deficient supply of oxy-gen. The previous night we had slept at 5,105 metres, so trudg-ing up the moderate incline of this scree was the equivalent of marching on a single lung at sea level. And that's how it felt. Not in a breathless way, nor in the sense that the muscles in my legs were tight. This was profound lassitude, a total-body tiredness. I felt completely drained of energy, and had to make frequent stops for rest.

Fortunately, Norbu felt similarly. Although he'd likened us to a couple of academics who had escaped from the library, he had not totally broken free of his books. He had brought along a volume of Tibetan mythology on Kailas and its region, a sort of pilgrim's field guide, that he stopped frequently to consult. Perched on a boulder, gazing off towards some distant peak or a high pass in the gigantic walls of rock, he'd divert my mind from the hurting ascent with tales of thunderbolts and magicians, enchanted yaks and mystifying deities.

Little by little we gained height. The valley was widening and we had left the river far below as we scaled great tongues of rocky scree. I devised a successful strategy for progress by tailing the yaks. They maintained a steady, unhurried pace, but to me it felt like being carried along in their slipstream. It worked for a period, until I could no longer put off a rest. Slumping down against a boulder, I pictured my body as a wilted leaf and could do nothing but watch as the yaks trundled slowly away. I couldn't begin to imagine how anyone could complete this journey in a single day.

We stopped for lunch on a ridge that looked down over a frozen torrent, perhaps twenty-five metres wide. Tashiduntub pointed across the ice-covered stream, his finger tracing our afternoon course through the air. The trail looked steeper than anything we'd yet encountered.

Coaxing the yaks across the ice was difficult. They stopped at its edge and turned their great heads, veering slowly away, as if they knew of a better route. But Tashiduntub and Tsetan took up position behind them, cutting off their retreat, and the leading animal, seeing no way back, gingerly placed a hoof upon the frozen surface. The ice was hard and treacherous. In other circumstances, a skating yak might have been amusing, but I willed them across safely, following behind cautiously.

The track wove its way into a slanting field of larger boulders. A side valley opened up to our right, revealing Kailas once more, its yawning flank smoothed by a glistening glacier. After just five minutes I reprimanded myself for not insisting on a longer lunchbreak. My rests didn't seem to achieve any regeneration, they were simply pauses in the eternal exertion. I was bringing up the rear. Norbu was plodding on ahead of me behind the yaks as they picked their way through the rocks with almost dainty steps.

I tried to banish all thoughts of the physical world around me, to focus on my inner journey. But I couldn't do it. I checked my wristwatch. We had passed 5,300 metres, more than 17,000 feet above the level of the oceans. I concentrated on the sun's rays. They warmed the skin on my head, creating a curious contrast with the chill in the air. As I sucked in the air, I could taste its fresh flavour. It was crisp and tangy, but lacking in nourishment.

Norbu stopped to rest and I joined him. We sat and drank in the silence. 'Just like on the moon,' he said quietly. A pure breeze murmured down from the distant glacier and brought a tear to my eye.

One circuit of the Kailas *kora* wipes away the sins of a lifetime, but for Tibetans this is just the start. Thirteen circuits are desirable because this gives the pilgrim access to certain shortcuts around the mountain and a high-status inner route that is rather shorter than the full fifty-two kilometres we were attempting. I suppose it works a little like a religious aficionados' frequent-flyer programme. But as Tenzin Wangdak, the lama at Guru Gyem, had tried to explain to me, the physical exertion alone is not sufficient for even one successful Kailas *kora* circuit. It is also essential to adopt the right mental attitude, and the pilgrim can check his progress in this department at various points along the *kora*.

Handily placed for this purpose are several sets of 'sin-testing stones', and we came across one such arrangement of boulders shortly before stopping for the night. Exhaustion had almost overcome me by the time I struggled up to join the others by the boulders. I sensed that something unusual was afoot when I saw Tashiduntub and Tsetan remove their hats and sunglasses. 'Now we see how worthy these men are,' Norbu told me with a mischievous glint in his eye. 'If you get through, you are a good guy. If not, this means bad karma.'

Tsetan went first. His physique resembled that of a string bean, and he easily crawled through the small gap beneath the first two boulders. The stones were positioned in such a way that after this first gap was negotiated, the pilgrim had to bend at an acute angle to wriggle through a second, longer and narrower opening. He slid through this one too, just like an eel. When he pulled himself out he gave us all a broad smile. Norbu slapped him on the back. 'Hooray, a good guy!'

Tashiduntub was next. There was more of him, but he managed the first gap without difficulty, and jack-knifed to squirm through the more restricted space. It was difficult for the rest of us to see how things were going through the second opening, but Norbu and I hurried round to the end to make encouraging noises. Tashiduntub's head and shoulders were visible, but it seemed that his hips were stuck. He looked up at us and grinned, grabbed hold of the underside of the largest boulder and hauled himself through.

I looked at Norbu. 'Who's next?'

'You, you,' he cried with a nervous laugh.

'But you're a Tibetan, Norbu. I think you should go before me.'

'I am a bit afraid,' he said, still giggling anxiously, 'and visitors always should go first.'

I wasn't really feeling up to it, and I also had a sneaking suspicion that Norbu wasn't going to do it at all, but my competitive side had been stirred. I took off my glasses, undid the tie round my sheepskin coat, and pulled off the hefty garment to lay it a rock. I got down on my hands and knees and poked my head under the first boulder. At first, it seemed that my shoulders were going to get stuck, but by angling my torso I managed to wriggle my top half through. Now my hips were wedged fast between the two immovable lumps of granite.

Grabbing hold of the rock, I tugged. Nothing happened. For an awful moment I thought I was stuck fast. I closed my eyes and dizziness came over me. Tiny pin-pricks of light flashed through the darkness of my skull and momentarily I slipped out of phase with the world of Kailas. Norbu was laughing when I lost contact, but his hand was on my shoulder when I returned to reality, asking me if everything was all right. Somehow I didn't think it was.

I considered easing myself back, but dismissed the idea as I seemed to be more through than not. So I thought small, flattened myself out and edged forward with the toes of my boots. I was through, but now came the difficult part, the jack-knife manoeuvre to realign myself for the second gap.

'I guess this means I'm half good,' I suggested to Norbu as I lay in the dust trying to dredge up a little more energy.

He was laughing again. 'Yes, yes, half-good guy.'

I struggled for a few minutes more. 'Are you ready for your attempt?' I called to Norbu, who had taken up position at the other end of the final gap.

'No, no,' he called predictably, 'I can't. I am too fat.'

After a couple more pushes, I gave up. I could see that there was no way I would get even my shoulders into the gap beneath the second set of sin-stones, and at least where I now lay offered a viable way out through an opening between the two sets of stones. Besides, my head was throbbing horribly. I just hoped that my good half was the part below the waist. At least that way it might help with the walking.

Things didn't get any worse that night, but they didn't improve either. While most of us were assessing our karma, a strong, biting wind had started to blow up the valley we had climbed that afternoon. It was still blowing when we gathered round a dung fire to eat a greasy yak stew. Norbu mixed *tsamba* into the broth, which was made from melted snow. We were camping within sight of the Drölma-la pass, the highest point on the *kora*. From there it would be downhill all the way, Norbu assured me. This was something to look forward to, I agreed, but first we had to cross the pass, and the route up to it looked terribly steep.

We were at 5,425 metres and I didn't sleep well. After popping a couple of aspirin, I snuggled down in the lee of a large rock, but woke with a start several times, gasping for breath. Although the wind dropped some time during the night, the yaks all had frosty moustaches the next morning. I wasn't hungry, but Norbu and the others all insisted I eat something before we set off to conquer the Drölma-la pass.

This was the part of the trek I'd been dreading most. Ekai Kawaguchi, the Japanese monk reduced to tears by Lake Manasarovar, had suffered a severe bout of altitude sickness on crossing the pass, and he'd done his *kora* on the back of a yak, despite knowing that it wouldn't count if he didn't make the pilgrimage on foot. Sven Hedin, the tough Swede, had also ridden most of the way round the Kailas *kora*. If neither a devout foreign Buddhist nor a hardened explorer had managed it on foot, what hope had I, I kept asking myself. But so far I'd resisted the temptation to ask for a yak ride.

It was an almost continual climb to reach the Drölma-la pass. That may sound obvious, but the relentlessness of the ascent was important to my mental preparation. As I sat half-heartedly chewing my dried-yak breakfast, I followed the trail with my eyes all the way to the top. I was examining it for any segment that looked even vaguely horizontal. There weren't many, but any horizontal stretch, no matter how short, represented a treat in store. Each would be a little oasis of *relatively* easy steps in what I could tell was going to be an otherwise utterly torturous morning.

I knew this was wrong. I knew I shouldn't be focusing on the physical aspects of the trek but that I should really be concentrating on my inner journey. I knew a lot of things, but none of them was helping.

For the first hour, the slope was gentle. My breathing was heavy, but I'd grown used to that by now. I took frequent rest-breaks, again now a familiar pattern. What I hadn't reckoned on was the loss of hearing. Norbu joined me on a patch of bouncy moss. When he asked how I was feeling it sounded as if he was talking in an echoing room located somewhere across the valley, although I could see him sitting right beside me. I swallowed a couple of times, but it made no difference.

I asked Norbu if he was feeling all right. 'Sure,' he said, a reply that reverberated across the airwaves. Didn't he feel tired? 'Yes, of course I am tired. But when we have crossed Drölma-la, it is downhill all the way back to Darchen.'

I told him I wished I had his confidence. I was feeling exhausted and light-headed. If there had been an easy way out, I think I'd have taken it. But the pass was more or less at the halfway point. It was as far to walk back as it was to continue. The only difference was the distance through the pass itself. It can't have been more than another two hundred and fifty metres higher than where we sat, but at that point it seemed that it might be two hundred and fifty metres too far.

Norbu looked away across the valley to where Mount Kailas stood, partially in the shadows of the early morning. 'Nobody can help you,' I heard his voice say. 'You are on your own. You must believe inside.'

We struggled on. By 10 a.m. we stood at the foot of the final ascent. This was the steepest part of the trek so far. I was finding it difficult to judge distance now, but the remaining increase in height can't have been more than a hundred and fifty metres.

The slope looked to me to be about a two-hundred-metre walk. It was rocky and strewn with mighty boulders, but generations of pilgrims had worn an obvious path and there was little snow to hamper my progress. It was just a very steep incline.

That final two hundred metres took me two hours. It wasn't simply that I was walking more slowly than I'd ever walked in my life, it was also the rest-stops. I began by taking ten paces between each rest. I'd count them in my mind, pushing myself forward, telling myself that each gruelling step was taking me closer to the point at which I could start my descent, to the point at which I could start breathing more easily, to the point at which my headaches would become a thing of the past. To the point at which I could take a drink of water without becoming breathless. Every few stops, I'd swallow a few slugs from my bottle, but any more than three gulps at a time left me gasping for air.

I started counting from one to ten, then switched into reverse, which was better. Each step became a countdown to the next rest-stop.

Norbu, the herders and their yaks were all ahead of me. Each was plodding upward at his own pace. They were drawing away, but not quickly. At least they too were finding it hard-going.

About halfway up the final incline I was overtaken. By several people. They were pilgrims doing the *kora* in a single day, a young man closely followed by two women, each with their prayer-wheels whirling. I was sitting down when they appeared from below out of nowhere. The three pilgrims soon caught me up and we all nodded hello. They were dressed in light pullovers and dark glasses; I looked down at their feet, expecting to see small wings on their ankles, but they were only wearing plimsolls. The pilgrims seemed both delighted and startled, in equal measure, when they noted that the *drokba* they'd seen taking time out on a rock was in fact a Westerner. But they probably weren't as surprised as I was to be overtaken by a trio of strolling day-trippers from another planet.

I was down to five paces between stops by the time I reached the pass. I was bent double, panting hard and pushing my knees with my hands to straighten my legs into making each step. I could see Norbu, Tashiduntub and Tsetan had stopped by a wall of flapping prayer flags and silk scarves backed by a pure cobalt sky. That was the important bit, the fact that all I could see behind the solid mass of pennants was sky. It meant there was no more climbing. My watch told me I was at 5,570 metres.

The yaks' reaction to the Drölma-la pass seemed to mirror mine. We were bewildered by the accretion of multi-coloured material strewn all over the ground. It was like a geological deposit of devotional ensigns, the largest collection of offerings I'd seen in all my time in Tibet, a truly cosmic accumulation. The flags and scarves were so dense that I couldn't see the rocks and, like me, the yaks were having trouble finding a way through. The poor animals had to pick their hooves up high to avoid being snagged in the vast tangle of bunting.

Norbu and Tsetan had tied together all the prayer flags we'd purchased in Darchen to make one streamer more than ten metres in length. They were attaching the ends of their contribution to those already quivering in the wind. The three pilgrims who had passed me were already on their way down the other side of the pass, skipping over the rocks, their prayer-wheels still whirling.

Norbu gestured towards the receding figures with an outstretched arm. 'They are amazed,' he laughed. 'You have climbed up here in your *drokba* coat. It is too heavy for the *kora*.' From somewhere deep down I summoned up just sufficient energy to generate a faint flicker of pride.

It was about another thirty-six hours before we arrived back in Darchen. Tufts of grass started to reappear shortly after the initially precipitous descent, which led us across a small glacier and down through more boulder-strewn slopes. It became more gradual once we'd reached a wide, perfectly U-shaped valley. Here the grass grew in peaty hummocks over a landscape sprinkled with granite boulders that sparkled in the sunshine. The route was marked every now and then by clusters of *mani* stones and yak horns. The going was definitely easier, but my exhaustion was still profound. Until, that is, we came upon two more pilgrims prostrating themselves.

One of the two women paused when Norbu greeted her. Like the figures outside the Jokhang temple in Lhasa, she had hardboard attached to the palms of her hands and was wearing tattered kneepads. The women were on day eleven of their circuit, she told us. They had another six or seven to go.

Up until this point, I'd thought that perhaps I'd got my head round the mountain. However, this level of devotion was beyond me. Did they not have food or warm clothing for the cold nights, I wondered? Norbu asked the woman and she explained. 'Every morning they bring their belongings to far away,' Norbu translated, 'then return to prostrate.'

His tone of voice was neutral, as if this was quite normal behaviour. It was, for a Tibetan. These people weren't simply prostrating themselves around Mount Kailas. Every day, they walked a section, deposited their stuff, walked back and then did the route again by prostration. Effectively, they were doing three circuits in one: walking the route twice, both ways, in addition to prostrating themselves over the fifty-two kilometres. My mind couldn't handle it.

The day after our arrival back in Darchen, Norbu took me to another monastery. Tirthapuri was a short drive out of town, a place always visited by pilgrims after they have completed the Kailas *kora*. There was a set-up here, similar to the sin-testing stones, which enabled you to assess the success of your devotion.

The procedure was simple. Up against the wall of the monastery compound was a deep hole, just wide enough to take an arm. Inside it were some stones, white ones and black ones, Norbu said. After completing a *kora* circuit, you put your arm in the hole and picked up a stone. If you pulled out a white one, this meant your mission was successfully accomplished. The sins of a lifetime had been washed away. You were a 'good guy', as Norbu put it.

If your hand emerged holding a black stone, this indicated bad karma. It meant your *kora* had not been successful and your soul was still tainted.

Norbu went first this time. He rolled up his sleeve and plunged his arm into the narrow opening. He pulled it out again, his hand clutching a white pebble. 'Good karma,' he said simply, with a huge grin on his face.

Now it was my turn. I bunched up the sleeve of my *drokba* coat, sank my hand into the hole, felt several stones with my fingers, selected one, and slowly pulled it out. I was squeezing the stone in my tightly clenched fist. I held it out towards Norbu. 'So . . . ?' he said.

I opened my fingers. The pebble was smooth and round and definitely not white. Norbu burst out laughing. 'Black! Bad karma.'

This was difficult to take in, but I felt terrible. It seemed that I'd made some sort of horrible mistake.

'You didn't do what lama says,' Norbu said. 'You always were thinking of your home and car.'

I'd assumed that because I'd made it round the *kora*, because I'd conquered the impossible height of the Drölma-la pass, I must have got my mental attitude right by default. I knew that I'd never for one moment come even close to the psychological strength of the women who prostrated themselves round the mountain, nor even to those day-trippers who had skipped past me on the final ascent to the pass. But in my own little way I must have vanquished my demons of doubt. If I hadn't, I wouldn't have made it. But apparently this wasn't enough.

I looked at the dark pebble resting on my palm. 'Does this mean that it was all for nothing?' The words were coming out of my mouth, but it was as if someone else was saying them. I felt numb. 'I have to do the *kora* again?'

'Yes, you must think of our *kora* as just practice. Next time you will be stronger in your mind.'

I couldn't imagine that there would ever be a next time. It was simply too terrible a prospect to visualize. Norbu threw his arms around me. 'You know, this is really a good sign,' he said. 'It means you will come back to Tibet.'

In a sense this was a kind way of putting it, but I thought it would be quite some time before I came round to the idea.

As I made my way with Norbu back to Darchen, where I would pack my bags and return to the world I knew, I thought about my time in Tibet. In a very real sense, this trip had been an introduction to a form of extreme environment that I'd not encountered before. The trials of life at high altitude were unavoidable and inexorable, and they were as much mental as they were physical. They didn't just entail the simple difficulties of survival on a reduced diet of oxygen, they also, I was now convinced, required a whole new mindset, a psychological out-look designed to make life possible on the roof of the world.

I'd toyed with the idea that adhering to a specially-adapted faith, be it Buddhism or Bön, was actually a necessity in this place, a theory that had been more or less confirmed to me by the monks I'd met along the way. Certainly, the vast majority of Tibetans I'd come across were steeped in a system of devotion that was far beyond anything I'd encountered anywhere else in the world. The chief exception was Norbu, but then his faith had been diluted through living half his life outside his country of birth.

I had somehow managed to complete the Kailas *kora* as a physical task, but the black stone at Tirthapuri had been a timely reminder of the fact that I'd failed the test of the inner *kora*.

Recognizing the need for mental strength had been a significant step, I thought, but on reflection I'd approached the whole enterprise from the wrong end. If I'd put the mental preparation first, the physical energy would have come as a matter of course. My mistake had been to believe, in a fashion that was probably typically Western, that physical needs came first.

REBIRTH ISLAND

I

In the early days, the Silk Road trade routes developed separately on the eastern and western flanks of Asia and eventually met somewhere in the middle. The network at the western end came into being rather earlier than its eastern counterpart due to the rise of the Achaemenid empire in Persia, which controlled large parts of the Middle East five hundred years before the birth of Christ, and its links with the kingdoms of India. Some suggest that the relatively easier terrain stretching from Syria to the Indian subcontinent helped in the early development of these lines of communication. This was a region subsequently conquered by Alexander the Great who, by the time of his death in 323 BC, had established an empire encompassing all the lands between Gibraltar and the Indus. After his conquests, Europeans hitched themselves on to the western end of the Silk Road. By the third century BC, the eastern portion of Alexander's territory had ripened to become a fertile meeting-place for Greek, Persian and Indian ideas, a crossroads for the exchange of goods, values and beliefs.

Meanwhile, at the other end of the continent, it was another hundred years before a Chinese envoy set out on a journey that would earn him the reputation as 'the father of the Silk Road'. The Chinese were having problems with their troublesome nomadic neighbours to the north and west, the Xiongnu, described in one contemporary Chinese account as 'the people abandoned by Heaven for being good-for-nothing'. In an effort to quell this good-for-nothing rabble, a palace courtier named Zhang Qian was sent forth from China in 138 BC on a mission to befriend some rival nomads to form an alliance against the Xiongnu.

Zhang Qian's trip wasn't a great success. He was twice taken prisoner by the Xiongnu and held captive for more than a decade. He also failed to forge any alliances and eventually returned, thirteen years after starting out, with only one of his original hundred men. But the indefatigable Zhang Qian's travels beyond the Tien Shan – the Celestial Mountains – laid the groundwork for the routes of the Silk Road from China. The report he delivered to the emperor about the lands and people he'd encountered made interesting reading. One aspect of Zhang Qian's testimony, an account of the amazing horses he'd come across, particularly fascinated his master. These creatures sweated blood, Zhang Qian claimed, and had been foaled from horses in heaven.

Zhang Qian's report suggested that the heavenly horses were far superior in strength and endurance to the small local breeds the Chinese had at the time, which were probably Przewalski's horses, or *takhi*. On hearing of these extraordinary animals and their blood-sweating – thought to be a sign of vitality but probably a result of seeping wounds left by parasites – the emperor decided he must have some. Other delegations were dispatched in search of them, resulting in further contact with neighbouring states. By the time Zhang Qian died, in 113 BC, he had become one of the most senior ministers in the emperor's court with the title Grand Messenger, his job being to organize the envoys to the kingdoms of Central Asia. These various missions led to the formalization of trade along routes that linked up with those established earlier on the western side of the continent. Along with heavenly horses came other exotica never before seen in China, including the alfalfa on which the new horses were fed, the grape – Zhang Qian gets the credit for these too – cucumbers, sesame and peas. The imperial court also became acquainted with a range of more novel beasts, including elephants, lions and ostriches. Luxuries such as silk, lacquer and jade started flowing out of China in return.

The heavenly horses that arrived in the country subsequently occupied a special place in Chinese culture and were immortalized in the art of the period. This elegant new breed came from two areas: the Ferghana valley, in modern-day Uzbekistan, where Zhang Qian had first seen them, and the Ili valley in today's Kazakhstan. Zhang Qian's last sortie was to the Wusun nomads, reputed to be the forefathers of the Kazakhs, who reared heavenly horses on the lush pastures south of Lake Balkash.

It was to Kazakhstan that I had decided to travel on the final leg of my Silk Road adventures. I was to begin among the heavenly horses in the south-eastern corner of the country where Zhang Qian travelled. From here I wanted to follow this northernmost limb of the Silk Road westwards, skirting the vast steppes of Kazakhstan, to the old trading city of Otrar. Otrar interested me because it is no more. Today its site remains as an archaeological reminder of better times in a region dominated by the Aral Sea, a great inland body of water that once marked the outermost edge of Persia's Achaemenid empire but which has hit the international headlines in more recent years as a scene of ecological catastrophe.

The Aral Sea has been gradually disappearing since the mid-twentieth century as thirsty Central Asian irrigation schemes, established during Soviet times, have resulted in a dramatic decline in the volume of water entering the lake from its two major tributaries, the Amudarya and Syrdarya. In 1960, the Aral was the fourth largest lake in the world, covering an area more than twice the size of Belgium. But since then it has lost four-fifths of its volume, its surface area has been reduced by more than half and its water level has dropped by more than twenty metres. The Aral Sea's remaining waters are now more than twice as salty as any ocean's.

Having spent the best part of a year exploring some of the Silk Road's most extreme natural environments, I thought it would be enlightening to investigate a man-made extreme, to see at first-hand how people have coped with such rapid and dramatic changes in a region's physical geography. There was just a chance that I might be able to gain access to an island in the Aral now abandoned by the military after decades of use as a testing-ground for biological weapons. Arguably, it is the most extreme human-induced disaster zone on Earth.

But down on the borders with China and Kyrgyzstan, the landscape was imbued with a timeless quality. The grasslands of the steppe were magnificently lush and unerringly level. They stretched for mile after treeless mile towards the sharp line of the Tien Shan's snow-capped peaks glimmering in the distance, creeping towards them to envelop their smooth foothills in a swathe of sweet green velvet. After Tibet, it felt good to be closer to sea level, where the grass was verdant, not the colour of dust, and the air tasted fresh and wholesome. I had left a land stocked with watered-down renditions of essential resources and entered another where the fundamentals were fully charged.

My companion on this stretch of my Kazakh journey was a man named Altai who had a Ph.D. in zoology. I'd found him through a zoologist friend in England. When I'd first met Altai he'd listened intently to my plans and then said that although birds were his speciality, he'd be happy to show me how traditional Kazakh life has always centred around horses. 'I know one place,' he told me, with a slightly furtive air.

We were careering along in an old Russian Uaz jeep, like the one Ganbaatar had driven through the Gobi B nature reserve in search of the world's wildest horse. Only Altai's vehicle was rather more the worse for wear. Directly in the sight line from the front passenger seat where I sat, its windscreen bore the jagged spider-web hallmark of what I'd initially thought might have been the impact of a bullet, but had in fact been caused by nothing more sensational than a stone, Altai assured me. At least the windscreen was still extant. The windows in the two doors, by contrast, were missing completely, and every now and then other more essential pieces of apparatus attempted to follow them. At one point, the accelerator came away and Altai was left pumping nothing into the engine until we came to a halt and he reconnected the offending article. This he did slowly and deliberately, exhibiting the sort of single-minded devotion you'd expect from a man who had dedicated his life to the observation of birds.

The roads here were arrow-straight, slicing their course across the pastures, flanked by lines of telegraph poles that tapered away to dissolve in the sunshine at a vanishing point somewhere in the far-off hazy foothills. These components of modernity eased my passage, but they seemed to be little more than trespassers on an everlasting landscape.

When we arrived at our destination in the Karkara valley, things didn't seem quite so ageless. The extended family that Altai had brought me to visit lived among the ruins of a large state sheep farm. Their homestead consisted of a permanently anchored gypsy caravan and a couple of houses with corrugated iron roofs and walls made of hard clay. Here and there it had flaked off to reveal wooden slats criss-crossed below the mud. Horses and chickens wandered in and out between the dwellings and the great pieces of rusting agricultural machinery that littered the yard.

No one seemed surprised to see us when we pulled up in the jeep and jumped out to greet a moustachioed man who had just dismounted from a large horse. Altai and I were invited into the yard through a battered gate and sat down for tea on cushions placed around a low table on the grass. It turned out to be curiously reminiscent of what I think of as a typically English spread. Although the tea itself came in bowls rather than cups, it was served with bread fresh from the 'oven' – the dough baked between two metal plates piled with smouldering animal dung – and great hunks of deep golden butter on chipped plates. Small bowls of thick yellow cream and thin cherry jam completed the feast. It soon became familiar to me: every meal we ate in the Karkara valley was a cream tea.

As the light faded, candles were passed around the stumpy table and we continued chatting into the chill of the night. Our host told us that the sheep farm had ground to a halt after Kazakhstan had ceded from the Soviet Union. The managers had left the area – he wasn't sure where they'd gone, probably back to the city whence they came – but they'd abandoned their houses and some of the workers' families had taken them over. He didn't appear too upset by the change in circumstances. He'd gained a house after all, and some of the sheep from the original herd to go with his horses. 'Before the Russians came, all Kazakhs were wandering herders,' he said. 'We still tend our animals, only now we don't wander very far.' It was just another attempt to modernize Central Asia's herders that had come to nought.

Throughout our conversation, down the valley, the horizon flashed with pulses of sheet lightning. They were accompanied by intermittent rumbles of thunder, occasionally answered by the whinny of a nearby horse. Our host told us that the area was renowned for lightning strikes, but that we weren't to worry because the cluster of houses we sat amidst was surrounded by conductors erected with the sheep complex. I'd seen a small forest of poles stuck into the nearby hill when we'd arrived. It was one legacy of the failed modernization drive that I was happy had survived.

★

The following morning, Altai and I accompanied our host's wife round the back of the homestead to milk the horses. They had been assembled on an expanse of grass that sloped gently towards a steeper incline, less than a minute's walk away, which plunged down to the bed of a stream. The sunshine was crisp and bright and the light breeze was good for the horses, Altai explained in hushed tones to avoid disturbing them, 'because not so many flies'.

Standing in a long line ready for attention were fourteen chestnut mares and their foals, all the progeny of one stallion, Altai said. The modus operandi for milking was the same as I'd seen employed in Mongolia, and unchanged from a description written seven hundred years ago by the medieval traveller William of Rubruck, a Franciscan monk from Flanders who had braved the Silk Road to visit the court of the Mongol Khans a couple of decades before Marco Polo. The foals were tied up at intervals along a rope stretched across the springy turf between two stakes stuck in the earth, and the mares allowed to stand beside their offspring. The leashes on the foals were too short to allow them to suckle, making it easy for the lady to progress from one peaceful pair of horses to the next, pushing each foal gently away to get at the underside of the mare. She wet her fingers in the milk before pulling the teats each time and calmly chanted, '*Sal, sal, sal,*' as the jets of liquid spurted into her pail.

'This means "give it to me,"' Altai whispered. 'Gimme, gimme, gimme,' the lady was intoning as she went about her morning's work.

The horses were tall and sleek and it was quite easy to understand how Zhang Qian would have considered such creatures to be heaven-sent when compared to the relatively stunted *takhi*. Horses have long been fundamental to Kazakh identity. Although in the country today most Kazakhs are sedentary livestock-herders, this settled lifestyle is less than a hundred years old. It was only in the 1920s that the Russians started encouraging them to give up their nomadic ways. The name Kazakh comes from an old Turkic word that is variously translated as adventurer, free-rider or outlaw. This was how they were viewed by the more settled Uzbeks who inhabited the areas to the south of the ancient Oxus river, today's Amudarya. 'In the past many Kazakh children, it is said, learned to ride before they walked,' Altai told me.

It was lunchtime and we were tucking into another cream tea. Kazakhs may no longer be nomadic in the literal sense, Altai went on as he helped himself to some more bread, but the traditions that have evolved over centuries, virtues born of necessity for survival on the steppe, continue. And most of these traditions involve horses. Mare's milk, served slightly fermented and known as *koumiss*, is everyone's favourite drink – one appreciated by William of Rubruck and Marco Polo in neighbouring Mongolia – while horsemeat is a common staple. A traditional horse race features in most Kazakh celebrations, as well as a number of national sports played from the saddle.

'There is *kyz kuu*,' Altai said. 'This you might translate as "overtake the girl".' It was a game for the younger generation that involved riding down the object of your affection. I plastered clotted cream over my hunk of bread as I listened. If the boy catches up with the girl by some predetermined point, he earns a kiss, Altai continued, but if she outrides him, his reward is a whipping.

'Pick up the coin', *kumis alu*, was another, though now it's usually played with a handkerchief, Altai explained. The purpose was to grab the object off the ground while at full gallop. I read later that this was a contest that particularly impressed Alexander the Great during his time in Central Asia. On seeing *kumis alu* for the first time, he's supposed to have exclaimed, 'That's a training worthy of a warrior on horseback.' Kazakhs even wrestled on horseback, Altai said, but the best game of all was *kokpar*.

'What's *kokpar*?' I wondered as I spooned cherry jam over my cream. A long dribble of the sticky concoction made its way down my wrist.

'It is played with a goat,' Altai said. I looked at him sideways, midway through licking my wrist. 'A dead one,' Altai added uncomfortably.

This was beginning to sound vaguely familiar. 'The goat is being held as a sort of a prize,' he explained, 'and when one rider has it, he has to run away with it.'

'*Run* away?' I queried.

'On horseback, of course,' said Altai. 'Others seek to catch him and snatch the goat from him. And then they all have a party.' Altai smiled nervously with a bowl of tea at his lips. 'This is very old, very traditional game. You will see it, because tomorrow they will play *kokpar*, very near to here.'

The following day, while our family all mounted their horses, Altai and I took his dilapidated jeep and drove a little further down the road we had arrived on towards the looming Tien Shan mountains. My map indicated that it led to the Kyrghyz border, just a few kilometres away, and thence to the town of Karakol where the great Russian explorer Nikolai Przewalski was finally laid to rest. He succumbed to typhoid in 1888 while in Karakol preparing for another expedition to Tibet.

I didn't get many more details about *kokpar* as we drove. It transpired that most of Altai's childhood had been spent in the city. His schooling had been in Russian, he told me, and he'd also spoken Russian at home until he was six, when his parents sent him away to a village for a year to learn Kazakh. Everyone in the village knew he was a city boy. They called him an asphalt Kazakh. Nevertheless, he still had fond memories of that year. This early experience of the countryside had eventually led him to specialize in zoology.

We stopped in an area where the Karkara Valley was released into a wide-open plain. Altai turned off the potholed road and we trundled across the grass to a gathering of horses and people. This was a place where *kokpar* was traditionally played, I was told. It was a reminder of the area's historic position as a meeting-place for nomads and Silk Road traders. Several dozen men, women and children were milling about, the men mostly on horseback. We were on a magnificent stretch of meadow with the silent Tien Shan mountains as backdrop.

While Altai had tried to explain the rudiments of *kokpar* over lunch the previous day, I recalled reading about a similar-sounding game, known as *buzkashi*, played in Afghanistan. A sort of early precursor to polo, it's played with a headless goat and it's not a game for sissies. Altai had confirmed that the goat is also decapitated for *kokpar*. After a few minutes waiting on the grassland, another small group appeared on their horses. They were three older men, all wearing Moslem skullcaps. One of them had a white, curly-haired goat slung in front of him across his saddle. It wasn't dead.

The men with skullcaps dismounted as the other riders gathered round and greetings were exchanged. The goat, meanwhile, was put on the ground and a youth was given the responsibility of holding it by the horn.

The elderly men with skullcaps knelt down on the grass facing the goat and everyone raised their hands, palms up, as one of them said a short prayer. The goat bleated. The riders sat in their saddles, arms outstretched, and watched.

Other than his skullcap, the man who said the prayer was dressed in western style clothes like everyone else. He wore a striped cotton shirt and a jacket with wide lapels. His trousers were blue and his black boots were scuffed at the toes. He had a white biro sticking out of the top pocket of his jacket. At the end of the prayer everybody did a face-washing motion with their hands, someone drew a knife and cut the goat's throat. I asked Altai what had been said in the prayer, and he told me it was basically a few words of gratitude. I suppose it might be summed up as, 'Thank you, God, for this goat. It's had a nice life, but now we want to use it for a game of *kokpar*.'

Its head and hooves severed, the carcass was ready. The man who had said the prayer grabbed it and walked towards where Altai and I were standing. We exchanged nods and I asked if I could hold the corpse. I wanted to see how heavy it was. The skullcap man said a few words in Kazakh as he passed me the

Above: Lhamo
working the bellows
to aerate the dung
fire

Right: Yangdzo,
one of Lhamo's
grandchildren,
taking time off from
corraling the goats

Left: A trio of *drokba* men

Below left: Tenzin Wangdak advising against all thoughts of family, office and car in his cave at Guru Gyem Bön monastery

Right: Mount Kailas, the 'nine-storey swastika mountain'

Below: Norbu and the author, two academics who have escaped from the library

Norbu launching prayers to the heavens at the Drölma-la pass

Above: Riders of heavenly horses breaking away from the pack during a game of *kokpar*

Right: The Golden Man, not quite what you expect of a supposedly barbarian society like the Scythians

Below: Bekmuhan with his golden eagle at the Charyn Canyon

Below and left: The ships' graveyard near Zhalangash

Right: The dust storm at Qulandy

Below right: Looters unloading the motorbikes on arrival at Rebirth Island

Below: Zhannat first laid eyes on the Aral Sea when she was 28 years old

Above: Dave Butler, veteran of the East Berlin sewage system

Left: Inside the laboratory complex at Aralsk-7

Below: So much for the clean-up operation on Vozrozhdeniye

goat. It was very heavy and I had to rest it against my thigh. 'We can only use a goat,' Altai translated, 'because the carcass of a sheep is not strong enough.' I gave back the goat. 'This is a rough game,' Altai added, unnecessarily.

The man walked away from us and deposited the dead animal on the grass as the riders, perhaps twenty or so, assembled a little further off, all facing the woolly carcass. The man backed away and the game began.

It started with a charge towards the decapitated goat, the leading three or four guys riding almost upside down, lurching over the sides of their mounts, each with an arm outstretched to pick up the dead animal. None of them managed to get a clean grip and the mêlée turned into a more or less static scrum of horses as they jostled for position. A man would launch himself downward, hand open, only to be pushed away by another ten riders all trying to do exactly the same thing.

Horses twisted and turned on the spot, while whips flew in all directions. A rider took hold of the reins of an opponent's horse and pulled it aside to make room for his own attempt to pick up the goat, but only for two other horses to squeeze into the gap he'd just created. I'd expected a blur of activity, but not all in one place. The seething mass of horseflesh was in perpetual motion all right, yet at the same time it was also entirely stationary. No one had yet managed to pick up the goat.

Altai was watching intently. 'What's the purpose of the game?' I asked him. He shook his head and I could tell he was only half listening. 'How do you win?' I asked again.

Altai turned his head partially towards me while keeping his eyes on the action in front of us. He was clearly thinking. Then he turned back to concentrate on the match. 'I don't know,' he said finally.

Horses were peeling off from the pack and trotting round to another side to rejoin the fray. The white carcass was now lost in the small thicket of horses' legs and human arms. A couple of riders nearest to where we were standing wheeled away and one of them momentarily lost his balance while half out of his saddle. The horse came towards the small crowd at some speed. I took flight with the women and children, who scattered in all directions, but the three elderly gents with skullcaps just stepped calmly aside as the rider, a young man wearing a rather smart stone-washed denim jacket, regained his composure. Pulling back on his reins, he wheeled round and returned to the scrum. The crowd reassembled.

'Yes,' Altai exclaimed, bending down and pointing into the throng. One of the men had got a grip on the beast and was trying to haul it up on to the front of his saddle, but immediately a tangle of other arms flew across him. Two other guys also had their hands firmly embedded in the fleece and a mounted tug-of-war ensued. The struggle continued for what must have been at least a minute before the man who had first grabbed the carcass gave an almighty tug and managed to get the decapitated goat into his lap. He leant low over the neck of his horse, broke free from the pack, and charged away. Everyone in the crowd disintegrated into helpless laughter, which seemed like a curious reaction to me until I realized that the man who had just burst out of the group no longer had the goat across his saddle. It was still inside the throng being tugged back and forth. Realizing his getaway was not a success, the rider aborted, grinned broadly and returned to the huddle.

I turned to observe the small crowd around me. They were watching excitedly, pointing and yelling encouragement at appropriate times. One small girl, who couldn't have been more than four, stood with her hands over her mouth. Behind us all and to one side, a little boy in long blue shorts and a T-shirt was examining the head of the goat which lay forgotten in the grass. He picked it up by one horn and raised it to his eye level for a closer look. Since he was holding it by a single horn, the head was at an angle, so the boy cocked his head to look at it eye to eye. He stood like that, eyeball to eyeball, for a little while. There was no expression on his face. He'd probably seen lots of goats' heads lying around in his short life. Eventually he dropped the head and ambled back to where his mother was watching the game.

A muscled youth with very short hair and an open-neck shirt had the goat across his saddle and was battling to exit the scrum. He had a wild man of the steppe on either side of him, each leaning across in an effort to grab what they could. These three broke away from the main body of horses and started to pick up speed, then, suddenly, the short-haired youth was free and galloping towards the Tien Shan. The other two gave chase, followed by a few more, and this breakaway pack made a mad dash for the mountains as the main body of riders huffed and puffed and wiped their brows.

A mixture of whoops and a small cheer had gone up from the spectators. 'He has won,' declared Altai, as if he'd known all along that this was how to win.

★

The *kokpar* match continued for most of the afternoon. Whenever a horseman broke away to score a victory, he'd ride back sooner or later and fling the carcass to the ground for another game. After a few more rounds of frantic activity, Altai asked if I'd like to join in. If he'd posed this question any earlier I wouldn't have even considered the offer. I'd arrived at the match expecting to witness one of the most hazardous sports on earth, but having watched for a while I was now not so sure. For the most part, *kokpar* appeared to consist of frenzied huddles in which nothing much actually happened. Several of the horsemen were looking weary, which might be to my advantage, and no one had been seriously injured. Not yet, at least.

Earlier I alluded to a football match of sorts in the Danakil Desert of Ethiopia. All the other players had arrived carrying Kalashnikovs and very long knives, and the game had been played in astonishing heat, though it'd been about average for the hottest desert on the planet. No one had seemed to know what the rules were but, like *kokpar*, it involved a lot of dashing to and fro, only on foot. These mad dashes, I was informed just before taking to the pitch, usually resulted in pile-ups. And these pile-ups sometimes led to fatalities. But only sometimes.

My survival instinct had kicked in on that occasion and I'd developed my own special gameplan: whenever a mad rush occurred, I madly rushed in the opposite direction. The strategy had proved very effective. My team won the match and no one was killed.

I decided to employ similar tactics for the *kokpar*, which vaguely resembled a kind of rugby on horseback, and looked like child's play by comparison. But as I climbed into the saddle,

I reminded myself not to get too cocky. This was still a danger-ous game and we were a long way from any hospitals.

Altai had spoken to the man who'd led the prayers and arranged for me to use his horse. It was a good-natured and obedient steed, he assured me. I took my place alongside the other competitors a few metres from the goat's carcass on the ground and received nods of acknowledgement. Then, without any further ado, the game began.

In a sudden surge of man and beast, everyone charged towards the immobile quarry. Everyone except me, that is. My horse was, perhaps, a little too placid. It just stood there, not even watching the proceedings. 'Go forward,' Altai urged. I dug my heels into the horse's flanks, and it took a step in the right direction, towards the seething horde. No one had yet managed to grab the goat. Riders were hanging down from their saddles while others jockeyed for position. Another couple of kicks took me to the edge of the fray.

Horses' heads bucked up and down all around me as whips flew and broad shoulders lurched back and forth. But almost as soon as I joined the party I was out again. A rider pushed the rump of my mount aside with his boot, and I found myself facing the wrong way, with my back to the action. Perhaps this wasn't such an easy game after all.

Hauling sideways on my reins, I managed to realign myself. Someone had succeeded in getting hold of the goat's hind leg and the frenzy intensified. The carcass was involved in the familiar tug-of-war. It changed hands a couple of times while the entire mass of riders edged slowly towards the crowd and I found myself being carried along in the turmoil.

Four riders broke free, charging towards the spectators who fled in panic. I saw that one of the guys had the goat's stunted leg in his hand. He took flight, the hefty carcass dangling down by his stirrup, the three others hurtling along behind. Several more took up the challenge, spurring their mounts into hot pursuit with a flurry of whips, but I took this as a cue to rein in my horse and head the other way.

The next round was similar, although this time I was immediately closer to the action. Nevertheless, I could only watch in admiration as, all around me, men hung upside down from their saddles trying to grab the headless goat. The scrum wheeled slowly around. I was enjoying this: it was like riding a merry-go-round with live horses. My major worry, that I might come off my mount, had disappeared. I wasn't too concerned after realizing that, amazingly, no horse ever trod on the goat. And whenever I felt my balance going, I could always reach out and steady myself on the haunch of someone else's horse. Everyone was doing it.

At length, the goat's headless carcass rose from the ground. All of a sudden I realized it was within my reach. This was so unexpected that it took me a second or two to appreciate what I should do. Leaning across a youth in a sleeveless T-shirt, I took hold of a leg and started tugging. The youth turned to size up his opponent and laughed maniacally. My efforts had managed to position the goat more or less across this guy's saddle, but two other men also had hold of it. There was a lot of grunting and straining, but it went nowhere.

As if in slow motion, it slid off the saddle next to me and a rider who was stretched full-length across the neck of my horse managed to haul the dead beast up and across me. I seized my chance, burying both fists in the thick fleece to halt its progress, while simultaneously digging my heels into my mount to make it move. My horse made a sort of skipping motion, edging forward a little through the throng of other mounts. Without even thinking about it, and almost by accident, I appeared to be on the verge of winning a round of this extraordinary game.

But only for an instant. Another guy was leaning across from some distance behind me. He had a firm grip on a leg and with an almighty tug the dead animal disappeared from my clutches. I was left with two clenched fists full of white goat-hair.

With the ferment continuing behind me, I steadied my horse. Altai had told me that one of the most important aspects of *kokpar* was the way it truly reflected the character of a people who had long aspired to live independently. For a brief moment, I'd felt the primeval thrill of life on the steppe.

II

The director of the falconry museum at Nura, a severe woman who took her job very seriously, rapped her long metal pointer smartly on the floorboards to make sure she had our attention. She gave me a stern look and began the guided tour. The museum wasn't large – it consisted of just one room – but it was filled with exhibits. We began with a detailed catalogue of the contents of the glass cases. There were ancient leather gauntlets, and neat little leather hoods used to calm the birds when at rest. Next to them was a display of small felt bags covered in embroidered fabric. These were used to keep scraps of meat in, the director explained, tapping the glass with her pointer. The scraps of meat, usually rabbit, were used to attract a flying bird during training.

Next came a series of wooden struts shaped like the letter Y; the fork fitted into your hip, she told us. At the opposite end was a curved strip of flattened metal that went under your elbow. The structure was used to support your forearm when a golden eagle was sitting on it. They were heavy birds, she added, just to clarify the matter.

★

Altai was a bird man and he'd insisted that, having witnessed the importance of horses to the national identity, we should stop off on our return journey to Almaty so that I could see some birds. Not just any old birds, he told me, but golden eagles. And although special enough in their own right, they came with an added edge. They were hunting birds, trained to do their master's bidding.

Among Kazakhs, the art of falconry stretches back to ancient times. Herders and their livestock shared the steppes with great numbers of birds of prey, Altai said, and Kazakhs soon realized that these birds could be used to obtain food and furs. Several species of falcon were trained, but golden eagles were the best.

'There is one legend,' he told me, 'about Mohammed, the founder of Islam. He came to Kazakhstan and saw hunting with predatory birds for the first time. He was amazed and ordered several such hunting birds to be sent to Islamic leaders in Arabia, where they did not know of this occupation. But his helpers did not understand what he said, so when they got the birds, they cooked them.'

We both laughed. 'But they obtained some more birds,' Altai went on, immediately serious again, 'and later this kind of hunting became widespread in Arab countries.'

We had arrived at the outskirts of the small town of Nura and turned off the road into a dusty courtyard. The director of the complex, a sort of raptor-training centre, had met us at the gate. Before we saw her birds, she told us, we had to visit the museum. I got her drift immediately. The subject was not up for discussion. She already had the metal pointer in her hand.

★

We had moved on to a set of wooden objects, the purpose of which was not entirely clear because Altai had mumbled the translation. I let it go because my concentration had begun to waver. I have an aversion to guided tours. There's something about being a captive audience that bothers me, and I'd encountered this particular type of museum director numerous times before in the old Soviet Union. I'd learned to identify the almost power-crazed glee in their eyes whenever a visitor appeared on the doorstep. I know that this woman was only doing her job, but she discharged her duties in a style now seldom encountered in the West. Her attitude indicated that I'd be well-advised to pay attention because there might be a test afterwards.

When we arrived at the last of the glass cases, I felt a palpable sense of relief. I'd take a quick look at the large number of paintings and photographs that adorned the walls, I thought, and then we could get outside and see the eagles. The director gave me a withering look. 'Not so fast,' I could practically hear her thinking as she gently tapped the pointer against the open palm of her hand. 'And now we will inspect the illustrations,' she said.

She led us back up the room to where the line of pictures began. I looked at my wristwatch. 'How are we doing for time?' I asked Altai.

He wasn't on my wavelength. 'Oh, no problem. We have lots of time,' he said.

To her credit, the director didn't pause over every one of the bad oil paintings and grainy black and white photographs – it just seemed that way. But actually I was glad when she did, because some of the stories she regaled us with, of famous birds and their owners, were attention-grabbing. There was the tale of the falconer who had lived to the age of 103. When he passed away, his eagle flew round his grave for two days before finally lying down on it to die too. Another old photograph showed a figure wreathed in a fur hat and heavy topcoat standing ramrod straight with his eagle on his forearm. The animals that this man's bird had caught fed an entire village throughout the Second World War.

Outside in the warm sunshine, Altai and I were escorted past a series of large cages towards an orchard on the other side of the courtyard. Most of the cages were empty, but one contained a display of pelts from creatures caught by the resident birds in recent months, the director told us. There were two different types of fox fur, some hares and a range of small wild cats.

A tree laden with plump apricots, their downy orange skins sun-kissed with flecks of red, stood at the entrance to the orchard. Further in, the sun glistened off dark plums and little green apples. The fruit looked good, but standing on a stout wooden perch, low down in the shade of a small pear tree, was something better. It was a very large golden eagle.

It squawked as we approached, twisting its neck to look at us. Its head moved through 180 degrees while the rest of its body remained motionless. I found the effect unsettling. Had a man been sitting there instead, any reaction to our approach would have involved a twist of the shoulders at the very least. The golden eagle's head just swivelled round like the gun turret of a tank, only much more smoothly and infinitely faster. It sat there and looked at us menacingly, its body still facing the other way.

'This is male golden eagle,' the director announced, suddenly revealing a command of English. 'His name Akbalak.' Akbalak squawked again, just to confirm his presence, but before I had time to take in the magnificent creature in front of me, we were moved on. A second bird, bigger than the first, was perched on another wooden block a little further into the orchard.

'This is female golden eagle. Her name Karager.' Standing beside Karager, stroking the smooth feathers on her head and chest, was her keeper, a man introduced as Bekmuhan. Karager appeared not to dislike the attention, but she was also interested in our arrival. She did a similar head-swivelling act and fixed us with the same impassive stare.

Bekmuhan, who was wearing a long leather gauntlet on his forearm, bent down to untie a leash attaching his eagle to her perch and held his arm out for her to stand on. Karager glanced down at his arm, hopped on to it and was raised up so that man and bird stood eye to eye. The golden eagle was the size of a small human child, maybe a four or five year old. She had brown plumage, with flecks of white on the wings and tail feathers. The feathers on her head were a lighter shade of russet.

She seemed relaxed yet totally focused, alert to everything going on around her. I had the feeling of being in the presence of a perfectly tuned machine, sleek and graceful but at the same time full of power and danger. Bekmuhan was still stroking his bird like a pussy cat, but Karager's bright yellow talons were huge and kneading his tough leather glove. She was more like a flying lioness.

That impression stayed with me in the evening when Altai

and I accompanied the two eagles and their keepers on a training session. We drove out of Nura to the Charyn canyon, a spectacular series of chasms that had been eaten into a sandstone plateau. Altai and I were back in the jeep, but the eagles travelled by motorbike and sidecar. They sat on the arms of their trainers quite contentedly, wearing their little leather caps to cover their eyes. The headwear made them look like executioners on their way to work as they sped into the canyon.

Training a golden eagle was a lifelong commitment, Altai told me. The first requisite was for the bird to grow accustomed to its keeper. In the initial phase, this meant spending several days and sleepless nights together. Both fledglings and adult birds are habituated in this way. This process is faster with a chick, Altai said, but it is worth persevering with an older bird because it usually makes a better hunter in the end since it has already learned its predatory skills in the wild. The eagle is taught to accept food from the hand of its keeper and thus trained to jump on his arm to get at the meat. After a mutual trust has been established, he will take his bird for walks in crowded places, such as a bazaar, to cement the relationship. The hunting itself, which often takes place alongside a horse and a dog, sometimes starts with stuffed foxes before proceeding to the real thing.

The display we witnessed was more of an obedience test than an actual hunt. The larger, female bird, Karager, was taken along a spur that looked out over one of the canyon's yawning gorges while Altai and I accompanied her handler, Bekmuhan, along a similar spur that ran along the other side of the ravine. The position we took up was a good two hundred metres from the bird's starting point and perhaps fifty metres lower.

Bekmuhan was wearing a plum-coloured tunic and a fur hat. The top of the hat was made of felt in the same colour as his tunic, and sewn on to it was a cut-out motif in a lighter colour depicting an eagle standing with wings folded. This was his training uniform, Bekmuhan explained, an outfit he always wore because the eagle was used to it.

Bekmuhan took a small pouch from his belt and selected a fresh piece of rabbit which he'd use to lure the eagle. He pulled on his leather gauntlet, positioned the rabbit titbit between the fingers, and held out his arm. Across the ravine, I could make out Bekmuhan's assistant unhooding the golden eagle.

With a few flicks of his wrist, Bekmuhan showed the distant bird that he had meat in his hand. Far away, I saw her drop off the assistant's arm and glide down towards us with a few effortless flaps of her mighty wings. She swooped momentarily down into the ravine and then up again, on a bee-line towards Bekmuhan's outstretched arm. With her wings spread, the huge bird appeared, talons first, over the crest of the gorge and landed on the gauntlet, where she set about the morsel of rabbit with her fearsome hooked beak. Bekmuhan stroked her bent head as she tucked into the snack.

After another similar exhibition flight, Bekmuhan suggested I might have a go at holding the scrap of meat. He told me that if I wore his hat and kept my gloved arm steady there was no chance of the eagle doing anything other than what I'd just seen. I had nothing to fear since she was only interested in the meat.

Altai had taken the eagle back up to the other side of the canyon, a lengthy walk up one spur and down the other. I extended my arm and flicked the new bit of rabbit back and forth in my armoured hand. Time seemed to stand still as I watched the eagle swoop down once more. Her flight was almost lazy. An easy swish of her great wings brought her across the ravine in a smooth arc and, before I had time to have second thoughts, she had landed on my arm to devour the meat.

I'd never really understood the phrase 'poetry in motion', but this was it. The golden eagle alighted with no more impact than a fly. If my eyes had been closed, I'd have barely noticed. There was the slightest brush of feather-tips in my face and no sound but for the faintest rustle of wings as she settled on my gauntlet. It was pure power and grace, a creature of beauty and splendour shot through with exhilarating precision and spine-tingling menace. Better than that, she was sitting on my arm to eat her dinner.

Altai said the relationship between Kazakhs and birds of prey dated back thousands of years. A tomb excavated in the east of the country had revealed the body of a man flanked by four eagles, one at each of the cardinal points. The tomb was thought to be at least two thousand years old, he told me. European visitors to the court of the Mongols in the thirteenth century had commented on the continuing popularity of hunting with birds across Central Asia. Marco Polo saw falconry being practised in Persia and noted that Kublai Khan's hunting parties included no less than ten thousand falconers.

*

The early affinity developed between the nomads of the steppes and its wildlife, particularly with birds and horses – both tamed and put to good use – led me to ponder on where things had gone wrong in human society's attempts to control nature and harness its forces to our advantage. I had left Altai in Almaty, a city with so many trees it appeared to be disguised as a park, and was continuing my journey westwards with one of his friends who had offered me a lift. The friend spoke no English, so I had plenty of time to myself during our two-day drive.

The road we followed took us along the course of the north-ernmost limb of the Silk Road, parallel to the ever-present peaks of the Tien Shan. Although I was still more than 1,500 kilometres from my ultimate destination, I had entered the Aral Sea basin, a two-million-square-kilometre swathe of Central Asia from which the great inland sea draws its sustenance. Tall reeds waving lazily in the breeze marked the path of streams that flowed down from the mountains into the plain. The wheat in the fields had mostly been harvested, whereas in the cut pastures burly men were wielding pitchforks to build great stacks of hay. Shafts of sunshine twinkled on sweaty brows and fops of black hair were swept back from noble foreheads. It was a view of the rural idyll I'd seen depicted in Soviet realist pictures, except that rust had engulfed the once shiny paintwork of the combine harvesters, and the honest workshirts had been replaced by vests sporting Western slogans and Disney-style characters.

Only the fields themselves remained unchanged from Soviet times. This is not to say that the fringes of the steppe hadn't been cultivated before the Russians arrived. Large irrigation systems were constructed on the Amudarya as long ago as the seventh and sixth centuries BC, but the scale of operations introduced by the Soviets had no precedents in the region's history.

The fields we passed appeared endless. They looked too big to have been the work of people. These were constructs on a scale usually associated only with nature. It was as if someone had driven a tractor to plough a roadside verge until the petrol had run out, so marking the edge of the cultivated area. Refilling the petrol tank, a second row of furrows was ploughed, returning parallel to the first, and so on until the entire steppe had become one gigantic field.

These vast tributes to human endeavour can be traced back to one man: Nikita Khrushchev, a former shepherd who did well for himself and in the process caught the modernization bug. Far away in the Kremlin, in 1949 he launched a drastic reorganization of agriculture. Khrushchev's campaign saw a concerted effort to increase the area of cropland in then Soviet Central Asia, ploughing up the steppes to plant wheat and dramatically increasing the volume of water diverted from the Amudarya and Syrdarya to irrigate fields, mostly of cotton.

It was manipulation of the natural world on the grandest scale, but also the control of nature gone awry. The results are still echoing down through the passageways of time. Ploughing the steppes was billed as a Virgin Lands scheme because looking from the outside the steppes appeared untouched. The groups who used them were those whom Khrushchev could once have called his own kind: the shepherds and herders and their livestock. It was the final nail in the coffin of the Kazakhs' nomadic lifestyle. And for other descendents of the nomads, the results have been equally catastrophic. I was on my way to see those left to cope alone on the receding shoreline of the Aral Sea. The stretches of irrigated farmland I was to pass on my continuing journey westward, as I joined the path of the Syrdarya, schemes that have their larger counterparts across the neighbouring states of Uzbekistan and Turkmenistan, had spelt doom for one of the world's greatest inland waters.

I'd received another reminder of when times were different during the days I spent in Almaty, the country's former capital, whose very name – Father of Apples – echoes the nation's rustic roots. Altai had urged me to visit the museum of archaeology to see the so-called Golden Man, a national treasure unearthed from a burial mound not far from the city.

It wasn't the man himself who was golden, but his clothing. A tailor's dummy had been dressed in his garb, a work of staggering detail: tunic and boots, each a fantastic patchwork of elaborate gold trefoils, and headdress bedecked with golden feathers and arrows. All over the costume were depictions of animals: a hat pin topped with a bird in flight and golden buckles in the image of a horseman. There were tiger heads and elks with huge horns, while snow leopards danced in front of the intricate peaks of distant mountains.

The Golden Man is thought to date from the fifth to fourth centuries BC, which makes him a Scythian. The stunning crafts-manship on his outfit is slightly at odds with what little we know about this ancient society of the steppe. To the best of our knowledge, the Scythian culture had no writing system, so most of our information about their nomadic way of life comes from ancient Greek and Roman texts. Their views on the Scythians were coloured by the fact that these people lived on the outer edges of the world as they knew it. Homer called them 'the mare-milkers', but Pliny reckoned they were cannibals.

Theirs was a mysterious, mobile society. They had a reputation as fearsome mounted warriors, but at the same time their behaviour was by no means always predictable. Herodotus describes a bizarre event in 514 BC, when Darius, the third of the great Persian kings, decided to invade Scythia. Actually, it wasn't really an event so much as a non-event. Darius turned up with an army of seven hundred thousand soldiers spoiling for a fight, and the Scythians retreated. The Persians pursued them, but the further into the steppe they marched, the further the Scythians withdrew.

Darius sent word that he had come for a battle, but the Scythians told him they weren't interested. They had nothing to defend, they said, no towns or cultivated lands. Why would they want to fight?

This was a pretty unusual way to behave, Darius thought, but he looked around him and realized the Scythians had a point. There wasn't anything to capture – no cities, no buildings, no plunder – in fact there was nothing here but endless steppe. It would be like fighting for the air, so Darius turned round and led his army all the way back home.

As far as the ancient Greeks were concerned, the world became stranger and stranger the further one travelled away from Greece. The ends of the earth were inhabited by all sorts of oddballs like the Scythians. There were people with dogs' heads, people with one big foot, and people who didn't wear clothes. The plantlife in the world's nether regions was equally extraordinary. Among Alexander the Great's more fantastical adventures is an encounter with a tree of talking heads. Interestingly, the Chinese entertained similar ideas about their unexplored hinterland. An encyclopaedia from around the same time as Alexander also describes a tree with human heads in place of flowers. In this case, the heads didn't speak when questioned, they just laughed. If they laughed too much, the account declared, they fell to the ground.

The stories of bizarre, monstrous races occupying the remoter parts of Asia were still fascinating enough in medieval Europe for the Franciscan monk William of Rubruck to keep an eye open for them as he travelled to Mongolia in the thirteenth century. The route he followed skirted the Aral Sea to the north and took him up the Syrdarya, then the Jaxartes river. He didn't see anything truly peculiar so he asked around when he arrived at the Mongol court. Having conquered most of the continent's nether regions, the courtiers had moved on rather faster than their European counterparts. William of Rubruck was astonished to hear that no one knew what he was talking about.

Not all the ancient Greeks bought into the marvels of the East and the monstrous races found therein. Strabo was a more down-to-earth type. In his great work *Geographia*, a mammoth seventeen-volume regional geography of the world, he concentrated on the more believable aspects of life at the ends of the earth. The barbarians herded animals and lived on a diet of meat and dairy products because that's all the environment would allow. It wasn't like the fertile soils of civilized countries, where arable farming was possible and people could eat bread.

In consequence, the Greeks and Romans could live in towns. They didn't need to carry weapons because they were living in peace with their neighbours, and their spare time could be devoted to relaxation and learning. Barbarians, by contrast, were forever on the move with their sheep and cows, and had to be constantly on their guard against animal rustlers, hence they were always armed.

The cultured citizens of the cities lived according to laws and ethics, concepts the poor old barbarians had missed out on. They didn't understand the divine laws of hospitality, so they couldn't respect them. The difference was clear-cut. If a stranger turned up in a Greek city, he was treated with civility. Barbarians faced with the same situation reacted in their own way. They ate their guests.

If you strip out the references to cannibalism, the patronizing arrogance of city-folk towards the nomadic herder hasn't changed much in the intervening twenty-one centuries. All across Central Asia I'd encountered recent attempts to civilize the supposed barbarians. If you couldn't manage it by bullying them, as the Communists had found in Mongolia and Tibet, you could always plough up their pastures as they'd done in Kazakhstan. They couldn't do this in the Gobi or on the Changtang because, as Strabo rightly pointed out, these places simply aren't suitable for arable farming.

Civilization is what the nomads have always needed, and few people have ever argued otherwise. Yet the argument doesn't stand up to scrutiny when you've seen the incredible finery of the Golden Man's costume. The minute detail of the gold work is so exquisite you need a magnifying glass to appreciate it fully. And this was made by so-called barbarians with simple hand tools and no means of magnification.

Ultimately, the Scythian kingdom was absorbed by other nomadic powers and disappeared from history more than two thousand years ago. No great loss, you might think. After all, what did these illiterate mare-milkers ever do for us? Well, hang on just a minute. I'll give the last word on the Kazakhs' barbaric ancestors to Herodotus. He informs us that the typical Scythian wore a curious outer garment covering the lower half of the body from waist to ankles. It was divided into sections to cover each leg separately. Some authorities suggest that this garment, which was particularly suited to a northern climate and designed to be worn when riding a horse, may be the Scythians' most important legacy to the world. As an article of clothing, it has been adopted by peoples all over the planet. You may well be wearing an example while you're reading this. In civilized parlance, the item's known as a pair of trousers.

III

The journey from Almaty to Otrar was about a thousand kilometres. Air travel concertinas geography, but following the
endless roads of the Kazakh steppes gave me a proper sense of
the territory's freedom and isolation. Kazakhstan is the ninth
largest country in the world and the largest of all that are
landlocked. The hours of driving bestowed the air with the
tang of distance.

At the end of the first day, we crossed the river Talas to enter
the city of Taraz where a small airfield looked as if it hadn't
seen much use for decades. Three sorry little biplanes stood
engulfed by chest-high weeds. Formerly a Silk Road stop, the
city was famous for its goatskins in the tenth century, according
to the Arab geographer Mukadasi. It was levelled by Chingis
Khan and didn't really recover as a significant settlement for
another six hundred years, but prior to the marauding Mongols,
somewhere along this river was the site of a battle that was to
have had perhaps even greater significance for the development
of Central Asia.

The precise location of the Battle of Talas was probably a bit
further up the course of the river, towards the mountains, but

no one knows for sure. In AD 751, a fierce struggle for control of the region took place on the banks of the Talas between forces of the Chinese Tang dynasty and an Arab Caliphate army. After five days of fighting the Chinese infantry were soundly beaten by their opponents' cavalry, a rout that spelled the end of Tang authority in Central Asia and effectively marked the western limit of Chinese cultural and political influence in the region. The defeat left Central Asia open to the Arabs and Islam.

The Kazakhs are Moslems but they wear their religion lightly. Mosques were thin on the ground and the general store in even the smallest village sold beer and spirits. The only omnipresent reminder of Islam came in collections of miniature grey-brick constructions located outside virtually every settlement. The buildings in these cemeteries, their domes topped by sickle-shaped moons, often looked more substantial that the dwellings in the villages themselves, the dead resting in more style than the living.

The battle of Talas is also recognized as a major event in the history of European civilization because it was the point at which paper-making technology was transferred to the Arabs and thence to Europe. The story goes that among the prisoners of war taken by the Arabs at Talas were a number of Chinese skilled in making paper. They were taken to Samarkand where they were ordered to start producing it. From there, the know-how spread westwards, arriving in Spain, Italy and the rest of Europe a few hundred years later.

Although the word paper comes from the ancient Egyptian writing material made from papyrus reeds, its invention is generally attributed to Cai Lun, a Chinese court eunuch who came up with a more progressive technique in AD 105. Cai Lun's recipe involved tree bark, old pieces of hemp and cloth rags, blended with bits of fishing net. His invention was immediately widely used in China.

Many authorities suggest that paper was a key ingredient in global cultural advancement. In ancient times, Chinese culture was less developed than that in the West because bamboo, which preceded paper as a writing material, was more awkward to use than papyrus. Civilization in China advanced rapidly after the invention of paper, and its transmission along the Silk Road to the rest of the world brought similar advancements, providing an inexpensive substance that would eventually facilitate the print revolution.

Soon after we left Taraz the next morning, the modern M32 highway we were following turned north at Shymkent, another stop on the old Silk Road, and the Tien Shan mountains faded in our wake to leave the splendid uniformity of the steppe. We were on the level floodplain of the Syrdarya where it meandered northwestwards to the Aral Sea, having left its source far behind in the Tien Shan.

I had arranged to break my journey for a couple of days with a team of archaeologists working on the ancient settlements strung out along the course of the river, the best known of which was Otrar. As soon as I arrived at the small modern town of Shaulder, where the archaeologists were based, the team leader took me on a tour of the area. Renato was a wiry Italian in his fifties. He wore a red T-shirt, baggy cotton shorts and bright pink flip-flops, not really the sort of outfit I'd expected of a serious archaeologist. With his shaven head, he looked more like Popeye or Pablo Picasso.

We set off from Shaulder in Renato's old Russian van. All of the previous settlements in this area, like the contemporary ones, were based on irrigation, he told me. 'The Syrdarya has changed its course many times over the centuries, and along these old channels we find ancient towns and cities.' We were driving through a present-day village, a small collection of whitewashed houses, their doors and window frames picked out in light blue paint. Around each house was a fence made from switches of tamarisk that resembled rows of inverted witches' brooms.

Renato stamped on the brake. 'Look!' he cried, 'From here you can see five ancient towns.' To me the landscape said nothing. It was flat and pockmarked with scrubby vegetation, but Renato was pointing vigorously in all directions. 'There, you see that mound?' Far off across the dusty plain I saw an innocuous rise. It wasn't high enough above the surrounding landscape to be a hill. It didn't even rate as a hillock. It was more like a low ridge, a bank of material like a pimple on the otherwise nondescript terrain.

'And there's another one.' He gestured towards a second, similar mound. 'And there, and there, and there.' I was still reeling from Renato's quickfire delivery, but we'd already set off again. 'It is a wonderful place to be an archaeologist. So many sites, so much digging to do.'

We turned off a road on to a dusty track that led us to Otrar, a site which like the others I'd seen on our drive, consisted of a raised mound some metres higher than the surrounding countryside. Otrar had flourished over a very long period, essentially from the first to the fifteenth century AD, thereafter slowly declining as its irrigation systems fell into disrepair. We were now trudging over hummocky ground, the accumulated remains of fifteen hundred years of occupation. Renato bent down to pick up something tiny from the dust. 'See this?' he said, handing it to me. 'A piece of a coin.' The shard, barely recognisable as a coin, had a tell-tale verdigris edge, Renato pointed out. They minted their own money in Otrar, suggesting a considerable degree of autonomy. The city was strategically located near the confluence of the Syrdarya and one of its tributaries, the Arys, and was an important trading post on a number of caravan routes. Coins from Otrar had been found in Tashkent and other Silk Road stops along the foothills of the Tien Shan.

Renato startled me by flicking the piece of coin back on to the ground. He saw my surprise and laughed. 'Oh, it is nothing,' he cried with a dismissive wave of his hand, 'there are thousands of pieces like that here.' I looked around my feet and swiftly realized that the ground we were walking on was also littered with pieces of pottery. I stooped to look more closely. Some were glazed, others not. This was an indicator of their age, Renato said.

In the fourteenth century, Otrar was the largest town in Central Asia. 'Maybe forty thousand inhabitants,' Renato announced as we trudged up a steep slope. 'All of these people were reliant on a complex system of irrigation.' From our vantage point on top of the mound, it was difficult to imagine a verdant landscape of irrigated farmland, but plenty of evidence was available, I was told. 'From the air you can see better how Otrar and the other towns in this area fit in with the relict river courses that they used.'

Otrar's pinnacle came after the arrival of the Mongols. 'Listen,' Renato told me, 'this was the town that brought Chingis Khan to Central Asia. Much of the rest of Asia and Europe might have been spared the Mongol hordes if Otrar's thirteenth-century governor had not murdered Chingis Khan's merchant-envoys here in 1218.'

The Mongols had already begun military operations in northern China when Chingis Khan sent a caravan of riches to Otrar to initiate trade. It consisted of about four hundred and fifty men and five hundred camels carrying gold and silver, furs and Chinese silks. At that time Otrar was an outpost of the Khwarazm empire which stretched across much of Central Asia, and trade with their settled neighbours was important to the Mongols. But when Otrar's governor, a man named Inalchik, saw the caravan, he became wary of the merchants' motives. He ordered the men to be detained as spies and eventually had them put to death. A solitary survivor, one of the camel drivers, escaped the massacre and carried word to Chingis Khan, who sent an army.

In the autumn of 1219, Mongol troops appeared outside the walls of Otrar. The city held out for five months but eventually fell after Inalchik had barricaded himself inside the citadel with twenty thousand troops. Their final act of defiance, having run out of arrows, was to bombard the Mongols with roof tiles. It did little to put off the inevitable. When Inalchik was captured the Mongols subjected him to an appropriately grisly end. They killed him by pouring molten silver into his eyes and ears.

And the rest, as they say, is history. The events at Otrar had ignited a wildfire of retribution from the steppe. The Mongols went on to take Bokhara, Samarkand and the rest of the Khwarazm empire in a hurricane of carnage that spread all the way to the gates of Vienna.

Yet after the slaughter wrought by the Mongols, Otrar had risen again. Chingis Khan's warriors had not actually caused much physical damage, Renato thought, unlike in many of the other towns in their path. They had simply killed most of the inhabitants and put their own people in charge. Renato took me across the site of the old city, but it wasn't until the following day that I could properly appreciate what he had shown me. Walking past a few relict mud bricks, peering into an ancient well and across an area enthusiastically described to me as the mosque, I'd had trouble getting a handle on what looked like a jumble of ancient earthworks to my untrained eye. But I was about to be shown a way in which the true scale of Otrar would be revealed.

Renato and his team had hired a couple of microlights and their pilots for a season of aerial surveys. Otrar wasn't really on their agenda, since it had been excavated several times over the past few decades. Their surveys were of more distant sites, but Renato took me on a flight over Otrar first.

We kitted up by the roadside in Shaulder. I was handed an old MiG fighter pilot's helmet and a padded jumpsuit against the cold. Our pilots, a Russian and an Armenian, spent most of their working lives spraying crops. They could dismantle their aircraft in less than an hour, load them on to a trailer and hit the road in search of the next job. I suppose they could be construed as modern-day nomads. They looked upon their time with Renato and his colleagues as an interesting diversion.

The microlights were homemade, said Renato, as we struggled into our jumpsuits. It was a comment that didn't exactly fill me with confidence. 'The wings are from Ukraine, the engine is taken from a Honda motor car.' I noticed the tyres were made in China and some of the tangle of tubes feeding the engine were stamped with the words 'Made in Iran'. I was about to take to the air in a contraption built with an assortment of contemporary Silk Road products.

The microlights needed only about fifty metres of runway in which to take off. The traffic on the road running out of town was stopped and one after the other we hurtled down the asphalt towards a man sitting on a cart pulled by a donkey. My pilot lowered the metal strut that he held in his hands and we lifted off to sail over the waiting donkey-cart. We had left the ground, but there was little immediate sensation of flight. My seat was directly behind the pilot's and raised above it, so I was already in mid-air.

Rising through the first hundred metres of altitude, we were buffeted by turbulence. It jostled us sideways, with harsh shoves quite unlike the smooth motion I had previously associated with flying. When it ceased, we simply hung in the air. I knew we were moving because of the roar of the engine, but other than the wind buffeting my face, there was little sense of progress.

Until, that is, I looked down and saw that the landscape

which had opened out below me was moving. Grand irrigation canals sprang directly from the wandering banks of the Syrdarya far to my left, carrying water to a patchwork of green cropland beneath my seat. We sailed over processions of sunflowers and cotton bushes, away from the river towards the ancient city, where the verdant fields gave way to patchy scrub. The mound I'd clambered across the previous afternoon was laid out like a giant sticking plaster on a tableau of semi-desert.

Renato appeared, his microlight hanging in the air to my right. He waved excitedly and pointed down to the ruined settlement. The walkie-talkie dangling from a cord round my neck crackled and he took me on another tour of the site: the central citadel, the mosque, the earthen fortifica-tions. From my birdlike vantage point, it was a layout that now made sense.

We veered away to the west, crossing the snaking course of the Syrdarya to penetrate the desert known as the Kyzyl Kum, or Red Sands. Former meanders of the great river twisted and turned across the substrate, vast sweeps of ancient river bed carved like wounds on the pinkish terrain. Shadows of other abandoned settlements appeared, towns and military camps that had risen and fallen with shifts in the river's path. They stood still and silent, forgotten sentinels looking out across the vanished watercourses.

Permanent settlements had thrived along the Syrdarya, as on its sister the Amudarya, for almost as long as nomads had been roaming the steppes. A constant supply of water, that most vital of all resources, underpinned these cities that provided pit stops along the threads of the Silk Road. Water didn't guarantee your future, but without it you had no chance.

Given the long history of irrigation on the two tributaries of the Aral Sea, I was drawn back once more to the simple issue of scale as the explanation for the ecological tragedy I was on my way to see. Effectively self-sustaining cities like Otrar had harnessed nature to sustain their populations, numbering in the tens of thousands, but the Soviet Union's Asian irrigation schemes had been designed to support an empire of hundreds of millions. The watering of Central Asia had been conducted at huge expense: its price tag was the Aral, and the tab picked up by those who lived along its shoreline.

My ride towards the vanishing sea took me further along the M32 highway in the company of a Kazakh archaeologist who had been working with Renato. We drove through Kyzylorda, a city hemmed in by its industrial past, its outskirts a jungle of rusting pylons, vast ramshackle silos and dilapidated factories quietly fading away into its forgotten history.

As the green fields slowly petered out, we passed a boy with his rod, setting off for an afternoon's fishing in an irrigation canal. Thereafter the colour faded away as the steppe and desert took over. It felt as though we were travelling back to the beginning of Soviet time.

Remote and appearing to consist of limitless space, Kazakh-stan had long served a function as Moscow's testing-ground for grand ideas. Khrushchev's expansion of irrigation and the Virgin Lands scheme had been just two. I'd passed endless wheat fields before arriving within sight of another, the oldest space launch facility in the world at Baikonur. The road, which followed the course of the Syrdarya, had taken us through all the towns and cities en route, but it bypassed the cosmodrome and its military garrison town, both still leased by the Russians. I knew they were near because they were marked on my map. More physical evidence bristled by the roadside: a forest of electricity pylons stretching far off into the distance to where satellite dishes like giant blown-out umbrellas were scanning the heavens above.

Solitude and distance had also combined to make Kazakhstan a handy spot for unwelcome elements in the Soviet regime. Dostoyevsky was exiled there to soldier in a line battalion. This was where Leon Trotsky passed his last years in the USSR before being expelled altogether. These outcasts were followed by entire races – Germans from the Volga and Ukraine, Chechens and Koreans from border areas elsewhere – banished to the steppes as suspected collaborators in the 1940s.

The hours slipped by. A wind had rallied and was moaning outside our vehicle's windows. The anticipation I felt on nearing the Aral, a region I'd written and taught about for years without seeing, was tempered by an increasing sense of unease at the prospect of reaching my ultimate objective. For seclusion was also key to the top-secret activities conducted within the Aral Sea itself. For nearly forty years, its principal island had been used for the open-air testing of biological weapons. Located three and a half thousand kilometres from Moscow, in the middle of a remote inland sea surrounded by sparsely populated desert, the island was the perfect proving-ground for a deadly array of airborne microbes. The name of this secluded spot deep in the heart of Central Asia, Vozrozhdeniye, appealed to me for its bitter irony: it means Rebirth Island.

Some of the biological agents tested there were genetically modified to make them resistant to existing medication. Plague, anthrax and smallpox were the ones I'd heard of; the others came with outlandish names – Q-fever, tularaemia, botulinum and Venezuelan equine encephalitis – to complete a lethal bill of fare.

I'd sought specialist advice at home in Britain and been informed that almost all of the agents responsible for these deadly diseases are quickly destroyed when exposed to ultra-violet light. The island's sparse vegetation, hot desert climate, and sandy soil – which reaches summer temperatures of 60°C (140°F) – all sharply reduced the possibility that pathogenic microorganisms would survive. The important exception was anthrax, a spore that outlives all the others. Anthrax can persist in soil for hundreds of years.

By way of preparation, I'd become familiar with the terminology, able to distinguish between bacteria, viruses and toxins, versed in which were transmissible from person to person and which were not. I had a booklet outlining symptoms and a stash of antibiotics and other medical supplies. But was I really prepared to expose myself to such self-evident dangers? A sliver of doubt was lodged in my mind, but the time was fast approaching when I would have to decide.

The trouble with anthrax is that its spores are very small. They're invisible to the naked eye. You need a microscope to see them, so you can't feel them either. They have no smell and make no sound. I didn't ask about their taste because ingestion is one of the ways they can enter your body. The other two are inhalation and absorption through open cuts or abrasions. Needless to say, the symptoms are unpleasant: sores, fever, intense pain and so on. And, of course, the prospect of death. If the spores enter your body through the skin or get into your intestines, there is hope. If treated, there's a 90 per cent chance of recovery. But if you breathe them in, if those imperceptible spores get lodged in your lungs, the chance of recovery is less than 10 per cent.

Anthrax spores are in the environment all the time. For most people this is not a problem because they are too large, relatively speaking, to breathe in. But the anthrax tested on Rebirth Island had been 'weaponized'. This means scientists ground up the spores so that they could get past nasal hairs. That was the whole point. These people had been testing special strains specifically designed to maximize their killing potential.

Packed in my baggage was a frightening array of protective equipment: oral and nasal masks, respirator, rubber gloves, protective suits and overboots. The gear had been checked and rechecked a dozen times. I'd brought it along to put off having to decide whether or not to venture across to Rebirth Island. Not bringing it would have meant admitting defeat before I started. I wanted to go, but the risks were clear. Pondering my options in the office of an anthrax expert employed by a consultancy company near Porton Down, a British Ministry of Defence research establishment, I'd asked in jest whether he would like to come with me. On hearing his response, I'd nearly fallen off my chair. 'I'd love to,' he'd replied.

The man was already leafing through his diary. The possibility was real but my dates were uncertain. I knew that, incredibly, people from the mainland sometimes sailed across the receding sea to visit the island, intent on scavenging any useful scraps they might find in its abandoned research buildings. Any visit of mine would depend on finding these looters and persuading them to take passengers. I'd agreed to ring the anthrax man, ex-military of course, when I'd appraised the situation. If he could rearrange meetings, he told me, he'd be on a plane like a shot.

I'd felt a great deal more secure on leaving Porton Down. With an expert in tow, my newly-acquired knowledge of bio-logical and chemical weaponry and its hazards could remain largely theoretical. I could assign responsibility for my safety to my partner. Whatever precautions he took, I'd take them too. But all still rested on my contact with the looters.

The very fact that there were looters seemed to be a good sign. Surely if any had succumbed to Rebirth Island's invisible dangers, future trips would be deemed too hazardous, no matter how desperate the scavengers. And I found it difficult to believe that these men, whoever they were, would have access to pro-tective gear like the stuff I was carrying. Not that I'd allow their continued health to seduce me into relaxing my guard. If I did manage to find the looters – I rated my chances at about fifty-fifty – and was able to cajole them into letting me tag along – probably less than evens – I would still be travelling in all my personal protective clothing, no matter what precautions they did or didn't take. As my friendly expert had put it, 'Having your head cut off is more tangible, but anthrax is more scary.'

As I closed in on my destination, though, I had to accept that it was all down to me. I still had a get-out clause: how hard I tried to make contact with the looters was my affair. And any conditions they might set for carrying me across the Aral Sea to Vozrozhdeniye might provide me with an excuse not to go. Only if I agreed to accompany them, only if I made the phone call to England and my anthrax expert rescheduled his meetings and boarded his plane, would I be committed.

As the sun was setting, I caught sight of a train on the tracks running parallel to the highway. The route stretches all the way from China, across the steppes of Kazakhstan, through Russia, Belarus, Poland and Germany to the Netherlands and the rest of western Europe. Extending across two continents, it's a modern-day version of the Silk Road, the iron horse replacing the camels and stallions of the past.

I counted the carriages. There were twenty in all. The last of the sunshine was reflected in their windows. By now the tufts of tired grass had become fewer and further between, the life of the landscape gradually seeping away into the sun and wind. And it was still some distance before I'd reach the disaster zone proper.

The receding vegetation gave the impression that the terrain had flattened further. I hadn't thought this was possible, but the ground became an immeasurable expanse of blank uniformity that defined the horizontal. Carriage by carriage the sun's dazzling glare flicked by, making the train seem like a glistening worm. Unable to burrow through the solid terrain, it was speeding across its surface instead. We were two lonely vehicles, both hurrying through a benighted country. This was a place where nature appeared to have exhausted her imagination, laid down to rest and fallen into a deep slumber.

IV

Aralsk surprised me. It was bigger than I'd imagined and not nearly as bleak. I'd been expecting to find a few hopeless inhabitants trapped in a wretched place that had lost its purpose. After all, this was a fishing port that now lacked certain basic necessities in that regard – sea and fish. Some time in the 1970s, the raison d'être for the whole town had disappeared without warning. It was as though the tide had gone out one night and never come back.

But the streets were full of people when we arrived in the early hours of the morning. It didn't feel as if we'd just gained access to a ghost town, which was more or less what I'd been prepared for after spending forty minutes at a police checkpoint on the town's approach road. A militiaman in shirtsleeves had waved us down at the roadblock with a luminous baton. He peered inside the car, demanded our passports, and carried them off into a nearby building, leaving us to twiddle our thumbs.

I got out to stretch my legs. The night was desert cool, with a warm, comforting breeze. Occasional flashes of lightning pulsed on the horizon directly behind the barrier blocking our progress. The sky glowed a deep, hazy orange colour, intermittently set alight by sheet-like flares and dramatic electrical zigzags. There was no accompanying thunder, just the light show. It was a suitably ominous reception at a town haunted by the phantom of a dying sea.

We had to ask several times before we found the only hotel. Even at 1.30 a.m. the concrete streets were wide and swarming with people taking the air and licking ice creams. When we finally pulled up at the Aral Hotel, I grabbed my bag and thanked the driver, who sped off to his home on the edge of town. I climbed the steps and passed through a metal swing door that took me into the grimy foyer. A swarthy, middle-aged woman sat slumped behind a chipped wooden desk, speaking on the telephone.

When she replaced the receiver, she looked at me blankly. My Russian was just sufficient to ask if she had a room. '*Niet,*' she said with the slightest shake of her head.

It used to be like this in the old Soviet Union. If you ever arrived unannounced at a hotel, it was mysteriously full. The woman, too, evoked a previous era with her hennaed hair and flower-print frock. I tried again, but to no avail. The receptionist just looked through me without interest. This was a large establishment, with four floors, situated in what was supposed to be one of the most godforsaken settlements in the whole of Kazakhstan. It couldn't be full; it didn't make sense. I asked a third time.

Wearily, the woman heaved herself out of her chair and emerged from behind the reception desk. She gestured that I should follow her and led me back to the metal swing door. We went out into the night and crossed the dirt road to a single-storey house with a red-brick façade. The woman flicked a light switch and showed me into a long room lined with two sofas and a number of large armchairs. She pointed at one of the sofas and left.

The following morning I awoke to find myself in a private house, but none of the family took any notice of me, so I assumed that their home regularly doubled as an overflow for the hotel. Later I discovered that more than half the hotel's rooms were derelict.

The streets of Aralsk weren't as crowded as they had been the previous night. Most of the houses were neat and white-washed, with eaves and window shutters picked out in light blue. The one in which I'd slept was conspicuous with its red brick façade, but it turned out to be just that: a façade. The bricks and mortar were painted on sheets of hardboard, although even in the light of day the effect was very realistic.

Across the main road at one end of my street, I passed a park that was unkempt and overgrown, and crossed a sizeable square flanked by the post office. People were popping in and out, going about their daily business. On the opposite side of the square, across the railway line, I came upon an open-air market, well stocked with fruit, vegetables and some stalls selling house-hold goods and carpets. I stopped beside a hardware stall where the proprietor told me in broken English that he was an engineer but couldn't find any work. He gestured at his selec-tion of spanners and hacksaw blades, electrical plugs and bicycle chains. 'So I can only sell these things,' he said simply.

The unemployed engineer and the dishevelled park not-withstanding, Aralsk still didn't mirror the place of misery and dejection I'd read about in newspaper articles before coming. The market was busy and the shops sold a wide range of products, though several did also come with sad little old ladies sitting on the pavement outside, each offering for sale the same dismal selection of matches and biscuits from upturned cardboard boxes.

The bright sunshine helped, but Aralsk lacked many of the signs of decay I'd been led to expect. There was no rubbish piled on the streets, the occasional bus indicated a system of public transport and most of the roads were in a fairly decent state. My hotel annexe, while hardly sumptuous, had offered both electricity and water.

I'd certainly seen worse on my travels through Central Asia. The grim town of Hor, in Tibet, had years of accumulated refuse. Although situated on the shore of Lake Manasarovar, it appeared to have had little connection to Tibet's most venerated stretch of water. Here, by contrast, Aralsk had been built to harvest the fruits of a sea that had disappeared. If any town had an excuse to be miserable, this was surely it.

It wasn't that I'd expected people to be living in hovels, or the burnt-out shells of buildings. My vision of the town hadn't been coloured by my reading the ancient Greeks' views of the Scythians. I wasn't thinking of Aralsk as a location at the end of the earth as they knew it, despite the fact that its inhabitants were hanging on in a place deemed expendable by the modern world. It was just that I'd been anticipating a stronger feeling of despondency, a greater atmosphere of desolation.

I found the desolation at the other end of my street, however. Returning past the Hotel Aral and its overflow, I wandered the opposite length of the dusty road and found myself at the defunct harbour. The road turned to run along its length, cordoned off by a stout metal railing decorated with motifs of stylized sailing boats and seagulls. The panorama from Aralsk's corniche was not the one envisaged by the designers of the railings. Beyond the wharf, where the sea should have been, there were no seagulls and no sailing boats. A small cow was grazing on some tufts of vaguely green grass growing on the former seabed. Otherwise, the waterfront looked like a barren wasteland.

I was standing on one side of the obsolete harbour. It was horseshoe-shaped and a couple of hundred metres across. Opposite, in the distance, I could make out the broken windows of dilapidated port buildings. I learned later that they constituted the redundant fish-canning factory. To my left, pieces of broken and abandoned machinery littered the wharf between some rusting cranes.

Below me, half a dozen corroded vessels had been lined up on concrete pedestals to face the wharf – an installation designed to remind the onlooker of times gone by. I clambered down some concrete steps and beside the redundant ships found a painted hoarding showing a map that compared the outline of the Aral Sea as it had been in 1960 with the shrunken coastline in the year 2000. From what I could make out, the nearest finger of the receding waterbody was about forty kilometres away. It was pointing forlornly at its departed port.

There's no doubt that the recent history of the Aral Sea is a textbook example of how to mess up the environment, which is why I found the relative lack of despair in Aralsk both a testament to human resilience and a glimmer of hope for the future.

Since long before people had started playing around with the Aral Sea's tributaries, the Amudarya and Syrdarya, the level of the sea had reflected a balance between the input of water brought by these two rivers and the water lost to evaporation in the hot desert sunshine. As the irrigation of cropland was expanded from the mid-twentieth century, the offtakes of water from the Amudarya and Syrdarya increased, and the volumes that remained to enter the sea were reduced to trickles. The sun kept shining, so the Aral Sea shrank.

As the sea contracted, its waters became saltier. Most of the fish and smaller organisms perished as a result. Commercial fishing soon followed suit. The repercussions I saw in Aralsk were repeated elsewhere around the once-great inland sea, with harbours left dry and their towns landlocked. The Aral Sea fish catch in 1962 stood at about forty thousand tonnes. Carp, bream, pike-perch, roach, barbel and a local species of sturgeon were loaded on to refrigerated wagons and transported all over the country. The cosmodrome up the road at Baikonur was a major customer. But the annual catch fell by half within the next five years. In 1975, landings barely reached three thousand tonnes and by 1980 the Aral Sea commercial fishery had ceased to function.

This is all bad enough, but it gets worse. Large areas of former seabed were exposed by the receding waters. The fine sediments of this desiccated, often saline territory were whipped up by the winds and blown in great dust storms across the region. I'd read academic papers citing evidence that deposits of this powdery salt were harming plant growth in agricultural fields and natural ecosystems far beyond the fringes of the seabed. Respiratory problems also plagued the residents of the area surrounding the Aral Sea. But atmospheric dust was only the beginning of their related woes.

The area's precious irrigation water was poorly managed, leading to waterlogging and the build-up of salt on the fields. The salt tolerance of most cultivated plants is relatively low, so salinization rapidly leads to decline in production. In an effort to maintain crop yields depleted by the effects of salt, massive amounts of agricultural chemicals were applied. In the 1980s, fertilizer use in the Aral Sea basin exceeded the average amount used in Russia by ten to fifteen times. The quantities of herbicides, defoliants and other pesticides applied was more than ten times the average for the former USSR. The managers of the state farms were fighting a losing battle: the yields continued to fall. But that was not all – the agrochemicals were seeping into the water draining from the plantations, contaminating drinking supplies for residents elsewhere.

Pollution by a cocktail of salts and agricultural chemicals has been linked to a range of health problems: gastritis, hepatitis, heart disease, cancers and anaemia. The people had not only lost their livelihoods, they were slowly being poisoned to boot. The situation was little short of cataclysmic.

But most survived and at least some efforts were made to cushion the blow. In an attempt to sustain the Aralsk cannery – at one time the largest in the former Soviet Union – fish caught elsewhere were transported to the town for processing. When that initiative finally collapsed, the workers were allowed to strip the factory in lieu of their non-existent salaries.

The Kazakh government had designated the Aral Sea an ecological disaster zone and offered redundant fishermen and their families the chance to leave, relocating them to other lakes across the country. Some moved west, to the Caspian Sea, others as far as Lake Balkash, more than a thousand kilometres to the east. Smaller, charitable bodies also did their bit, and I'd been given the name of a woman who worked for one of these non-governmental organizations.

I found Zhannat in her office on the first floor of a building not far from the Hotel Aral. She was a local woman in her early thirties who had lived all her life in Aralsk, like her parents and grandparents before her. Her mother had been born at sea, she said, on a trawler in the Aral in 1943. While the town's menfolk were away at war, the women had been left in charge of the fishing.

Zhannat had grown up during the region's downward spiral. She told me she hadn't even laid eyes on the Aral Sea until she was twenty-eight years old. This staggering revelation left me open-mouthed in disbelief. I sat there as Zhannat kept talking. 'I was amazed,' she said. 'At school in Aralsk we always learned we lived in a region of ecological disaster. There was a very big promotion that we don't have a sea any longer. I remember I went to Almaty once and people asked me, "So, how is your sea?" and I would answer "What sea? We don't have one any more."'

Zhannat saw her mother's birthplace for the first time when she started working for the organization in whose office we sat, a charity established in the 1990s by fishermen in Denmark.

I'd thought that all the fish had disappeared, but not so apparently. A few species that could cope with the high salt levels have survived. In the 1970s, Soviet scientists had looked into the problems of the Aral Sea. As its native species were declining, the experts came up with the idea of introducing fish from other parts of the Soviet Union in an effort to maintain employment in the area. One of these new species was flounder, a flat fish from the oceans. Although the flounder didn't become established in time to save Aralsk's commercial fishing industry, it offered some hope to individual fishermen. The problem was that they didn't have the right equipment to catch it. That was where the Danes came in. They called their project 'From Kattegat to the Aral Sea'.

A couple of days later, Zhannat took me to the village of Tastubek. It was a long and bumpy journey across a landscape that resembled the Gobi with its sparse vegetation and dusty tracks. Tastubek had once been famous for its sturgeon. The name of the village means 'stone peninsula' and the stony bed along its shallow shoreline provided an ideal breeding ground for the mammoth fish. From a fishing village with a population of a thousand people, just a few families had hung on, Zhannat told me, refusing to abandon their homes. Before the Danish project started no one had fished from Tastubek for eighteen years, the survivors turning instead to animal husbandry as the only alternative livelihood. Now a few men had begun again.

About sixty people currently lived in Tastubek. The village was a small collection of mud houses – some derelict – and wooden paddocks where goats were corralled in the evenings. As we drove in we saw a few Bactrian camels sitting in the shade of the buildings. The solid dwellings were lined up along a shallow embankment, a ridge of perhaps a couple of metres depth, no more than a crinkle in the desert topography. It took me a minute to realize that this was the former shoreline. Zhannat shielded her eyes from the late-afternoon sunshine, thrust out her arm and pointed into the distance. Shimmering on the horizon was the vanishing sea.

It was a poignant moment for me. For years I've been reading about the Aral Sea catastrophe, even penning the occasional commentary piece about the steady deterioration of an eco-system in decline. My first view of its waters, no matter how distant, sent a shiver of exhilaration down my spine. The buzz lasted no more than an instant, but occasions like that make travelling to remote regions worthwhile. It's one of the few means I've discovered that come close to recreating the tingle of excitement you feel as a child at Christmas.

But I couldn't imagine how much more moving that first sighting must have been for Zhannat. This was the spot from where, a few years before, she had seen her sea for the first time. She shook her head and laughed. 'I was so amazed when I saw it,' she told me again. 'For all my life I was thinking that we do not have a sea any more. I thought it had gone for ever.'

And so it still might, though possibly not this part. In 1990, the declining water levels meant that the Aral split in two to produce a 'Big Aral' in the main lake basin and a 'Little Aral' to the north. The Little Aral was the one we were looking at. 'Little' is a relative term; it's still more than a hundred kilometres across, and it has a chance of survival. Zhannat had explained the situation to me as we'd lurched across the desert towards

Tastubek. The Little Aral is totally within Kazakhstan and fed by the Syrdarya, while the Big Aral, split between Kazakhstan and neighbouring Uzbekistan, is fed by the Amudarya. There are fewer irrigation schemes on the Syrdarya so some water still reaches the northern segment. Although the size of the Little Aral has been more or less stable since 1996, the Big Aral is still receding and no one holds out much hope for it.

The two water bodies continue to be linked, however, by a narrow, ephemeral channel. The Kazakh government had tried to dam this overspill, which threatened to drain the Little Aral into its hopeless big brother. Their first effort, an earth dam, had collapsed. But a more solid, concrete structure was under construction. The plan was to allow the Little Aral to be replenished. It wouldn't be enough to reinstate Aralsk as a port, but it might just return the waters to the mini-cliff at Tastubek.

In time, the authorities hoped that freshwater fish could be reintroduced to the Little Aral, but meanwhile a number of fishermen were catching flounder. Tastubek had been one of the first villages where trials with the new Danish nets had been conducted. Their success was reflected in the fact that a couple of former fishermen had recently returned to the village with their families after years of town life in Aralsk. Zhannat proudly indicated a couple of newer wattle-and-daub houses on the edge of the village.

Just before 8 p.m., we accompanied a man named Nurbolat to the edge of the sea with his nets. He travelled by motorbike, with his small son in his lap and a neighbour sitting behind. Zhannat and I followed in her jeep. The shore was several kilometres away from Tastubek across stony ground. It didn't look like the former seabed, having been colonized by scrawny bushes, but the rounded pebbles were testament to its previous services as a spawning ground for sturgeon.

The pebbles accumulated to form a steep, grey bank that ran along the shoreline, a small grandstand from which we looked out across the still-great expanse of water. It was calm and unruffled, a glassy plane shining in the evening light.

Nurbolat started to unravel one of his nets while his neighbour began to undress. His job was to carry one end into the water, Zhannat told me. Stripped down to his underpants, the young man took hold of the hefty anchor to which the net was attached, stepped into the Aral Sea and waded out at right angles from the shore.

When they'd first begun to catch flounder no one wanted to eat it, Zhannat said. It wasn't like the freshwater species they used to catch. It was a curious-looking fish: flat with both eyes peering upward. Some thought it was a freak of nature, a consequence of the area's pollution. But slowly people had come round.

Nurbolat was gradually feeding out the net, which was about a metre in width, as his colleague waded further away from the shore. Meanwhile, Nurbolat's little boy had settled on his haunches and was throwing stones into the water. I stepped down the pebble bank, dipped my finger into the sea and licked it. The water had a saline tang, but it didn't taste as salty as the ocean.

By the time the net was fully extended, the man in his underpants was forty to fifty metres away, though his head and shoulders were still visible above the waterline. Nurbolat took a metal stake and fastened his end of the net to it in the shingle as his colleague began the long wade back to shore. The little boy was still throwing stones.

We all walked up the coast a little way for the fishermen to repeat the procedure with a second net. Zhannat and I removed our shoes and socks and paddled the short distance. During the spring and summer, fishermen like Nurbolat caught enough fish for their daily needs, she told me. Aralsk was several hours away and there wasn't sufficient ice to keep it fresh for such a journey during the hotter months. Most of the ice machines at Aralsk had ceased to function, along with the processing factory, some years before.

Many more fish were caught in autumn and winter, when trucks drove down to the shore from Aralsk to pick up the catch. It was during the colder period that Nurbolat made some money from his exploits. But still, no one in Tastubek was giving up their livestock. In a sense, Zhannat explained, those villagers who had stayed on in their homes and coped with the fisheries disaster were more resilient as a result. Some could now fish again, but they had camels and goats to fall back on.

'This is not actually a very good way to catch flounder,' Zhannat said. Her comment surprised me. 'Flounder like deeper water. Nurbolat already put most of his nets further out, by boat.' Then why was he placing these nets so close to the shore? 'To catch carp,' said Zhannat. This surprised me even more. I'd thought all the freshwater species had disappeared. 'This year some carp have been found. We are maybe thirty kilometres from the mouth of the Syrdarya here. They enter the sea from the river.'

The faintest breeze had begun to stir, disturbing the glassy surface of the sea with gentle ripples. Standing ankle deep in what was left of one of the world's worst environmental disasters, I realized that there was some hope for this part of the Aral Sea. If the overspill to the Big Aral could be dammed successfully, it seemed likely that carp could be re-established permanently. Finding some early arrivals from the Syrdarya was a definite sign that things could get better.

We made the long and uncomfortable journey back to Aralsk the following morning after watching Nurbolat bring in his catch. He'd caught half a dozen carp in the nets running out from the pebble bank and a few flounder in those anchored further off-shore. They weren't exactly rich pickings but it was enough for his family's immediate needs.

A few hours after leaving Tastubek, we took a detour. Zhannat had suggested we visit what she called a ships' graveyard near another former fishing village at Zhalangash. The harbour there had been particularly deep, she said. In the 1980s, when everyone saw that the Aral Sea was receding fast, many trawlers had been anchored at Zhalangash in the hope that the disappearing waters could somehow be reined in. The village turned out to be their last resting place.

A long, straight, sealed road took us over a ridge topped by the miniature grey buildings of a human graveyard. The domes of the tombs and their sickle moons flicked past the window to reveal an open panorama of scrubby desert laid out beneath us. The village of Zhalangash, which seemed larger than Tastubek, shimmered in the heat haze directly ahead. As we descended

the long, gentle slope, a scattering of tiny dots to the left gradually took on the shapes of ships languishing in the arid wilderness. From this distance they looked like a collection of ancient
toys abandoned in a sandpit by a distracted child.

When Zhannat and I arrived at the ships' graveyard, we
wandered among the rusting hulks where desiccated shells
crunched underfoot. The former sea floor had been claimed by
tough grasses and salt-tolerant shrubs. Here, as at Tastubek, the
inhabitants of the village had turned to livestock when the sea
had gone away. The thick, rubbery bushes gave their camel's
milk a briny flavour. People in Aralsk really enjoyed the salty
taste, Zhannat told me.

A couple of camels were grazing some distance off. The other
ships of the desert, stripped of anything worth salvaging, lay
forsaken. They had no ropes, chains or cables, and even their
paint had all but surrendered to the wind and the sun. Their
iron hulls were now burnished to the dull colour of burnt sugar.
Some had gaping holes which had been cut at ground level to
access their machinery. These ships had been wrecked in an
unusual manner, not by rocks or a storm, but left forlorn and
useless by a sea that had ebbed away. It was now nowhere to
be seen. The water had simply absconded, leaving a cohort of
forgotten bridges where a generation of sea captains had been
cheated of the honour of going down with their vessels.

'Aral' means island in Kazakh. The sea is like an island surrounded by desert, and here at Zhalangash the full impact of
the receding waters was brought home to me. Backed by an
old sea cliff left to fester over a waterless wasteland, I counted
thirteen ships slowly decaying beneath the hot desert sun.

I'd seen the desolation at the dry harbour in Aralsk, while in Tastubek I'd sensed the hardships, now leavened by the hope of flounder and a few carp, but as the wind whispered through the towering skeletons of these discarded vessels, I appreciated the true scale of wretchedness brought about by human folly.

As if in a cemetery, we continued drifting through the ghostly collection of trawlers in silence, and my thoughts turned once more to the prospect of visiting Rebirth Island. I had outlined my plan to Zhannat when we'd first met. She'd asked me why I wanted to go there and I'd described my fascination with extreme environments. She had listened carefully, without comment, and had not mentioned it since. During our days together, I had turned over the possibilities time and again in my mind. The sliver of doubt and anxiety was still there, gnawing away at my resolve. Part of me reasoned that I'd seen enough; I'd witnessed the aftermath of this unnatural extreme. Was there really any need to go further? On the other hand, I'd come so far that to give up now seemed foolish. Why lug all that protective gear from England and let the chance to use it slip through my fingers? I knew my doubts were rooted in fear but if I took the necessary precautions there was no reason to believe I wouldn't survive. If the chance arose for me to set foot on that forbidden terrain and I refused it, I knew that in my heart of hearts I'd always regret the decision. After several restless nights spent tossing the idea back and forth, I'd finally reached a verdict. If Zhannat could put me in touch with the looters, I'd accept any offer they made for me to accompany them to the epicentre of this eerie disaster zone.

The camels had stopped grazing. They were heading towards

the village, ambling past us at a safe distance. We paused in the shadow of one of the battered wrecks and watched them go by. As if privy to my thoughts, Zhannat turned to me and asked, 'Do you still want to go to Vozrozhdeniye Island?'

I said I did. She nodded thoughtfully. 'There is another former fishing village, far from here,' she said. 'It is near the shore of the Big Aral. The people there, they go to Vozrozhdeniye.' Zhannat's eyes had gone back to the camels on their long walk back to the village. 'I called them by radio before we came to Tastubek,' she went on, adding that they had no telephone. 'They agreed to let you join them on a trip. If you want, I can take you there.'

I thanked Zhannat. I don't know why she'd waited before relaying this information. Perhaps she'd been testing my resolve, or quietly assessing the sort of person I was.

V

If Zhannat had been considering my motives for an excursion to Rebirth Island, her caution was understandable. During the height of their secret research programme into bioweapons, the Soviets had stockpiled hundreds of tonnes of anthrax for use against the USA and its western allies. When they shut down the programme, large quantities of weaponized anthrax were shipped to Rebirth Island in the Aral Sea for disposal. The anthrax spores, stored as a slurry, were mixed with bleach and buried in stainless-steel containers.

All well and good, you might think. But not quite. Anthrax spores tend to clump together, and this coagulation means that some spores were protected from the bleach and remained viable in the soil. We know this because in the early 1990s a senior Kazakh scientist from the Soviet programme defected to the USA and spilled the beans. In the aftermath of the terrorist attacks on New York in September 2001, the American intelligence community sat down and surveyed the world scene for possible sources of nasty substances that could be used against them. They looked at Vozrozhdeniye and saw the problem. It seemed that any international terrorist worth his salt could make an excursion to the island with his bucket and spade and dig up some anthrax. The local government was consulted and US decontamination teams were dispatched to sort out the difficulty.

So that's it, problem solved, I thought to myself when I read this. But not quite. Dave Butler, my anthrax expert, wasn't totally convinced: the Soviets weren't the only ones to experiment with biological agents as weapons of war. During the Second World War the British had conducted tests with anthrax spores on the island of Gruinard off the west coast of Scotland. The island remained uninhabited by government decree until 1988, but even now complete decontamination is difficult to guarantee. As Dave explained succinctly, it had taken more than sixty years to decontaminate Gruinard. 'They pumped formaldehyde over the entire island. You have to kill every single spore, and they can live for centuries.'

He'd never heard what exactly the Americans had done on Vozrozhdeniye, but spending a mere few months cleaning up the island's dumps wasn't good enough for him. There was also the matter of spores left lying around over a wide area after the atmospheric tests. 'There's a very good chance that some have survived,' he said. That was all I needed to hear.

I was confident that Dave knew what he was talking about. Shortly after the events of September 11, the USA experienced an anthrax attack in which weaponized spores were delivered by post to employees of a publisher in Florida. David Butler was the man they called in to examine the envelopes.

I'd telephoned him on my return to Aralsk and he had eagerly set about making arrangements to join me. At the same time, I began taking the antibiotics he'd recommended. I wasn't intending to give up my protective equipment; I was simply taking all the precautions available. The course of antibiotics provided additional protection in case of exposure to anthrax.

Biological weapons were first tested at Vozrozhdeniye in the mid-1930s, and in 1954 a secret base for about a thousand people was built. It was known in official circles as Aralsk-7. The Kremlin's research into biological weapons received added impetus in 1972, the year the Soviet Union endorsed the international Biological Weapons Convention. By signing the convention Moscow had pledged 'not to develop, produce, stockpile or otherwise acquire or retain' biological agents for offensive military purposes. The Soviets did precisely the opposite. Endorsement of the convention was seen as an excellent opportunity to get ahead of the opposition.

The facilities at Rebirth Island were part of a nationwide series of covert installations for research, production, storage and testing of biological weapons. Knowing that their rivals would be keeping an eye on them, the Kremlin bosses arranged for many of these operations to be run not by the military, but by various other government ministries like health and agriculture. A major branch of their bioweapons effort was given civilian cover by setting it up under the guise of a state pharmaceutical agency.

Secrecy was, of course, all important to the concealment of one of the darkest conspiracies of the Cold War. Rebirth Island's Aralsk-7 base reported to a larger unit located across a series of clandestine military settlements dotted around the civilian port of Aralsk. All were now abandoned, but Zhannat had pointed one out in the distance as we'd driven back into town. There had been four in total, she said: Birch, Seagull, Falcon and Aralsk-5. None of these places ever appeared on any maps. As far as the outside world was concerned, like the Aralsk-7 base itself, they simply did not exist.

The network was so secret that even its employees weren't told what colleagues in other branches of the organization were doing, or where. The veil of silence that enveloped these ethereal places extended into the civilian world. Local residents had their suspicions, but everyone knew the unwritten rule: displaying the slightest interest in such goings-on was detrimental to health. On occasion, the use of an open-air testing ground on Rebirth Island was also detrimental to the health of residents on the mainland.

The island had been chosen in part because of its geographical isolation. It was easy to protect from trespassers. Special fast patrol boats guarded Vozrozhdeniye against intruders throughout the decades of testing, and fishermen knew not to venture too close to its shores. The insular location prevented the transmission of dangerous microorganisms to neighbouring mainland areas by animals or insects, and the surrounding stretches of water were considered large enough to prevent biological agents being blown to the mainland.

Most of the time, the island's seclusion was enough, but it wasn't always easy to conceal its secret purpose. Despite being kept in the dark about the activities conducted on Vozrozhdeniye, local suspicions were aroused by some ominous misfortunes. Three people died in a smallpox outbreak in Aralsk in 1971. In 1976, a mass death of fish occurred in the Aral Sea. Outbreaks of plague hit the region in 1986 and entire flocks of sheep lost their wool. In May 1988, a huge herd of saiga antelope mysteriously died in the Turgay steppes north-east of the Aral. About half a million animals dropped dead in just one hour.

The authorities came up with their own reasons for such events. They displayed a fertile imagination in this respect. The mass death of antelopes, for example, had been caused by a spacecraft from Baikonur that had been forced to jettison its fuel. Not many people were convinced.

Outbreaks of plague, one of the oldest identifiable diseases known to mankind, were more easily accounted for because the disease is endemic to parts of Kazakhstan. It's carried by wild rodents and usually transmitted by their fleas. People in this part of the country also sometimes contract plague through infected camel meat. Zhannat told me there was a ban on its sale in western areas of Kazakhstan between March and September.

During my time in Aralsk I lived on *manti*, steamed dumplings filled with minced lamb and served in a hot broth with a dollop of sour cream. They were essentially the same ravioli-type affair I'd eaten with Lao Gao in the Badain Jaran in China. In fact, it struck me that the basic concept of wrapping dough around a savoury filling was common to innumerable people across the continents of both Asia and Europe. As a diversion from having to think about my imminent trip to Rebirth Island, I spent a whole afternoon making a list of all the similar foods I'd come across in my travels. There were *buudz* in Mongolia and *wonton* in China. I'd also eaten a very similar dish in Tibet, where they're called *momo*. All have much in common with the *kreplach* of Jewish cuisine, Russian *pelmeni*, Polish *pierogi*, and the numerous forms of stuffed pasta served in Italy. In fact, you could probably retrace the highways of the entire Silk Road without once having to vary your diet.

On returning from my trip to Mongolia and China and investigating the myth that Marco Polo introduced pasta to Italy from the East, it had seemed likely that the origins of this dish were located somewhere in the Arab world. Wheat is thought to have been first cultivated in the Middle East around nine thousand years ago. Al-Idrisi, the twelfth-century Arab geographer, noted in his *Book of Roger* that this flour-based food could be kept for a long time without going off. Some food historians speculate that the earliest experimentation with hard wheat was carried out by nomadic Arabs who needed easily transportable supplies that wouldn't spoil.

My sudden obsession with pasta reflected the anxiety I was feeling now that I'd made my arrangement to visit the most dangerously extreme place imaginable. But interesting though this diversion was, it wasn't going to be much help to me on my outing to Rebirth Island. I was enjoying the steamed dumplings while I could because there was no food of any description on my list of vital supplies for the trip to Vozrozh-deniye. In my meeting with Dave Butler in England, he'd made it quite clear that neither my nose nor my mouth should be exposed once we'd set foot on the island. Never. 'There's no such thing as a little sniff,' he'd said. We would wear oral and nasal protection: small facemasks like the ones surgeons wear with elastic strings over the ears, and a respirator, just in case. This meant that eating was out of the question.

Other details of our trip were revealed to me one morning

while sitting with Zhannat in her office. We had a map of the Aral Sea area spread out on a table. She indicated the former fishing village from which we'd set off. Qulandy was on the other side of the Little Aral, near the shoreline of the Big Aral. It was a long day's drive from Aralsk, Zhannat told me, on a very bad track, much worse than the one we'd taken to Tastubek. From Qulandy, it would take another couple of hours to reach the shore where the villagers kept their motorboats. The trip across the Big Aral should take two hours, depending on the weather. On reaching Vozrozhdeniye, we'd transfer to motorbikes. It was a three-hour drive to get to the Aralsk-7 base.

I was doing the sums in my head. 'So from Qulandy it'll take us a total of seven hours just to reach the research base?' Zhannat nodded. Judging from the map, the distance as the crow flies looked to be about a hundred kilometres. 'Yes, seven hours if all goes well,' Zhannat confirmed. 'But the sea can be stormy sometimes, which slows the boats down. Also, the boats are very old. Sometimes they don't work so well.' She smiled. 'The motorbikes are old too, of course.'

She'd already said that the Qulandy villagers didn't like staying on the island overnight. Their crossings, made maybe once or twice a year, were usually scavenging day-trips. They were long days by the sound of it, but I was quite happy to hear that no one intended to spend the night on Rebirth Island. Zhannat ran her finger along the coast of the island to show me where we'd land.

It was a good map. The shape of the Aral Sea has become a yardstick of cartographic dependability in my mind. Many maps continue to be stuck in the 1950s as far as the Aral is concerned. When I'd flown to Kazakhstan several weeks before, I'd checked the route map in my in-flight magazine. It had shown a bulbous water body split in political terms almost equally between Kazakhstan and Uzbekistan. But in reality the once-chubby inland sea has become fragmented into Little and Big, and the Big Aral has a large wedge stuck in one side, which is Rebirth Island. Vozrozhdeniye appears on the outdated maps too, but as a barely perceptible sliver. As the waters have receded, the island has grown. In 1960 it was about two hundred square kilometres. Today it is more than ten times that size. Both countries have been gradually expanding their national territory as the Aral's waters ebb away.

The modern-day, much larger Vozrozhdeniye was clearly depicted on the map we were using. In fact it indicated that it was now no longer an island at all. The Big Aral had shrunk to such an extent that it had become connected by a land bridge to the southern coast and now stuck up into what was left of the sea like a big fat finger. At home in Oxford, I'd looked into driving on to the former island from Uzbekistan, but found it would be difficult politically. It also seemed unwise to approach the derelict research base from the south since the southern portion of the island had been where the biological weapons were tested. The prevailing winds over this part of the world are from the north-west, hence Aralsk-7 had been sited to the north of the testing ground.

The map we were using showed that the northern third of Vozrozhdeniye was part of Kazakhstan, but the major portion of the former island was in Uzbekistan. The location of the border was one aspect of our trip that worried me. In England, when I'd been looking into the viability of reaching Rebirth Island, I'd initially found it almost impossible to discern where on the island the research base was. Few maps even showed a settlement, for obvious reasons. Until the end of the Soviet Union, Aralsk-7 didn't officially exist.

I'd managed to track down some satellite imagery of the region in a report on the American proposal to decontaminate the anthrax disposal sites in 2001. The images, taken by a spy satellite in 1970 and now declassified, showed Aralsk-7 clearly: the bioweapons laboratory and its small town about two kilometres further north. But was this north or south of the new international border? There was no indication because the border wasn't marked. Back in 1970 it hadn't mattered: it was all part of the USSR.

Zhannat's map showed the international borders. It also depicted the former research settlement with a small dot. The dot was south of the border – in Uzbekistan. This was a problem for me because I didn't have a visa to enter Uzbekistan.

I asked Zhannat whether the border was marked.

'Yes, here it is,' she said, pointing to the map.

'No, is it marked on the ground?'

She hesitated. 'What do you mean?'

'I mean, are there border guards or patrols?'

'I think sometimes.'

My heart missed a beat. 'Sometimes?'

'Yes, sometimes. I think so. Not always.'

Zhannat's answers were hesitant. I don't think she really knew. But I could imagine the sort of reception Dave and I would get if we were caught by a military patrol trying to cross an international border illegally, dressed in respirators and protective clothing.

I should have been addressing these questions to the villagers in Qulandy rather than Zhannat, and I would do just that. But meanwhile I pressed on.

'Do you know if any looters have ever been arrested going into Uzbekistan?'

'There are rumours,' she said. 'Rumours that some people have disappeared.' She wasn't being hesitant any longer, which worried me even more. 'But I've never met such people,' she added more brightly, as if this might draw a line under the matter.

No, I thought to myself, if they'd disappeared nobody would have met them.

Two days later, Dave Butler arrived in Aralsk. I'd spent the intervening time worrying whether or not to tell him about the added risk involved in our illegal entry into Uzbekistan, an issue I didn't think he was aware of.

When he heard the news, Dave was full of bravado. 'Well, I know what to do if we're caught,' he told me. 'We put our hands in the air and, when asked, claim ignorance. I just hope my name's not on their list,' he added thoughtfully. I gave him a puzzled look. 'Well, I'm ex-military, aren't I?'

All of a sudden, Dave's desirability as a travelling companion lost its edge. I couldn't decide which scenario was worse: being arrested as a spy or as an international terrorist. Then again, I didn't suppose it would make that much difference.

After the first hour on a paved road, the drive to Qulandy was as uncomfortable as Zhannat had promised. We turned off at a place called Saxaul, named after the virtually leafless desert shrub I'd first encountered back in the Mongolian Gobi with Aldaraa. The thought of that sub-zero night in the desert somewhat paled in comparison to the present situation.

Saxaul was full of poachers, apparently. As if to prove the point, a man on a motorcycle drove by with a large gun on his lap. Hunting saiga antelope was an alternative approach to surviving the region's ecological crisis, while adding to it at the same time. Saiga hunting was banned in this part of the world in 1920 when the species had been pushed to the brink of extinction. It's still illegal, but a law is meaningless if it's not enforced.

The saiga is a weird-looking antelope, equipped with a large proboscis-like nose, that inhabits the open steppe grasslands and semi-arid deserts of Russia and Central Asia. When the spacecraft from Baikonur had supposedly jettisoned its fuel over the region in 1988, instantly killing half a million, about a third of the world's saiga population had been wiped out in an hour. The disintegration of the USSR has been mirrored by another precipitous collapse in the antelope's numbers. Thought to have totalled around a million in 1990, now only about thirty thousand of these curious creatures survive. Poachers eat the meat and export the horns to China where they are used in traditional fever cures. Such a large number of males have been shot for their horns in the last decade or so that conservationists fear the antelope population may not be able to recover unaided. Zhannat thought that poachers pay off the local police with a share of the profits. It was sad for the saiga, but people had to live somehow.

The remainder of our journey to Qulandy took us through a landscape of dusty desert scrub. The atrocious track skirted the Little Aral, occasionally offering views of its distant waters across wide plains of former seabed. We bounced along in the lee of huge cliffs that had once marked the coastline but now stood lonely, dejected and crumbling in the arid scene.

The long drive gave me the opportunity to get to know Dave. Much of his work was in advising large corporations on security issues and surveying their buildings for weak spots in case of attack by terrorists using biological and other forms of weaponry. He said he enjoyed his civilian job, but it involved a lot of time indoors, often in tedious meetings. Hence the attraction for him of our visit to Rebirth Island. That and his particular interest in anthrax.

Dave had spent the last years of the Cold War engaged in various forms of undercover work in Eastern Europe. He was very open about his job at that time, which surprised me. The work involved surreptitiously hanging around military camps and training grounds on the look-out for bits of equipment that he could pinch and take back for British military intelligence to study. On several occasions he had spent lengthy periods crawling round the sewers beneath the Stasi buildings in East Berlin looking for secret documents. There were always plenty available, he told me. Since toilet paper was often hard to get hold of, even in East Germany's secret service, Stasi employees frequently used top-secret memos to wipe their bottoms. Dave was evidently pretty good at his job, usually coming back from a mission with something of interest, if often somewhat lacking in the fragrance department. Among the officer corps, he was known as Velcro.

By mid-afternoon Zhannat announced that we had left the Little Aral behind and were approaching the Big Aral. The sun was low in the sky by the time we finally pulled up in Qulandy. It was a fairly large, prosperous-looking village; most of the houses were freshly whitewashed, finished with the customary light blue trim, and sported new corrugated-iron roofs. Some of them even boasted a veranda of sorts, a zone where you could sit outside on rugs in the shade. Near each family's dwelling was a corral for their camels, and a wooden shed positioned over a hole in the ground for the private things in life. I never found an identifiable centre to the village, but roughly in the middle they were midway through building a mosque. This seemed to be the only public building – there being no shops.

When the Aral Sea had left them with no fish, the inhabitants of Qulandy, like those of Tastubek and Zhalangash, had diversified into livestock. These people had very large camel herds, Zhannat told us. In some measure they were the product of a lucrative sideline in smuggling, though of what, she wouldn't say. Aralsk, the nearest town, was a long way off, as we knew, so no one in authority took much notice of Qulandy's residents. In consequence, they did more or less as they liked, and seldom paid any taxes.

We met the looters who had agreed to ferry us across to Rebirth Island the following morning. They were a motley crew, not very interested in our concerns about possible Uzbek border patrols. When I asked the question, they took it as a cue for a lot of posturing about how much faster their motor-bikes were when compared to the Uzbek military jeeps. I took this to mean that they simply ran away. Were they ever caught, I wanted to know? 'Don't worry,' came the reply. How often did they encounter border guards? 'Sometimes,' was the response. None of this was very satisfactory but, having come so far, it was a bit late to pull out now. We'd just have to take our chances. Departure time from the village was set at 3.30 the next morning.

But when we were woken at three o'clock, I had to cancel. This wasn't because I'd finally lost my nerve, though I'd come close on several occasions over the previous few days. No, my reason for calling off the trip was much more prosaic. I had the shits.

Dave and I had spent the remainder of the day checking our kit. Catering for all eventualities, we each had two of every-thing, including the protective suits. These were lightweight and came in one piece. They had elasticated cuffs and leg-ends, and zipped up over our clothes. How could I go to the toilet in one of these? 'You don't,' Dave told me. It was going to be very hot out there, he said, so we'd lose a lot of moisture sweating inside the suits. Neither of us was likely to want to urinate, and defecation was totally impractical. 'If you unzip the suit and squat down, who knows what you'll pick up,' he said, quite reasonably.

When just before 11 p.m. I'd been forced to visit the wooden shed over the hole in the ground for the first time, I'd assumed it was just nerves, but two more trips before 3 a.m. persuaded me otherwise. It must have been something I'd eaten. There was no way I was going to risk a visit to Rebirth Island with such an obvious disadvantage.

It was only much later that day that I realized the good fortune of my having to postpone. I spotted the dust storm on my seventh visit to the wooden shed. It didn't look like a dust storm. It just seemed that something strange was happening on the western horizon. Up above me the atmosphere was crisp and azure, but far off in the distance was a long, curious smudge in the sky. It looked unreal.

Having spent the entire day in semi-slumber, laid out in the cool of the house where Dave and I were staying, I thought perhaps I was hallucinating. Puzzled, I stood and watched. The smudge was real. It had a milky texture and didn't appear to be moving. I ran through the options. The phenomenon it resembled most was a bank of fog, but I didn't think that was likely. You need a lot of water vapour for fog to form, and although we were near the Aral Sea, I'd never heard that it was a source of serious fog. Besides, the smudge wasn't in the direction of the Aral. It was in the west, not the south where the sea lay, so there was no source of water over which it could have formed. It was also mid-afternoon, the hottest part of the day, not the time when fogs develop. The blur was coming from the direction of the Ustyurt plateau, a desert clay plain that stretched from here to the Caspian Sea. It is a vast source of tiny dust particles.

I ducked back into the house to grab my camera. When I emerged, the smudge had grown larger and more distinct. Slowly, I started walking towards it. By this time the phenomenon had become quite discrete from the sky: a great, lumbering, dirty bank of ground-level cloud. At the edge of the village, where I had a building and a single small tree as visual markers, it was clear that the bank was moving. Extremely slowly, the dust cloud was arriving. Its movement was virtually imperceptible, but at the same time it was gradually becoming bigger and more distinct.

A couple of camels tied to the wooden fence of a nearby enclosure were groaning loudly as the great wall of dust crept closer. Sand whipped past my ankles as gusts caused a pair of trousers to billow, hung out to dry on a clothesline. The air had a dry taut feeling. The wall of dust towered above me, several hundred metres into the sky, blotting out the sun and overwhelming the edge of Qulandy with a dull, yellowish haze.

Abruptly, the atmosphere became full of dust and I was engulfed by the miasma of flying dirt. Violent eddies of wind tugged at my shirtsleeves and invisible particles invaded my being, clogging my nose and filling my hair. I ran to take shelter with the family standing in their doorway. They laughed as I coughed and spluttered, and offered me tea as we stood and stared at the open-air display of ethereal grime. We watched a flock of small birds flapping their tiny wings above the branches of the tree without going anywhere. It was the best they could do just to remain stationary in the blustery wind.

The atmosphere remained choked and swirling for hours. It took me a while to realize it was a good omen. If we'd made our trip to the island as planned, this fierce monster would have engulfed us on the return boat journey. It was the first time I'd ever considered a bout of diarrhoea to be serendipitous.

★

The air was calm and clear again at three the next morning, and I hadn't visited the wooden hut since the dust storm had hit. Confident my problems in that department were over, I joined Dave and the half-dozen looters to clamber into one of three jeeps that careered down to the sea's edge. Driving at high speed across the bumpy terrain in the darkness seemed like a good way of having an accident almost as soon as we'd set out, so Dave insisted that our driver slow down. The rest of the convoy soon vanished into the night and, guided only by the tunnel of light from our vehicle's headlamps, we lost our way several times. This surprised me. The Aral Sea may no longer be the fourth largest lake in the world, but it's still a very large body of water.

Two and a half hours later, when at long last we arrived, the looters were already busy loading their motorboats. Dave and I took off our boots and waded into the black nothingness as motorbikes were revved up and driven into the shallow waters, where it took half a dozen people to heave them into the two small boats. The orange glow of dawn was seeping into the horizon when the boats' engines finally spluttered into life and we pulled away from the shore.

To me the thrill of setting off on a trip across water is unrivalled. No start to a journey can compare with a passage across the sea, no matter how polluted and depleted the waters may be. The trace of salt in the air is the flavour of freedom. I closed my eyes to enjoy the pungent wind of adventure buffeting my face, and felt more alive than I had in weeks. Probably this was just an instinctive attempt to allay my fear of the dangers that lay ahead, but it was good while it lasted. The distant shore was a thin dark line behind us by the time the sun rose slowly to spread its rays across the swell. The boat's engine chugged with a sound like bubbling fat. Perched astride the fibreglass hull with my bare feet resting on the torn plastic seat of a motorcycle, I watched as little by little the dark waves took on the golden glow of daybreak.

But as the sun continued to climb in the cloudless sky, the aquatic scene was transformed into something other-worldly. The Big Aral was unmasked to take on a green colour that was unnatural in its intensity. Its deep, oily, emerald sheen defied the laws of nature. The sea was revealed as the cocktail of man-made chemicals I knew it to be.

Time passed. Dave said we ought to eat something as we'd have to go about eight hours on the island without food. He dug into his rucksack and produced two vacuum-packed camping meals. I chose beef stew and dumplings and ate it out of the silver envelope with a plastic spoon. It filled me up, though the cold dumplings tasted like lumps of chalk, but it was just as well that we had some nourishment while we could. The looters had confirmed that the journey by motorbike from our landing point to Aralsk-7 should be three hours each way. They would not stay at the derelict base longer than two hours maximum, since the boats had to make it back to the mainland before nightfall. Finding the right spot in the dark was very difficult. Hence my relief that we'd not made the journey the previous day. We'd certainly have got lost in the pall of dust, perhaps even gone down in the waves whipped up by the storm.

An hour and a half after we'd left the mainland, the youth at the helm stood up, peered into the distance in front of us, said something and pointed. Hovering on the horizon, far across the dead green sea, I could make out the hint of dry land. 'Vozrozhdeniye,' the youth said, and sat down. He didn't continue directly towards the island, but veered away for some time before turning again and heading straight for the land. I assumed this was to avoid some hidden obstacle like a sandbank, but I learned later from Zhannat that the course he chose was more likely to be calm. The two boats were simple fibreglass vessels, solid enough, but each had a heavy load: two motorbikes, fuel drums and four or five people. The sea wouldn't need to be very choppy for its waves to slosh over the sides. If the boats filled with water, they'd sink like stones.

As Rebirth Island loomed larger before us, my mouth became dry and the knot that had been growing in my stomach for the past half-hour gradually tightened. Although the coast where we were landing was far to the north of the weapons testing-grounds, and almost certainly consisted of land that had been under water during the lifetime of the Aralsk-7 base, neither Dave nor I had been able to discover exactly where the caches of weaponized anthrax had been buried. We'd both agreed that we should treat the entire landmass as potentially dangerous.

Mentally, I reminded myself of the nature of the threat. As far as I was concerned, anthrax spores were undetectable, but if any became lodged in my lungs the chance of death was likely to be more than 90 per cent. And, as Dave had quipped earlier, I'd do well to remember that 'death can be fatal'. But now, as our boat neared the beach, the joking was over. We dug into our rucksacks to pull out our face masks.

The boats came to a gentle halt as their hulls became wedged in the sand a few metres offshore. The boatmen jumped out, hauled their vessels as far in as they could and then set about unloading the motorbikes while Dave and I walked up the soft sandy bank to break out the rest of our protective clothing.

In many other places this would have been a nice beach. It had plenty of sunshine and a lot of fine sand, dotted with the occasional wispy clump of grass. But it also had its drawbacks: it contained a few things you wouldn't expect to find on a good beach. There were rusting pieces of machinery, old wheel hubs and a large fuel tank with white stencilled Cyrillic lettering still visible on its corroded flank. Two long-wheelbase lorries stood axle-deep in the sand, their cabs tipped forward to reveal their butchered engines. Of course the other problem with the beach was its location on Rebirth Island.

Six of us set off for Aralsk-7 on four motorbikes. The looters looked us over with interest when Dave and I approached wearing our white suits, black rubberized overboots and face masks. We had offered them our spare suits before leaving the mainland, but no one had been interested. Now they cracked a few jokes at our expense – revealing a lot of shoddy dental work as they laughed – and proceeded to argue over who should have two people on their bike. It felt nice to be wanted.

I was assigned to a youthful character in a bush hat, padded army jacket and tracksuit trousers. He had a sneer on his lip and a bandolier of cartridges across his chest. He was the only one of the group who carried a gun. We tore off at high speed along the beach, initially swerving our rear wheel in the sand before it gained a grip. I had to sit on the rifle, which dug into my backside.

We kept the seashore in view for the first hour of driving,

speeding alongside the abnormally green water of the Big Aral. There were no gulls and no other signs of life. The beach was wide, tranquil and deserted. It didn't look as if anyone had ever sat on it or would ever want to.

Turning away from the coastline, with me still clinging to the jacket of the unnamed gunman, we bounced across broad drifts of looser sand where the grasses were thicker and higher. We swished through the long swards and continued inland, stopping when we reached a ships' graveyard. I was glad of the opportunity to stretch my aching legs. Military speedboats that had patrolled the waters around Vozrozhdeniye during the decades of weapons-testing lay half engulfed by drifting sand. They were equipped with willowy antennae instead of masts, but the radio equipment had disappeared, leaving just tangles of wire. I recognized the low, broad hull of a defunct fuel tanker among them. As the Aral Sea had dwindled, the Russians had been forced to relocate Aralsk-7's port several times. This was the place where they'd finally given in.

From our position, the Aral Sea was nowhere to be seen. But, as the presence of our scavenging friends testified, this place could still yield some useful leftovers. My driver wandered over to a giant metal container situated a little further inland from where the bikes were parked. He lowered an old plastic bottle on a piece of string through an opening in its side, then passed round the black bottle of oil for everyone to fill their motorbike engines.

Half an hour later, we all stopped again. The gunman and I pulled up beside the lead motorcyclist, who had paused to examine the ground. A conversation ensued. Dave arrived a few minutes later. 'What's up?' he asked when he saw the men gathered around the interesting patch of earth. One of them walked away from us with his eyes fixed on the ground, as if he were searching for something. We joined the main group and I made gestures to ask what was so fascinating. The terrain here was still sandy, but there were also early signs of soil. Thick grass and reeds spread out in all directions across the flat landscape around us. The gunman lowered himself to his haunches, his signet ring flashing in the sunshine as his thick finger pointed.

The tiny ruts of tyre tracks were visible in the sandy soil. One of the men made a driving motion with his hands. He was grinning from beneath the peak of his baseball cap. His mimicry wasn't the action you'd make with the handlebars of a motor-cycle: he was miming a driver with a steering wheel. Dave gave voice to my thoughts: 'Christ, a patrol.'

We hadn't passed any indication of the border with Uzbekis-tan, but I hadn't really imagined that we would. I hadn't expected to see stop signs or a frontier post, customs buildings or a duty-free shopping zone. This was an uninhabited island, and we were yet to see even a road. But the indication that a jeep had passed this way was unnerving. An encounter with a military patrol was the last thing we wanted.

Now I regretted I hadn't tried harder to persuade Zhannat to join us on Rebirth Island. Neither Dave nor I spoke anything more than a few words of Kazakh or Russian, so we were reduced to hand gestures for communication. They weren't sufficient for more detailed exchanges of information. Like, when did the men think the jeep had passed this way?

I made an attempt by pointing to my wristwatch. The guy with the baseball cap traced a circle round the face indicating, I think, that we still had an hour to go before reaching the research base. That wasn't what I'd wanted to know.

Tucked away in one of the magnificent imperial rooms of the Hermitage museum in St Petersburg is a marble slab bearing an archaic Russian inscription nearly a thousand years old. It's called the Tmutarakan Stone and harks back to a principality that existed long ago on the edge of the Black Sea.

Over the centuries, historical facts about Tmutarakan have become so intertwined with legends that today the ancient principality has taken on a shroud of mystery. The name has been translated as the Place of Howling Darkness or the Kingdom of Cockroaches. In contemporary times, Muscovites have adopted the title as a nickname for any place that is both repugnant and remote. Each April during the later decades of the twentieth century, a secret team of Soviet scientists set out for a season of bioweapons-testing in a place they referred to in jest as Tmutarakan. Its real name was Vozrozhdeniye.

We approached the military town where the scientists had lived on a long, straight paved road that we joined a short time after finding the tyre tracks. My first sight of the settlement was a series of rooftops, but as we drew nearer it became clear that the roofs were skeletal. For a strange moment, it almost seemed as if we were approaching a building site, where the edifices were still under construction. But in truth many of them had lost their slates. The rafters had been picked clean and now stuck up like the bare ribs of carcasses drying in the sun.

On the edge of the town, we sped past a dump of rusting vehicles and an assortment of other machinery. The terrain here was uneven, a series of shallow craters, one of which was an abandoned ammunition dump. I saw the cases of shells and the ends of discarded missiles poking out of the earth.

The road leading into the town had been built of concrete sections. The slabs were for the most part still solid, though we had to slow down and weave past incipient potholes. We stopped in the shadow of a large, three-storey apartment building. I looked up and saw that all the windows in its towering wall had been smashed.

We left the looters to do whatever they'd come to do and walked round the corner of the apartment block into the sunshine. We had an hour to look round before we'd agreed to rendezvous and continue on to the laboratories a couple of kilometres further south. Another moment of pantomime with my watch and the guy wearing the baseball cap had confirmed the arrangement.

Weeds and straggling bushes lined the concrete pathway that took us past the chipped walls and broken windows of the derelict buildings. A battered road sign, the international one for children crossing, leaned drunkenly towards us as we entered what had been a playground. Remnants of rusting swings, their seats long gone, stood forlorn and forgotten in a mass of shattered planks of wood. I could still make out the faded yellow painting of a cartoon bird on a nearby wall.

We were undisturbed. As Dave set about recording the scene on the little video camera he'd brought, I walked a few paces away from him to stand still for a moment and listen. There were no sounds whatsoever. No birds, just an eerie silence. It was truly a deathly hush.

We ventured into one of the buildings, a civic centre or school judging by the wide set of steps, now partially destroyed and littered with debris, that took us up to a pair of huge doors. They hung limply from their hinges, opening the way to an interior that had been hacked apart by looters. The level of destruction appeared to have gone beyond the scavengers' call of duty, and I sensed an element of straightforward vandalism, fuelled by the desire for revenge. The smithereens of hundreds of smashed tiles lay strewn across the floor, gaping holes pock-marked the walls and shards of broken glass lay everywhere. Gingerly, we picked our way across the debris, wary of punctur-ing our rubber overboots, to gaze at yet more destruction in other rooms.

In spite of the damage, the building still had the air of a place that had been deserted in a hurry. Books lay open on the floor, and parts of posters were still attached to remnants of the walls. Instinctively, I wanted to crouch down and turn the pages of the books, but Dave's golden rule was not to touch anything. Despite the dangers of anthrax echoing like a mantra through my skull, I was surprised at how much willpower it took to obey this simple instruction.

Having arrived with people who took no precautions what-soever, I felt a strong temptation to shed those we had adopted. But as Dave had explained, it was as well to be cautious. People had lived here once, but nobody knew what had happened since. The looters had made their own decisions. We should stick to ours.

The feeling of hasty abandonment was common to all of the parts of Aralsk-7 that we saw. It was as if someone had blown a whistle and the entire population had grabbed what little they could carry and simply walked out, forgetting to shut the door behind them. As we left the gutted building, I passed a wall map that depicted the Soviet Union as it had been: a great swathe of red dominating Eurasia. Although torn, the map was otherwise complete, but the red colouring had faded badly. It depicted an empire that had come and gone. Like the capital of the Kingdom of Cockroaches, it was now consigned to the annals of history.

But the history of Rebirth Island is still with us, and it's an evil and dangerous one. Down in the research zone, we saw the tools of the bioweapons scientists' trade. Dave was astonished when the looters led us to the gutted remains of a small building littered with petri dishes and glass test tubes. It didn't have a roof, and the rafters seemed to have been burnt, but scattered across the floor and in neat stacks along lines of metal shelving, most of the glassware was undamaged. There was no way of telling what foul concoctions it had contained. Dave shook his head in disbelief. 'So much for the clean-up operation,' he said.

A collection of wire contraptions was piled up near a heap of test tubes. I'd read that experiments had been conducted on horses, sheep and donkeys, but that monkeys, our closest relatives, made the best subjects. These pieces of equipment looked like their feeding trays. The scientists who worked on Rebirth Island used to joke that the condemned monkeys were the luckiest inhabitants of the Soviet Union because they lived on fresh fruit. Bananas, oranges and apples were rare delicacies for most human residents of the USSR, but the test animals needed to stay in the prime of health right up to the moment when they took their last breaths, usually while strapped to poles out on the testing-grounds just to the south of where we were. The cream of Soviet science, who conducted the atmospheric tests, lived on hunks of bread and fatty sausage.

We investigated the laboratory complex only after shedding our surgeons' masks and donning our respirators. This we did one at a time, in a carefully rehearsed sequence: a deep breath, pull off the mask over the head, replace with the respirator, chin first and over the face, then exhale with a forceful puff to expel any new air in the mask through the filter. The moulded black plastic enclosed our faces. It felt strangely comforting to go through such a mechanical routine.

Most of the building's interior was relatively intact, suggesting that even the looters were wary of entering this nerve centre of the evil star. We progressed down a long corridor looking into the rooms that opened off, the sound of breathing through the respirators' filter systems adding to the surreal atmosphere. It was like wearing aqualungs and, just as if we were under water, our respirators allowed us to steal a glimpse of a secret world. We passed rooms full of electrical apparatus and others equipped with work-benches and metal cages. One room contained a bed with the sheets still on, and posters on the wall offering pictorial reminders of the importance of wearing all the necessary protective clothing. The sheets were rumpled, as if their occupant had risen one morning and forgotten to make his bed. Now it would never be made because he was never coming back. It was a long, sinister, murky corridor, worthy of the Place of Howling Darkness.

The phantom military patrol never materialized. It was only on the long journey back to Qulandy that my mind began to process the full magnitude of what I'd experienced. On the back of the motorbike, my arms wrapped round the stomach of an unidentified gunman, I could ponder the awfulness of this aberrant plague-spot. The faded wall map, the unmade bed and that deathly hush would stay with me for a long time.

As Dave dug a hole in the sand and buried our potentially contaminated clothes and protective equipment some distance from the shore, I watched the looters heave their bikes back on to their fibreglass vessels. They'd brought back some plunder, hidden inside rough tarpaulins. I never discovered what it was. I was happy to be leaving the most extreme place I'd ever set foot in, but it was the circumstances of the looters that really struck me.

Theirs was a more fantastical story than any of the tales of bizarre and monstrous races peddled by the ancient Greeks. Marooned in a region devastated by human mismanagement, these men, deprived of their livelihood by the annihilation of an entire inland sea, now braved the waters of this chemical soup to pillage scraps of debris from the Kingdom of Cockroaches. Land, sea and air, the Soviets had poisoned them all, month after month, year after year, for decades. As regular as clockwork. They'd used the deadliest materials known to mankind and, just occasionally, when they thought they weren't deadly enough, they had worked on that too. Now all that remained here was a toxic island in a dying sea, and the guys from Qulandy were left to pick up the pieces. Of all the sagas of survival in extreme environments that I'd come across in my travels, theirs had to be placed at the lowest point on the scale. To brave the dangers of Rebirth Island took a very special blend of courage and desperation.

Endnote

In the two thousand years since the Romans became obsessed with the soft, luxurious fibres of a new cloth brought to them from a little-known land far to the East, civilizations all along the network of trade routes now known as the Silk Road have waxed and waned. New ideas and materials that wound their way between the benighted territory of Asia's most extreme environments fuelled numerous advances in culture and commerce. Islam and Buddhism spread to envelop great swathes of Central Asia, while Christianity seeped into Europe. Europeans adopted paper and passports, they learned to count using new numerals from Arabia, and eased their aches and pains with medicinal rhubarb from Tibet. In turn, the peoples of China adopted the chair, harnessed the *karez* to irrigate new farmlands and were awestruck by a novel breed of horse from heaven.

The harsh conditions and forbidding terrain spread out across the heart of Central Asia dictated the tracks of this iconic system of highways. Rugged mountains and fierce deserts limited the paths that travellers could follow, and added to the romance of the Silk Road. Coming from a world clogged with congestion, I'd found it refreshing to traverse such vast, raw tracts of physical geography, expanses of the natural world that remain largely untamed.

None of the goods, peoples and innovations could have flowed along the celebrated caravan routes without the inhabitants of these desolate topographies. The nomadic societies of Mongolia, Tibet and Kazakhstan were the masters of movement who provided the necessary beasts of burden: the horses, camels and yaks that made up innumerable caravans through the ages. These peoples also took part in the commerce itself. Tibetans, who once controlled the Eurasian trade routes, have long exchanged salt, rhubarb and yak tails for the barley they're unable to grow. Mongolians, too, have been keen traders ever since imperial China first seduced them with silk. That link with their settled neighbours to the south has endured through the centuries: every Mongolian still fastens his *del* with nine metres of China's finest. Indeed, it was the rejection of an attempt to initiate trade with his western neighbours that brought Chingis Khan's horsemen down on Otrar and thereafter the rest of Asia.

Although more than seven centuries have passed since the terrible carnage wrought by the Mongol hordes, the images remain in the minds of settled peoples, colouring their view of wandering nomads to this day. In one sense, little has changed since the time of the ancient Greeks: we still think of the world as becoming more mysterious and less familiar the further we travel from home. Central Asia's nomadic citizens and the inhospitable territories they occupy remain unnervingly different. They are peoples and places made strange by distance.

These herders have learned to live with the vagaries of their extreme terrains, developing their own culture by adapting successfully to the unforgiving conditions. Nomads have never been interested in signing up for city life, or in most of a city's supposedly civilizing features. It's difficult to avoid this conclusion. These offroad societies have had access to modernizing influences, courtesy of the Silk Road, for more than two thousand years. They have chosen only a few innovations from their settled neighbours, such as the solar panels I'd seen throughout the Gobi. As for the rest, they've been content to watch them pass by. While the inhabitants of towns and cities across two continents have been dazzled by the trinkets supplied by centuries of commercial exchange, those who cohabit with the immensity of nature remain content with a minimum of possessions. And this is why nearly all the recent attempts to change their ancient ways, by meddling socialists intent on updating the herders' lifestyle, have failed. It's not what the nomads want.

Nomads are pragmatic, unsentimental people. The Buddhists among them eat meat, and some *drokba* willingly kill yaks by suffocation for the purpose. I remembered Aldaraa's look of incomprehension when I asked if the camel I'd just mounted had a name. This view had been encapsulated by Renato, the archaeologist who'd shown me round Otrar. I'd asked him to sum up the relationship the Kazakhs had with their horses. 'If a horse is no good, they eat it,' he'd said. 'A good horse a shepherd will use. If it is very good they will use it for *kokpar*. The best horses they race. And they bet. They love horses.' While trucks, trains and ships have taken over from the beasts of burden along the trade routes of Eurasia, the nomads still prefer to trust their livestock as insurance against the harsh voids they have made their home.

Of all the lessons I'd learned on my adventures off the world's oldest superhighway, one stands out. It seems that these traditional societies have successfully resolved the age-old conflict between man and nature, while modern social orders continue to make mistakes in their ceaseless struggle for progress. This message was clear in the blank uniformity of the Kazakh steppes, the only place I visited where the nomads' lifestyle has been effectively displaced. In ploughing the pastures to make way for arable farming, a tragic chain of events has been unleashed. The region's voracious irrigation schemes have sucked dry the waters of the Aral, leaving the descendants of the nomads to eke out a living as best they can from a dying sea. This, the most extreme human-induced disaster zone on Earth, should stand as a warning to all the 'civilized' people of the planet.

But beyond the condemned shores of the Aral, away from the Silk Road's still vibrant corridors of progress, most of the windswept lands of the nomad remain little changed. My appetite for extremes had been sated once more by the Gobi's endless gravel plains, the sandy peaks of the Badain Jaran and the rarefied heights of the Changtang. These terrains linger like lost samples of an unfettered world, occupied by none but the hardy herders. Above all, I'll remember the austere splendour of a desert studded with stones, and the stark beauty concealed within an ocean of steppe grass. I shall hark back to the wind spraying great trails of sand from the crests of giant dunes, and the dream-like summit of Mount Kailas twinkling in the sunshine. These places remain the exclusive domain of the nomads, free-roaming peoples tucked away in the forgotten folds of the Wilderness of Silk.